Principles and Practice to Help Young Children Belong

This vital resource for early years and primary school trainees and practitioners explores a range of social and therapeutic strategies and interventions that will successfully support all children's sense of belonging.

A sense of belonging is vital to children's physical, emotional, psychological, mental health and wellbeing. This book considers social and therapeutic strategies and interventions that support all children's sense of belonging and can be adopted by practitioners. It addresses the interrelated factors that impact children's sense of belonging such as race, gender, expression of sexual orientation, religion and disabilities. It will help develop practitioners' awareness of current social and educational issues including LGBT+ topics, the changing family unit, relationships, misogyny and toxic masculinity, meditation and mindfulness as well as the importance of children connecting with nature and transformative activism. The chapters adopt a theoretical and practical approach, presenting case studies of good practice, which will create positive and inclusive outcomes, supporting individual growth and community wellbeing.

An essential reading for practitioners, including teachers, teaching assistants (continuing professional development), lecturers and social workers, working in early years and primary educational setting, this book would also be suitable as a core and supportive text for students studying on a variety of undergraduate degree courses within the scope of education, pedagogy, mental health and wellbeing, social work and child development.

Estelle Tarry is presently an assistant professor in postgraduate teacher education in the Middle East. She was previously a lecturer at the South Devon University Centre, Plymouth University, UK, and authored *Challenges in Early Years and Primary Education* (2022) for Routledge.

Principles and Practice to Help Young Children Belong

Therapeutic Approaches to Support Pupils in the Margins

Edited by Estelle Tarry

Taylor & Francis Group

LONDON AND NEW YORK

Designed cover image: © Getty Images

First published 2025
by Routledge
4 Park Square, Milton Park, Abingdon, Oxon OX14 4RN

and by Routledge
605 Third Avenue, New York, NY 10158

Routledge is an imprint of the Taylor & Francis Group, an informa business

© 2025 selection and editorial matter, Estelle Tarry; individual chapters, the contributors

The right of Estelle Tarry to be identified as the author of the editorial material, and of the authors for their individual chapters, has been asserted in accordance with sections 77 and 78 of the Copyright, Designs and Patents Act 1988.

All rights reserved. No part of this book may be reprinted or reproduced or utilised in any form or by any electronic, mechanical, or other means, now known or hereafter invented, including photocopying and recording, or in any information storage or retrieval system, without permission in writing from the publishers.

Trademark notice: Product or corporate names may be trademarks or registered trademarks, and are used only for identification and explanation without intent to infringe.

British Library Cataloguing-in-Publication Data
A catalogue record for this book is available from the British Library

ISBN: 978-1-032-71615-2 (hbk)
ISBN: 978-1-032-72363-1 (pbk)
ISBN: 978-1-032-71619-0 (ebk)

DOI: 10.4324/9781032716190

Typeset in Galliard
by SPi Technologies India Pvt Ltd (Straive)

Contents

List of Contributors   *vii*

Introduction: Living in Worrying Times   1
ESTELLE TARRY

PART I
Tackling social inequality and social justice   5

1 Social Inequality and Social Justice   7
KATRINA PERKINS AND MOLLIE BELL

2 Anti-racism in Early Childhood Spaces: Transformative Activism   19
EMEL THOMAS

3 Religion, Belonging and Childhood in the Primary Classroom   36
MATTHEW VINCE

4 Unmasking Toxic Masculinity in Early Years and Primary Schools: Exploring the Impact on Children's Socialisation and Development   53
ALISON MILNER

PART II
Social interaction; social beings and relationships   69

5 Supporting Children's Sense of Belonging and Feelings of Mattering Through Relationship-Rich Pedagogies   71
ELEONORA TESZENYI

6 (LGBT+) and Different Family Structures:
   What Is a Family? 86
   HELEN HUGHES AND CATHIE BURGESS

7 Fostering Belonging Through Compassionate Care
   in Education 105
   EUNICE LUMSDEN

8 The Modern Iliad: Asylum Seeker and Refugee
   Children's Search for Belonging 123
   ESTELLE TARRY

9 Ecology and Embodiment: Engaging Children
   and Young People with Nature 140
   MARIE HALE

PART III
All Schools and All Practitioners 157

10 Towards a Needs-Led Approach to Inclusion: Questions
   and Challenges for the Ideology of Inclusive Practice 159
   CATHIE BURGESS

11 Developing a Mentally Healthy Culture for All
   in Schools: Issues and Possible Solutions 182
   ANDY SMITH

12 Wellbeing in the Modern World 199
   JODIE ROSSITER

   Conclusion 216
   ESTELLE TARRY

   Index 218

Contributors

Katrina Perkins is a lecturer at the University Centre South Devon and specialises in development and society. She is a programme leader and teaches on a variety of psychology and sociology programmes. Currently Katrina is undertaking a PhD in education, focussing on global citizenship.

Mollie Bell is a social science lecturer at South Devon College. She specialises in psychology and sociology. She has assisted in the running of groups for perceived disadvantaged individuals including those linked to young adult carers and has co-run a Ukrainian support group for individuals fleeing the war in Ukraine.

Emel Thomas is a senior lecturer in education at the University of Northampton. Prior to this, she taught in a variety of schools in England and has also conducted research for charities that support disengaged young people. Her main teaching and research interests include migration, identity, race, families and communities, intercultural teaching and learning.

Matthew Vince is an honorary research fellow of Cardiff University's Islam-UK Centre. His research covers sociological approaches to religion, education and childhood. His work includes projects that support teachers in the classroom, such as Discovering Muslims in Britain for Key Stage 3 course.

Alison Milner has over 20 years of higher education sector experience, with research interests around creative methods and personal and professional identity in the learning environment. She has previously written chapters about professional reflexivity and research dissemination. Currently she is researching the kindness of practice on a BERA funded project.

Eleonora Teszenyi is an academic at the Open University, and works both nationally and internationally. Her collaborative projects reflect diverse ways of knowing and values local knowledges. Practice still underpins her work, and her research focuses on children's rights and early childhood pedagogies, in particular, practice in multiage environments.

Helen Hughes is a lecturer at the University Centre South Devon and specialises in education psychology and counselling skills. She has an ongoing passion for child development with a specific interest in gender and family support.

Cathie Burgess is an experienced lecturer in childcare and education, Forest School Leader and Beach School practitioner, her master's in education focused on supporting learning using technology. She is a strong advocate for child-centred approaches and believes in the potential to meet children's needs through a flexible and dynamic approach to education

Eunice Lumsden is professor of child advocacy and head of childhood youth and families at the University of Northampton. Nationally, she has advised the government of early years qualifications and was an academic adviser for Best Start for Life. Her research interests include child protection and poverty.

Estelle Tarry is presently assistant professor in teacher education. She has been a PhD supervisor and taught on undergraduate and master's degrees in universities in the UK. Previously she was a primary school teacher in the UK and Head of British International Schools in Sri Lanka, Thailand and the Netherlands.

Marie Hale is a lecturer in social sciences at South Devon University Centre and lecturer at Schumacher College on the MA in movement, mind and ecology. As a human geographer, Marie's research interests focus on people and their relationships to place across a range of contexts and the interweaving of social and ecological landscapes. She has a deep interest in transformative learning and how embodied practices can lead to a deeper understanding of our world.

Andy Smith has been involved in education for more than 47 years by teaching/lecturing and leading in a range of schools, colleges and local authorities. Andy retired from his role as senior lecturer in special and inclusive education at the University of Northampton in 2022. He continues his interest in school improvement, developing teachers as school-based researchers and supporting special educational needs coordinators (SENCos).

Jodie Rossiter is an NCPS accredited counsellor, psychology lecturer and doctoral candidate in counselling psychology and psychotherapy with the Metanoia Institute. Employed by the Shekinah charity in Devon, she leads a team of counsellors and trainees, offering low-cost counselling to the wider community, specialising in therapy for victims of crime.

Introduction
Living in Worrying Times

Estelle Tarry

The world, countries, societies and individuals have recently faced many environmental, political, economic, technological, social and educational challenges. The cost-of-living crisis, post-Covid adjustment, fractured societies, immigration, forced displacement of large populations and movement such as Black Lives Matter and #MeToo have highlighted that social injustice is still being exacerbated and perpetuated. As a result, there has been an increase in the marginalisation of children through no fault of their own. Living on the outside of socially accepted norms or facing social exclusion affects children's sense of belonging, their sense of who they are, and their feeling of being valued and respected, and it impacts their relationships and connectedness of being part of a family and community.

These children, Generation Alpha children (born 2010–2024), arguably generation Covid, are the first generation that is fully immersed in digital technology and permanently connected, with unprecedented access to online information, content, news and social networks. One would think what an advantage these children have, with access to a wide range of knowledge sources and opportunities for learning new and advanced digital skills and making connections with diverse people—with differing backgrounds, cultures, religions, values, beliefs, thoughts and opinions—from around the world, and being globally minded. However, this comes with many caveats. These children are also experiencing screen saturation in their formative years, with an increase in the exposure to race-based violence, natural disasters, war and conflict trauma, misinformation, relentless change, loneliness and isolation from lack of direct human connections and relationships—all leading to an increase in anxiety and depression.

Like never before, a sense of belonging is vital to children's physical, emotional, psychological and mental health and wellbeing. And our role as practitioners is to support these children and reduce social marginalisation in schools, enabling children to flourish and thrive.

This book blends social workers', counsellors' and education practitioners' perspectives, working together with children and drawing on concepts from psychology, sociology, philosophy and education. It examines the importance of children's sense of belonging and its relationship with mental health and wellbeing. The book addresses interrelated factors that impact children's sense of belonging and specifically targets children who face social inequality; those who face prejudice and discrimination through race, gender, expression of sexual orientation, religion and disabilities; and those whose mental health and wellbeing are affected by social injustice and life chance. This book develops an awareness of contemporary and ongoing social and education issues that are often neglected and rarely considered with children, including transformative anti-racist activism, asylum seeker and refugee children, LGBT+ children and the changing family unit, and misogyny and toxic masculinity. This book supports the underpinning knowledge and understanding of teaching and learning, supporting mental health and wellbeing, and principles of working with marginalised and vulnerable children, families, communities and other professionals.

What is this book about?

There are three sections, with chapters that examine good practice in the development of transferable knowledge and skills that will create positive and inclusive outcomes and that prepare children to be able to respond to possible future challenges and support their individual growth and community wellbeing. The chapters adopt a theoretical and practical approach, giving advice and guidance with interventions, activities, case studies, suggestions and opportunities to reflect that will support all children's sense of belonging, mental health and wellbeing. All the chapters are of our times, specifically addressing contemporary topics and issues.

Part A, 'Tackling Social Inequality and Social Justice', highlights and explores growing social inequality and the impact this has on the most marginalised and vulnerable groups of children, who may be experiencing prejudice, isolation and fear due to class, gender, age, ability, race, ethnicity, religion or citizenship. These chapters include transformative anti-racist practices and approaches, the effect of toxic masculinity and its educational implications and the impact of religion and spirituality on children's identity and their sense of belonging. The reader is encouraged to reflect on their own practice and cultivate children's true sense of belonging.

Part B, 'Interactions: Social Beings and Relationships', examines the importance of positive relationships and interconnectedness in fostering belonging and the consequential impact on mental health and wellbeing. These chapters focus on the importance of more compassionate practitioners, leaders and policy makers by encouraging them to adopt a holistic, caring and empathetic child-centred approach. This section gives the reader activities and guidance on the development of nurturing environments, the complex concept of what a family is, relationship-rich pedagogical practices and children's reconnection with nature through meditation and mindfulness to ensure that children are happier, motivated and engaged in their learning. With the continuing global displacement of populations and some having travelled great distances, children are finding themselves in unfamiliar countries and societies. Practitioners are encouraged to reflect on their own cultural lens, to consider their own prejudices and biases and to be more open minded and culturally responsive when supporting children, parents and communities.

Part C, 'All Schools and All Practitioners', addresses the challenges practitioners face and adopts a positive needs-led and whole school approach to inclusive practice and the development of a supportive mentally healthy culture for children and practitioners. It embraces restorative classroom practices to redress power imbalances in the classroom by encouraging mutual respect, collaboration, joint problem-solving, open communication and trust. Not only should the mental health and wellbeing of all children be the heart of education and schools, but this section also examines the stress and pressures practitioners are under, including the role of the education mental health practitioner, and the implications and benefits of positive psychology in schools through self-discovery, healing, empowerment and connection.

Who is this book for?

The book is suitable for experienced practitioners, practitioners in the early stages of their career and students who are studying within the scope of teaching, education studies, social work, child development, mental health and wellbeing and social and therapeutic interventions.

Contributors

This book is written by higher education lecturers, from social work and education backgrounds, with extensive practical experience and expertise in their topic. They are dedicated practitioners who, for whatever reason, have entered their profession because they have been inspired and overwhelmingly driven to support and help children to be resilient and perseverant in the ever-changing world.

Part I
Tackling social inequality and social justice

1 Social Inequality and Social Justice

Katrina Perkins and Mollie Bell

Introduction

In the midst of global challenges evident in contemporary society, a surge in attention towards understanding and tackling social inequality has materialised. Described by Shiller (2015) as the 'greatest social threat of our time', 'inequality' is a notoriously difficult term to operationalize and remains debated because it covers a variety of dimensions of human experience. Inequality can be separated in terms of equality of opportunity, where people have equal chances to succeed in life unhampered by artificial barriers (Hatibu and Hafidh, 2021), and equality of outcome, where people appear in institutions in society in the same proportions in which they appear in the whole of society (Wilkinson and Pickett, 2010). Social inequality occurs 'when people frequently receive more of society's "valuable goods" than others, owing to their position in the social network of relationships' (Hradil, 2001, p. 29, cited in Hoffmann, 2008). People can be treated differently based on class, gender, age, ability, race, ethnicity or citizenship among other factors, ultimately affecting quality of life. Ferdinand and Mount (2008) identified five broad areas in which inequality overlaps: Inequality of wealth, inequality of participation in society, inequality of access to power, inequality of outcome, and inequality of opportunity. Hoffmann (2008) suggests that the determinants of social inequality likely denote social positions which in turn limit 'chances for conversation' or the convertibility of economic, social and cultural capital as noted by Bourdieu (1986). It is only in the last 200 years or so that society has really begun to question whether inequality is indeed natural and inevitable, or whether a more egalitarian society is realistically possible.

Despite Tony Blair's ambitious aim to eradicate child poverty by 2020 (Blair, 1999), and the UN Sustainable Development Goals (SDGs) prioritising addressing poverty (SDG 1) and reducing inequality (SDG 10) as a goal in itself (UN, 2019), discontent with growing social inequality is evident in contemporary society with the Covid crisis and rising cost of living impacting the most vulnerable. The World Inequality Report (Chancel et al., 2022) presents a synthesis of international research efforts to track global inequalities to inform democratic debate worldwide. Their 2022 data suggests that global wealth

DOI: 10.4324/9781032716190-3

inequalities are even more pronounced than income inequalities. While the poorest half of the global population owns just 2% of total wealth, the richest 10% of the global population own 76% of all wealth (Chancel et al., 2022). Similarly, on a more local scale, research published as part of the Institute for Fiscal Studies (2022) postulates that education in the UK is not tackling but preserving inequality. Research suggests that children who are eligible for free school meals (which corresponds to roughly the 15% poorest pupils) in England do significantly worse at every stage of school. The unequal gaps continue to translate into differences in qualifications as adults (70% of private school students are university graduates by the age of 26, compared with less than 20% of children from the poorest fifth of households), meaning that today's education inequalities become tomorrow's income inequalities (Farquharson et al., 2022).

Social inequality can therefore impact child health and development, socio-emotional development, cognitive development and education opportunities, persisting across childhood and into adulthood (Pearce et al., 2020). Naturally this could lead to potential consequences for a country's economic and political stability (Mdingi and Ho, 2021; Malikov and Alimov, 2022). As such, the reduction of inequality is crucial not only to improve the welfare and living standards of nations but also for addressing wider obstacles to personal development and overall economic growth and stability.

Globalisation and inequality

A significant factor influencing social inequality is the rise of globalisation. Globalisation is a powerful discourse that has the potential to impact how society views inequality and thus how it behaves and responds. In its most simplistic sense, globalisation can be described as capturing the increasing interconnectedness of societies (Papanikos, 2024). Globalisation transcends boundaries, increasing the interdependence of nations. Societies and nations are connected socially and culturally through the internet, media, travel and communications; economically through trade; environmentally through sharing one planet and politically through policies and regulations (Oxfam, 2017). With the expansion of trade and global investment and barriers of distance being broken down at a rapid rate, consequences of globalisation for social inequality are far-reaching and varied. Hui and Bhaumik (2023), for example, found small to moderate increases in inequality as a result of globalisation, with developed and developing nations seeing an average increase in inequality as a result of globalisation. Equally, their research suggests that technology and education mitigate the effects of globalisation on economic disparity.

For some, globalisation is a fruitful phenomenon that expands the horizons of the poor, generates increased awareness of diversity and hybridisation, stimulates international markets and wealth and helps towards a more universal humankind (Hirst, Thompson and Bromley, 2015). Pro-globalists argue that trade openness and foreign direct investment play a key role in lessening inequality among developing economies (Tabash *et al.*, 2024). For others, a key feature of the modern world is that it is organised through capitalism, private ownership of property, pursuit of personal profit and free competition (Hirst, Thompson and Bromley, 2015), resulting in exploitation, marginalization of impoverished populations and increased social inequality (Tabash *et al.*, 2024). Jameson (1998) suggests there is a paradoxical dichotomy when it comes to cultural globalisation. On one hand, globalisation has the potential to empower and act as a force for good. On the other hand, it can disempower and result in colonization and the promotion of western ideals (Amadi and Agena, 2015). Given the undoubtable significance of globalization for everyone, global governance, institutions and policies have a role to play in creating a fairer society.

Social inequality is arguably not an inevitable consequence of globalisation but a reflection of how global governance and social policy respond to the new dynamics that globalisation generates and represents. Policies and interventions that address structural inequalities that can have devastating long-term consequences for children are critical for reducing social inequality and therefore improving children's health and wellbeing, fulfilment and sense of belonging.

Global governance

Global governance refers to a purposeful order that derives from institutions, normal agreements and informal procedures that are regulated to benefit society on a global scale (Benedict, 2001, pp. 6232–6237). It comprises of a range of concerns, including the development of the economy, human rights and trade, ensuring protection of the environment, peace and security. The main aim of global governance is to coordinate behaviours of transnational actors and reduce combined action problems that transcend national borders (GCF, 2024). Within this framework, activities are incorporated that extend further than national boundaries and are rooted on rights and rules that are implemented through an arrangement of economic and moral incentives (Benedict, 2015, pp. 151–161). Within global governance, the public and private sectors, their methods and specific elements are included. These elements include standards in consensus among states, the development of norms deriving from shared values and the commands issued by authorities and implemented by states (Solesin, 2020). The United Nations Convention on the Rights of the Child (UNCRC, 1989) is the most widely ratified international human rights treaty in history with 54 articles that cover all aspects of a child's life and set out their civil, political, economic, social and cultural rights. Global governance is not a static order; it is consistently adapting to contend with the emergence of new actors and the development of new challenges across a global level (Elfert and Ydesen, 2023).

To tackle inequality on a global scale, global governance is imperative and can be used as a tool to identify solutions to the issues associated with globalisation. Markedly, in regard to education, acts and reforms that enable the development of inclusive policies and practices to reduce inequality are mitigating factors of educational attainment. In terms of education, there are multiple accounts of the conceptualisation of international relations and how developing and emerging theories of global governance can be, and have been, applied within the realm of international and comparative education (Mundy and Manion, 2014; Tikley, 2017). Global networks have become a progressively more important aspect of educational governance. Developing from starting points, distributing research and policy-linked knowledge and creating best practices and global education assessments shape the global understanding of education, learning and teaching (Mertanen, Vainio and Brunila, 2021). Global assessments have been implemented globally to measure the quality and effectiveness of the transnational education systems (Hinke Dobrochinsk Candido, 2020).

Education governance

Education governance is not an abnormal concept. It concerns parents, the school experience of children and the effectiveness and equitability of the education provision. There have been major adaptations in the model of education governance over the last decades. Governments can be seen to embody one actor in the governance of education. This is due to the educational decisions and policies being widely promoted within developing and emerging global spaces and influenced by nonstate actors (Solesin, 2020). International education and development improved markedly in the year 2015, due to the experiences of the 2009 (EFA) and Millennium Development Goals. Education communities at the World Education Forum in May 2015 declared the Education 2030 Act. This act aims to enable inclusive and equitable quality education and lifelong learning for all (UNESCO, 2015). The main intention of the act is to ensure that all children are provided with quality education, no matter their socioeconomic background or the social inequalities they face, which in turn should enable children to develop a sense of belonging to a wider learning and developing educational community. Under this consensus, a plan for sustainable development and international cooperation was outlined in the form of the Sustainable Development Goals, a collection of 17 global goals adopted by all United Nations member states and intended to be a 'blueprint to achieve a better and more sustainable future for all'. It was based on the global education community's shared outlook for the future of education, based on the right to education framework, lifelong learning paradigms, inclusiveness, equity and quality (UNESCO, 2015; Solesin, 2020). The development of these frameworks has been suggested to be a key movement in reducing social inequality (Tikley, 2017), recognising that inequality and strategies to reduce the ramifications go hand in hand.

The main intention of governance in education is to consolidate accountability and provide people with a voice in conversations that have a significant effect on their lives; to enable the provision of quality services, it is strongly connected to social justice and fairness. Due to this, tackling inequality within education should be at the core of discussions. Education for All (EFA), at its core, is rooted in citizens having the equal right to quality education regardless of their background or perceived level of inequality. To do this, arrangements within institutions need to embody the practices that enable communication between children, parents, schools, local education departments and national ministries (EFA, 2009).

Intersectionality

Different groups respond to particular arguments for and against tackling inequality, questioning the extent to which social inequality is mediated by individuals or wider social structures. Regardless of the root cause, social inequality can result in significantly impaired life chances for children. Given that there is progress still to be made on tackling social inequality, understanding interactions between different identities and social positions (intersectionality) is key to making sustainable progress on reducing inequality. Central to understanding these complex phenomena is the importance of adopting a multifaceted approach. Originally developed by Kimberlie Crenshaw, the term 'intersectionality' refers to 'the critical insight that race, class, gender, sexuality, ethnicity, nation, ability, and age operate not as unitary, mutually exclusive entities, but rather as reciprocally constructing phenomena' (Collins, 2015). Challenging the deep-seated structures of discrimination, intersectionality acknowledges multiple overlapping aspects of social inequality, understanding that inequalities are 'interdependent and indivisible from one another' (Bond, 2021). Using an intersectional approach to examine social inequality is useful not only to show where social inequality intersects but as a way to create more effective interventions to tackle the complex reality of social inequality. The National Governance Association (2023) attempts to do this by widening the lens on understanding disadvantage in schools, looking beyond pupil premium measures and instead considering five broader drivers of disadvantage:

1. Poverty
2. Special educational needs and disabilities (SEND)
3. Vulnerability (including looked-after children and young carers)
4. Certain ethnic groups
5. Mental health and wellbeing

As education is often a domain where social inequality manifests, broadening the lens or parameters and considering the way in which drivers of disadvantage can intersect allows a wider scope where learners can be supported.

> **Case Study: Tackling inequality**
>
> Research from Jamatia (2023) puts forward the examples of youth-led organizations and youth activists who have been fundamental in tackling social inequality. Considered as potential powerful agents of change, their successful interventions involve advocating for inclusivity and equal rights and providing support to those most affected by social inequality by engaging in youth empowerment initiatives that in turn foster leadership skills, critical thinking, and a sense of agency. Specific examples that have proven to be successful include youth engaging in established mentoring programs, tutoring initiatives and scholarship schemes. These require learners to be proactive in championing social justice, engaging in advocacy campaigns and rallies and using social media platforms to amplify voices and effect change. Creating safe spaces for dialogue, establishing networking platforms and engaging in skill-building workshops offer valuable examples for others to use to be empowered in addressing social inequality and reshaping a more positive future for children and young people.

It is clear that global education with weakened global governance includes underfinanced institutions, service providers and government agencies that do not respond and meet the demands of the needs of their learners, and the difference is most clear with participation, completion and low levels of attainment. Therefore, it could be suggested that developing a strong global governance would enable support in relieving the impact of inequalities within education and enable children and young adults to feel a sense of belonging (Elfert and Ydesen, 2023). However, it would be naïve to assume that this was not already one of the predetermining factors. EFA is a key framework, as mentioned prior, that aims to ensure that fair, quality education is provided for all. However, many of the deepest barriers to EFA are embedded beyond the education system and are derived from poverty and social inequality or disadvantage. However, it has been suggested that to achieve EFA, effective embedding of education planning in reduction strategies for poverty should be incorporated. This is due to many factors; poverty, ill health and diminished nutrition are significant factors in disparity between attainment (UNESCO, 2008).

There have been recommendations put forward by Dakar (UNESCO, 2005), suggesting that multiple governments do not provide sufficient weight to policies that aim to overcome inequalities within education. To alleviate some of the constraints linked to social inequality, setting equity targets that aim to reduce differences based on wealth, gender, language and multiple other markers seen to be significant factors of disadvantage would enable the focusing of political attention. However, UNICEF (2008) suggest that progress in education is linked closely to other areas, including the reduction of poverty and increase in public health, and while the education sector has become stronger, it cannot develop past the constraints within society. Therefore, to improve social inequality and children's sense of belonging within education, inequality within society also needs to improve. Global governance is important to reduce inequality as it has been identified that whether main stakeholders are involved in education might be a driving factor for mitigating the impact of inequalities on the life chances of the younger generations (Melhuish, 2020).

Inequalities in education

Inequalities in education settings are responsible for over half of the inequality in opportunities experienced in the United Kingdom. Inequalities can be based on many factors, including the nine protected characteristics of age, disability, gender reassignment, marriage and civil partnership, pregnancy and maternity, race, religion or belief, sex and sexual orientation under the Equality Act 2010 (UN, 2024). Sustainable development cannot be achieved for all if individuals are excluded from developing a better life. There are moral, social and economic constraints within societies, as those individuals experiencing inequality and poorer skills are less able to adapt to the living expectations within society. The aim of equality and future productivity can be seen as interlinking; if equality is not addressed within education, productivity within society can be stunted. Heckman (2006) suggested that policies that recognise learning potentials should be developed within childhood, specifically within early childhood, to improve life chances. Global governance is important to reduce inequality as it has been identified that whether main stakeholders are involved in education might be a driving factor for mitigating the impact of inequalities on the life chances of the younger generations (Melhuish, 2020).

The skills seen to be imperative for ample life chances in contemporary society are becoming more complex and vaster. However, there are large disparities between individuals that link to disadvantage and inequality. Those experiencing disadvantage are less likely to be successful within education (Sylva *et al.*, 2004). It has been widely researched that the socioeconomic background of the family has a direct impact on educational outcomes within primary and secondary education. However, it is not just socioeconomic status that impacts inequalities within education; children and young people from ethnic minorities also experience marginalisation and discrimination, thus diminishing their sense of belonging to education settings (Nurse, 2013).

Poverty and education

Children's view of daily life differs greatly from that of an adult; this has been suggested to be amplified when the focus is on inequality and hardship (Bierman, 2004). When adults, particularly those who are parents or guardians, are asked about inequality or poverty, they may denote extended workdays, insufficient pay and being unable to support members within their family. However, children see it as not seeing their family members for long periods of time, feeling marginalised within school and having a weakened childhood due to needing to support adult tasks within the home (Chapman, 2005).

Poverty and education are interlinked and are significantly difficult to dissemble. Young people living in poverty may stop attending education settings so they can work to support their family's socioeconomic status. However, this often leaves them without literacy and numeracy skills needed to further their careers. Their children, in turn, are in a similar situation years later, with little income and few options but to leave school and work (ChildFund, 2024). It has been widely proposed that the relationship between poverty and education is multidirectional. Individuals experiencing poverty lack access to a decent education, due to the outside responsibilities; however, without an education, those individuals are deemed to be constrained to a life of poverty (Van Der Burg, 2008). Children experiencing poverty can also be vulnerable to bullying and social exclusion within education, due to the stigmatisation of living in poverty (Tureysky, 2021). Children experiencing poverty are often prevented from partaking in school activities due to the associated cost, which in turn can further reduce the children's sense of belonging and increase their sense of marginalisation or social exclusion (Seligman, 2010).

Alongside the social impact experienced by children and young people experiencing poverty and inequality, there are also specific academic implications. The disparities between education attainment appear early in childhood and are seen to develop throughout an individual's lifetime. Prior to beginning school, differences can be seen in children who are experiencing poverty; this can emerge in their cognitive and socioemotional skills. During school years, the educational disparities solidify (IFS, 2024). The Institute of Fiscal Studies (IFS) (2022) stated that in the United Kingdom only 57% of children eligible for free school meals were assessed as having an acceptable level of development when related to their early learning goals. This was compared to 74% of children who were not entitled to free school meals and did not experience the same levels of inequality. When pupils are not eligible for free school meals, they are three times as likely to achieve grades surpassing expectations than those who are disadvantaged. These inequalities are seen to develop through primary school, into secondary school, and throughout an individual's lifespan (Shepherd, 2011). This suggests that the inequalities apparent in disadvantaged families has a direct impact on the attainment of qualifications, which further outlines the economic disparities that individuals experiencing inequalities within childhood would experience (Nurse, Melhuish, 2021). While at school, individuals who experience disadvantage or inequality are likely to face a multitude of challenges that coexist alongside attainment issues; these include excessive levels of exclusion, poor mental health and weakened attendance (NGA, 2023).

The impact of inequality on belonging

Belonging has been defined in multiple ways in relation to school settings. However, Libbey (2004) suggests that the concept of school connectedness, like belonging for school-age children, can be described using a variety of terminology, including school attachment connectedness, school bonding and learning communities. Although it is notable that the definition of belonging may change among societies, there are consistent factors that surface. Positive interventions include the supportiveness of the teaching practices, developing social bonds with peers, engagement in academic progress and fair discipline. The Wingspread Declaration (2004) depicts that belonging in school settings is rooted in the idea that students believe the adults within their educational community care about their learning and have specific interests in them as individuals. It suggests that positive teacher relationships can enable the feeling of belonging within education, which can in turn alleviate some of the impact that inequality has on educational attainment. Research into the impact of belonging in educational settings has highlighted significant benefits, demonstrating that a sense of belonging can significantly increase academic outcomes and reduce absenteeism (Roeser, Midgley and Urdan, 1996). Although significant, there is a clear absence of effective working policies related to social connectedness or belonging. Seligman (2010) suggests that this absence may be due to the lack of a clear framework or model. However, due to the emerging popularity within positive areas of psychology, global governance may be more forthcoming with policies or frameworks that can foster belonging to reduce inequality.

Reflection

What can teachers and practitioners ask themselves?

- What do you think affects children and young people who live in poverty the most?
- How do your policies and practices promote inclusive education, aiming to reduce the impact of inequality?
- How does your approach to education ensure that your teaching and education practices are inclusive and reduce equity issues?
- How can partnership working with parents, community and family learning be developed further to mitigate factors of inequality and manage the impact it has on children's education?

Considering the five driving factors of disadvantage proposed by the National Governance Association (2023):

- Which do you believe to have the largest impact, and how would you reduce this within your educational practice?

References

Amadi, L. and Agena, J.E. (2015), Globalization, culture mutation and new identity: Implications for the Igbo cultural heritage. *African Journal of History and Culture*, 7(1), pp.16–27.

Benedict, K. (2001), *International Encyclopedia of the Social & Behavioral Sciences*. Pergamon: Science Direct.

Benedict, K. (2015), *International Encyclopedia of the Social & Behavioral Sciences*. Pergamon: Science Direct.

Bierman K.L. (2004), *Peer Rejection: Developmental Processes and Intervention Strategies*. New York: Guilford Press.

Blair, T. (1999), "Tony Blair's full speech," https://www.theguardian.com/politics/1999/sep/28/labourconference.labour14

Bond, J. (2021), *Global Intersectionality and Contemporary Human Rights*. London: Oxford University Press.

Bourdieu, P. (1986), The force of law: Toward a sociology of the juridical field. *Hastings LJ*, 38, pp. 805.

Chancel, L., Piketty, T., Saez, E. and Zucman, G. (eds.). (2022), *World Inequality Report 2022*. Harvard University Press.

Chapman, D.W. (2005), The search for quality: A five country study of national strategies to improve educational quality in Central Asia. *International Journal of Educational Development*, 25(5), pp. 514–530.

ChildFund. (2024), 5 ways ChildFund advances digitalization and Youth empowerment. https://www.childfund.org/stories-and-news/2024/august-2024/5-ways-childfund-advances-digitalization-and-youth-empowerment/

Collins, P.H. (2015), Intersectionality's definitional dilemmas. *Annual Review of Sociology*, 41, pp. 1–20.

Education for All (EFA). (2009), Overcoming inequality: Why governance matters. *EFA Global Monitoring Report*, 119–63.

Elfert, M. and Ydesen, C. (2023), *Global Governance of Education*. London: Springer Cham, pp. 1–22.

Farquharson, C., McNally, S. and Tahir, I. (2022), Education inequalities. *IFS Deaton Review of Inequalities*. Available at Education Inequalities https://cradall.org/sites/default/files/education-inequalities_0.pdf (Accessed April 10, 2024).

Global Challenges Foundation. (2024), What is global governance? Available at https://globalchallenges.org/global-governance/what-is-global-governance/ (Accessed April 14, 2024).

Hatibu, S.H. and Hafidh, H.A. (2021), Equal opportunity factors for youth unemployment in the EA countries: Data and policy analysis. *Management Studies and Economic Systems*, 6(1/2), pp. 29–45.

Heckman, J.J. (2006), Skill formation and the economics of investing in disadvantaged children. *Science*, 312(5782), pp. 1900–1902.

Hinke Dobrochinski Candido, H. (2020), Datafication in schools: Enactments of quality assurance and evaluation policies in Brazil. *International Studies in Sociology of Education* 29(1), pp. 126–157.

Hirst, P., Thompson, G., and Bromley, S. (2015), *Globalization in Question*. New Jersey: John Wiley and Sons.

Hradil, S. (2001). *Soziale Ungleichheit in Deutschland*. Opladen: Leske + Budrich.

Hui, Y. and Bhaumik, A. (2023), Economic globalization and income inequality: A review. *Asia-Pacific Journal of Management and Technology (AJMT)*, 3(4), pp. 1–9.

Institute for Fiscal Studies (IFS). (2022), The UK education system preserves inequality–newreport.https://ifs.org.uk/articles/uk-education-system-preserves-inequality-new-report

Institute of Fiscal Studies (IFS). (2024), Education inequalities. *Education Inequality: The IFS Deaton Review*. Available at https://ifs.org.uk/articles/uk-education-system-preserves-inequality-new-report

Jamatia, P.L. (2023), The role of youth in combating social inequality: Empowering the next generation. *International Journal of Social Science, Educational, Economics, Agriculture Research and Technology*, 2(8), pp. 229–238.

Jameson, F. (1998), Globalization as a philosophical issue. In F. Jameson and M. Miyoshi (Eds.), *The Cultures of Globalization* (pp. 54–80). Durham: Duke University Press.

Libbey, H.P. (2004), *School Connectedness: Influence Above and Beyond Family Connectedness*. United States: UMI.

Malikov, A. and Alimov, B. (2022), Income inequality and political instability. Available at https://iariw.org/wp-content/uploads/2022/08/Malikov-Alimov-IARIW-2022.pdf

Mdingi, K. and Ho, S.Y. (2021), Literature review on income inequality and economic growth. *MethodsX*, 8, art. 101402.

Melhuish, E. (2020), Does an integrated, wrap-around school and community service model in an early learning setting improve academic outcomes for children from low socioeconomic backgrounds? *Early Child Development and Care*, 192(5), 816–830.

Mertanen, K., Vainio, S.E. and Brunila, K. (2021), Educating for the future? Mapping the emerging lines of precision education governance. *Policy Futures in Education*. E-pub ahead of publication.

Mount, F. (2008), The social evils series: Five types of inequality. *Viewpoint Informing Debate*. Available at https://policycommons.net/artifacts/1896234/the-social-evils-series/2646768/ (Accessed April 12, 2024).

Mundy, K. and C. Manion. (2014), The Education for All initiative. In *Education and International Development: History and Prospects Post-2015*. Oxford: Bloomsbury.

National Governance Association. (2023), Widening the lens on understanding disadvantage. In *Widening the Lens on Disadvantage*, pp. 2–10. NGA for Schools and Trusts.

Nurse, L. (2013), Biographical approach in the study of identities of ethnic minorities in Eastern Europe. In J. D. Turk and A. Mrozowicki (eds.), *Realist Biography and European Policy. An Innovative Approach to European Policy Studies*, pp. 115–140. Leuven: Leuven University Press.

Nurse, L. and Melhuish, E. (2021), Comparative perspectives on educational inequalities in Europe: An overview of the old and emergent inequalities from a bottom-up perspective. In *Contemporary Social Science*, 16(4), pp. 417–431.

Oxfam. (2017). Global citizenship in the classroom – A guide for teachers. https://oxfamilibrary.openrepository.com/bitstream/handle/10546/620105/edu-global-citizenship-teacher-guide-091115-en.pdf?sequence=9&isAllowed=y

Papanikos, G.T. (2024), The future of globalization. *Future*, 10(2), pp. 87–108.

Pearce, A., Mason, K., Fleming, K., Taylor-Robinson, D. and Whitehead, M. (2020), Reducing inequities in health across the life-course: early years, childhood and adolescence. Available at https://www.euro.who.int/en/health-topics/health-determinants/social-determinants/publications/2020/reducing-inequities-in-health-across-the-life-course.-early-years,-childhood-and-adolescence-2020 (Accessed April 12, 2024).

Roeser, R.W., Midgley, C. and Urdan, T.C. (1996), Perceptions of the school psychological environment and early adolescents' psychological and behavioral functioning in school: The mediating role of goals and belonging. *Journal of Educational Psychology*, 88(3), pp. 408–422.

Seligman, R. (2010), The unmaking and making of self: Embodied suffering and mind–body healing in Brazilian Candomblé. *Ethos*, 38(3), pp. 297–320.

Shepherd, D. (2011). Constraints to school effectiveness: What prevents poor schools from delivering results? Stellenbosch Economic Working Papers.

Shiller, R.J. (2015). *Irrational Exuberance: Revised and expanded third edition.* Princeton: Princeton University Press.

Solesin, L. (2020), The global governance of education 2030: Challenges in a changing landscape. Available at https://unesdoc.unesco.org/ark:/48223/pf0000372895 (Accessed April 12, 2024).

Sylva, K., Melhuish, E., Sammons, P., Siraj-Blatchford, I. and Taggart, B. (2004), *The Effective Provision of Pre-School Education (EPPE) Project: Findings from Pre-School to End of Key Stage 1.* London: DfES.

Tabash, M.I., Elsantil, Y., Hamadi, A. and Drachal, K. (2024), Globalization and income inequality in developing economies: A comprehensive analysis. *Economies*, 12(1), pp. 23.

Tikley, L. (2017), The future of education for all as a global regime of educational governance. In *Comparative Education Review*, 61(1), pp. 25–53.

Turetsky, K.M., Sinclair, S., Starck, J.G., & Shelton, J.N. (2021). Beyond students: How teacher psychology shapes educational inequality. *Trends in Cognitive Sciences*, 25(8), pp. 697–709.

United Nations (UN). (2019). *The Sustainable Development Goals Report 2019.* https://unstats.un.org/sdgs/report/2019/The-Sustainable-Development-Goals-Report-2019.pdf

United Nations (UN). (2024), *Equality and Non-discrimination.* https://www.un.org/ruleoflaw/thematic-areas/human-rights/equality-and-non-discrimination/

United Nations Children's Fund. (1989), *Convention on the Rights of the Child.* https://www.unicef.org.uk/wp-content/uploads/2016/08/unicef-convention-rights-child-uncrc.pdf

United Nations Educational, Scientific and Cultural Organization (UNESCO). (2005). Education for all: The quality imperative. *Global Monitoring Report.* Paris: UNESCO Publishing.

United Nations Educational, Scientific and Cultural Organization (UNESCO). (2008). Comparing education statistics across the world. *Global Education Digest*, pp. 17–39.

United Nations Educational, Scientific and Cultural Organization (UNESCO). (2015), *Education 2030 Framework for Action.* Paris, UNESCO.

Van Der Burg, S. (2008), Poverty and Education. UNESCO 10(15), pp. 12–34.

Wilkinson, R. and Pickett, K. (2010), *The Spirit Level: Why Equality Is Better for Everyone.* London: Penguin.

Wingspread. (2004), Wingspread declaration on school connections. *Journal of School Health*, 74, pp. 233–234.

2 Anti-racism in Early Childhood Spaces

Transformative Activism

Emel Thomas

Introduction

Racism is evident in all spheres of life, and tackling it is of great importance. Addressing racism is not just about the experience of an individual, but rather it must be on 'creating a fairer society for marginalised people, which is a better world for us all' (Williams, 2020, p. 13). At an early age it is crucial that educators address processes, actions and conversations that are one dimensional. Otherwise, there will always be an inequality gap on a range of measures from birth, early childhood, and youth on into adulthood. To understand how such inequalities emerge and thrive within early childhood spaces, this chapter accounts for the terminology of race and racism. Viewed within an educational framing, it is presented that the formation of an early year's anti-racist pedagogy must reflect on history, current affairs and theory. It is also argued that such pedagogy cultivates a deep sense of belonging among both the marginalised and the majority in early years spaces. Change takes time and can be challenging, but in early childhood education and care (ECEC) anti-racism should involve some form of critical engagement. According to Akala (2019, p. 308), it is asking and tackling questions in relation to the shape of the world that children are born into that will determine whether racism (in all its formations) is challenged and eliminated. Consequently, transformative anti-racist activism is proposed in this chapter as the prioritisation of race and belonging in ECEC, deep historical reflections, contemporary listening agency, critical progression and restorative compensation. These elements of activism enable the nourishment of babies, young children, and their immediate and wider communities in a holistic manner.

Race and anti-racism in education

In the social sciences race is identified as a problematic concept that warrants action(s) against racial discrimination. Conceptually, Gillborn (2008, p. 3) identified that for education 'far from being a fixed and natural system of genetic difference "race" is a system of socially constructed and enforced categories that are constantly recreated and modified through human interaction'. Racial constructs in ECEC settings can be identified through social systems, structures and communication (Smidt, 2020). Racism is not the opposite of race but rather a byproduct that is experienced diversely by children and adults. Therefore, racism can be defined as discrimination that takes the form of prejudice and partiality to manifest itself both overtly and covertly and at any time. According to Wolgast and Wolgast (2024, p. 2), racism is 'intimately tied to how value and profits are created and distributed, [and] the exclusionary mechanisms of racism have been central to the acquisition of land, raw materials and other resources of central importance to the accumulation of wealth'. In other words, within society and social relationships, racism has a history, a description, and a value. Within the sector of ECEC in England, race and racism are acknowledged as operating and influential (Seltzer and O'Brien, 2024; Smidt, 2020; Tembo, 2021). Seltzer and O'Brien (2024) allude to research indicating that children as young as three years old are negatively influenced by racialised views and experiences. On the one hand, exposing racism in ECEC usually involves drawing attention to the meaningful differences between individuals and groups, while tackling racism requires action for justice. Exposing and addressing racial inequality in ECEC can be initiated through the application of activities, critical theories and social justice activism. For example, first by applying critical race theory (CRT) to research projects one can explain, frame and justify the lived racial experiences of the marginalised against five principles (Tembo, 2021; Thomas 2012). This includes accepting the normalisation of racism in everyday life, showcasing stories and counter stories on race, exposing liberal agendas and convergence of equality, acknowledging white supremacy, and accounting for intersectionality (Thomas, 2024). Hence the organisational changes that need to take place in an educational setting become clearer. Second, enacting an anti-racist approach to ECEC practices would require active change on an institution and individual level (Brown et al., 2010; Escayg, 2019). Anti-racism is action for adjustment that must confront, reflect, dismantle and compensate in its process. In ECEC anti-racism is not merely about providing diverse resources for teachers and children but is about disrupting attitudes, practices and policies. Reflective paradigms, such as the MANDELA model created by Tedam (2012), and applied by Lumsden (2023a, 2023b), provides a firm grounding for early years settings and care practitioners who seek to be anti-racist in their work. The core elements of the model applied in early childhood spaces seek to frame questions around 'Make time; Acknowledge; Needs; Differences; Education experiences; Life experiences; and Age' (Lumsden, 2023b). This is so that through using a reflection template the facilitation of conversations will contribute to the engagement and inclusion of all in ECEC. Considering Escayg (2019, p. 13), transformative anti-racism 'lay[s] bare the mechanisms of racism and encourages children [and adults] to question and critique systems', resulting in institutional and social change. However, to be truly transformative, anti-racist approaches in the early years must be activated in a sustained and tolerant manner that is forward-thinking.

Anti-racist pedagogy in English early childhood education and care (ECEC)

Contemporary theories provide a framing for the analysis of experiences, concepts and processes, yet they have been criticised for not substantially creating change in relation to the racialised experiences of children and adults (Borsheim-Black, 2015; Leonardo, 2018; Rodman, 2020; Saul, 2021). Since Gloria Ladson-Billings' seminal works on the operation of racism in education within the United States of America (USA) (Ladson-Billings, 1998; Ladson-Billings and Tate, 1995), there have been several English studies that applied the tenets of CRT to policy agendas and children and educator experiences (Barron, 2014; Gillborn, 2006; Tembo, 2021; Warmington et al., 2018). However, inclusive and equitable measures are still largely popular in educational management teams across England as they are practice and resource focused (Cumbria County Council, 2024; Devarakonda, 2016; Riddell, 2009; Wandsworth Borough Council, 2024). Therefore, equality targets and measures are a positive match to pedagogical developmental agendas in the early childhood stages. In fact, such targets and measures are short sighted in relation to creating long-term and sustained change of attitudes and beliefs on race and racism, that themselves are embedded and often unidentified. It has become apparent that race terms and political agendas are influential in the perception and values adopted by various early childhood providers when seeking an equitable learning environment for babies and young children (Clarke and Watson, 2014; MacNevin and Berman, 2017; Tembo, 2021; Warmington et al., 2018). For example, in the USA there has been an active demonisation of CRT in educational settings (Rufo, 2023; Smith, 2021; Waxman, 2022), while in the United Kingdom (UK) politicians have been outspoken against teaching CRT in curriculum (Nelson, 2020; Warmington, 2020). Whatever one's position on the use of theory versus the reality of its application for early childhood developmental curriculum, addressing progress and developmental markers is often the focus of teaching input and engagement within ECEC. It is widely accepted that the environment around the child is of critical importance and takes priority in all pedagogical planning and actions (Bradbury and Swailes, 2022; Bradford, 2012; Bronfenbrenner, 1979; Tudge et al., 2021).

Pedagogy is the methods, practice and theory of teaching (Hall et al., 2008). By its nature pedagogy embeds strategies, techniques and philosophies to guide the learning and development of children. To understand how pedagogy aligns with anti-racism, it is important to account for legislation and historical events that deeply impact culture and identities. By considering the influence of significant incidents, it is possible to acknowledge why educators use various activities to address racial inequality in their settings. In England there was first recognition of race and racism in legislation that sought to tackle discrimination in public places (Race Relations Act, 1965). The later Race Relations Act (1976), although not directly focused on ECEC, provided the backdrop in which some early childhood providers accepted the need for employment initiatives and policies that attempted to address racism in the lived experience of teachers and children. More recently, following the recorded death of George Floyd in the USA on May 25, 2020, heightened awareness of the treatment of diverse groups in society rapidly grew in countries around the world. The social movement for change escalated against a compassionate global viewing of the inequalities that manifested in the life and murder of George Floyd, a black man, at the hands of police officers. Consequently, numerous organisations and institutions recognised the need for introspection and change in relation to race-related policy and practice (Tedam and Cane, 2022). In ECEC settings in England there was a re-embracing of diversity and equity policy with recognition of both children and teachers from varying ethnic backgrounds (Batty et al., 2021; Boyle, 2022; Capita, 2020; Tembo, 2021). Anti-racist approaches came to the front of the psyche of early childhood professionals and the wider public. This compassion sprouted again from a stagnated era of racism reporting and race equality promotion following the implementation of recommendations from the Stephen Lawrence Inquiry (Macpherson, 1999) and the Race Relations (Amendment) Act (2000); both had previously significantly impacted early years settings in England. The substantial influence of McPherson's inquiry, following the murder of the black teenager Stephen Lawrence at a bus stop in London in 1993, meant that all educational providers had a role in addressing 'institutional racism' alongside the police force. Consequently, anti-racist approaches in early childhood education and care settings are evident today. For example, these include the development and accessibility of anti-racist policy (now widely known as equality, diversity, and inclusion [EDI] policy), the recording all racist incidents (zero-tolerance action against racist behaviour and language), equitable access for all children, culturally relevant teaching, and diverse community engagement. Yet these are by nature professional methods or activities in early childhood settings that can be criticised as neglectful of a third aspect of pedagogy, which is critical theory (Freire, 1970). To be tolerant and truly equitable, anti-racist pedagogy by its nature must have method, practice and theory combined in ECEC. Anti-racist pedagogy is not tokenistic and should still operate long after racialised incidents of public interest have been forgotten in current affairs.

Anti-racist pedagogy is a framework aimed at challenging systemic racism and promoting inclusivity and belonging within education, including early childhood settings. The core principle of an anti-racist pedagogy acknowledges that an organisation or institution plays a core role in perpetuating and/or dismantling race-related inequalities (Escayg, 2019; Smidt, 2020). Therefore, for early childhood settings in England, an anti-racist pedagogy contains elements that challenge racism, promote cultural awareness, work towards equity and create a form of social justice for children and educators. The updated Early Years Foundation Stage (EYFS) statutory framework includes learning and development obligations for children from birth to five years old in England (DfE, 2023). Much like its predecessors, the EYFS framework establishes goals for promoting equality diversity and anti-discrimination in early years practice.

However, it fails to mention key pedagogies for addressing race and anti-racism in ECEC. On their own, such curriculum frameworks (DfE, 2023), which are goals based and legally orientated, are limited in ensuring system-wide initiatives for forward-looking social movements of racial justice. Consequently, anti-racist pedagogy must at its core seek to ensure that babies, children, educators and stakeholders in early childhood settings feel heard, valued, respected, and included, all consistently. First, anti-racist pedagogy in the early years seeks to ingrain content that celebrates the diverse racial and cultural backgrounds of the children and babies in their care. This includes creating visibility of different cultures, languages and traditions in the learning environment. Anti-racist pedagogy does not merely operate this as tokenistic gestures but emphasises the importance of acknowledging and showcasing diversity all the time. Second, anti-racist teaching and instruction adopts cultural resources and experiences so that practices are responsive to improving learning processes. For example, in some English early years settings, teachers used dual language books within their lessons to meet the needs of Punjabi and Urdu speaking children to encourage simultaneous reading (Conteh, 2011, p. 216). Third, anti-racist pedagogy in early years settings encourages children in their formative years to develop critical and questioning skills including on aspects of race and privilege. Although this involves deep consideration of theory in relation to practice, ECEC providers work best at creating distinctive opportunities for children to discuss and examine race and racism using language that is accessible to them. In age-appropriate ways, acknowledging children and educators' identities is crucial within an early years anti-racist pedagogy. As Urbani *et al.* (2022) suggest, this is the formation of an anti-racist critical consciousness that educators from majority ethnic groupings must embed in their early years work. Finally, an anti-racist pedagogy in the early years commits to the creation and maintenance of an inclusive environment. This inevitably is a long-term endeavour that can only really be recognised when a child of any race and cultural background has an intense sense of belonging in an educational setting. Although many ECEC institutions have the words *inclusion* and *equity* in their policies and plans, many do not develop that sense of true belonging (Arndt, 2018), and this is often because of the limitations that arise in implementing activities only. In anti-racist pedagogy in the early years there should be embedded all the fundamentals of teaching: method, practice and theory of race. However, frameworks in England mention only 'race and anti-discrimination' in the context of the Equality Act (2010). This legislation brought together anti-discrimination laws to advance equality across public organisations through identified protected characteristics. Yet there is arguably now scope for the explicit inclusion of 'anti-racism' pedagogical terms to go further than current law dictates, ensuring the ongoing celebration of diverse races and cultures, enacting anti-racist teaching for learning, cultivating critical skills and maintaining inclusivity and belonging. Anti-racism must be transformative because it demonstrates a commitment to working against racism rather than simply not being racist, because it is a requirement by law and a policy guidance document.

Implementing anti-racist pedagogy in early years education in England

As discussed, earlier anti-racist pedagogy has four core identifiable features that demand time and commitment from early childhood educators. These are to celebrate diverse races and cultures, enact anti-racist teaching for learning, cultivate critical skills and maintain inclusivity and belonging. These four elements must be rooted in the curriculum, classroom environment and educators. The latter in many cases requires personal education that challenges belief systems and is by far the most difficult to implement. Hence actions for implementing anti-racist pedagogy in English early years settings have resulted in changing resources such as books, toys and classroom physical displays to reflect the full diversity of children and staff that attend a setting (Cumbria County Council, 2024; Letterbox Library, 2024). A significant challenge of this type of action is that it is perceived as a gesture that is minimum effort or nonchalantly included after a period of racist trauma, uncertainty or race-related events of public interest (such as after the deaths of Stephen Lawrence and George Floyd) (Ang, 2010; Tedam and Cane, 2022). Indeed, when considered through a race theoretical lens such as CRT, these changes align to the concept of interest convergence and compound the perspective of the majority rather than the minority. For example, in English educational settings incorporating aspects of fundamental British values led to concerns from many Muslim families that they were not wholly accepted or represented (Vincent, 2019). Claims of racialisation and prejudice were raised when the religious ethos of families become problematic for early years settings seeking to showcase diversity (Johnson, 2019). Such criticisms will arise for ECEC leaders that adopt race diversity initiatives without wider community engagement and an anti-racist pedagogical framing. It can be easy to polarise the experiences of anti-racism in early years environments when the limits of the advancement of justice and equality are not forward looking and enduring. Therefore, when implementing anti-racist pedagogy in the early years, three core methods must be adopted.

One primary method of implementing anti-racist pedagogy in the early years is through culturally responsive teaching. In ECEC this takes on the form of inclusion and equity by centering, valuing, integrating and respecting the culture and identity of babies and children as they grow and develop alongside their parents or guardians. This is crucial in terms of acknowledging the differences each child brings to the early learning environment. According to Kellett (2011), this can be easily achieved through a mosaic approach of child and parent friendly activities as part of a cultural discovery process. This fits with current policy and guidance in England in relation to fostering an understanding of the world (DfE, 2023). Culturally responsive teaching is not just changing teaching materials as part of tokenistic measures but rather looks for materials and co-creates them to showcase languages and identities of difference (Dwivedi, 2005). Lesser-known elements of culture are explored and centred as learning for both the child and the educator. This is a route to making the unfamiliar familiar for all. To this end educators and children in early childhood settings share stories and counter stories in respect of their different cultures (D'Arcy, 2017; Matebekwane, 2022). This is a learning process. Language is not a deficit for development but for early years educators and their stakeholders it is the mindful incorporation of skills that can be shared and encouraged. Indeed, culturally responsive teaching of language in the curriculum is a way to practice new skills and behaviours by adults and children. Historically, the deficiencies of children's English language development have caused many educators to stereotype and label early years children who have accents and bilingual speaking parents or guardians (Coard, 1971). Some early years practitioners have prioritised English speaking and neglected to consider contemporary neurological research that suggests young children have silent periods and are highly competent if speaking and hearing more than one language (Cambridge Assessment, 2013; Costa and Sebastian-Gilles, 2014; Goswami, 2011; Siraj-Blatchford and Clarke, 2000). There must not be a fear of slow language development in culturally responsive early childhood teaching; but rather and awareness and sensitivity towards norms and stereotypes of those speaking a non-English language. Modelling respectable behaviour in these aspects is critical. Likewise, in culturally responsive teaching early childhood educators must ensure that assessment with young children is well considered. It is vital that routes of assessment demonstrate the strengths of the child alongside giving meaning to future developments so that resilience and contribution is established. The standards of assessment in early years curriculum guidance must be flexibly applied (DfE, 2023) and not surmised by educators in a rush to target set. Comparing children and early childhood providers is harmful to children and the progression of anti-racist pedagogy. It is well known theoretically that a hierarchy and systems of inequality exist in education within England. At such an early age, simplifying targets establishes harmful educational practices and can result in the labelling of children as slower learners (Clark, 2022). Culturally responsive teaching also requires ongoing professional development and reflection by early years educators. Training and development of all staff in relation to race related matters and on establishing a culture of reflection and consideration is important. Continuous professional development and the reflection of staff on their own biases and assumptions in an open and invested manner results in a culturally responsive early years setting (Henry-Allain and Lloyd-Rose, 2021; Lane, 2008; Lumsden, 2023b). Budgets for race, anti-racist responsiveness and professional development must be protected if any ongoing anti-racist pedagogy is to succeed (Eardley and Gilder, 2024).

A second method of implementing anti-racist pedagogy in the early years is through critical conversations. This method involves shaping the early years environment and creating it as a safe and respectful space where children, their parents/guardians and educators can explore and challenge their own beliefs and privileges. Although it is challenging to enact critical conversations, by involving teachers, children, administrators, parents/guardians and community members in becoming active listeners, demonstrate a level of compassion and empathy (Williams, 2020). In early years settings this will result in conversations (that are also age appropriate) and transparent in order to build and sustain understanding and individual responsibility. For young children in early childhood settings this is providing them with opportunities to ask questions and express their thoughts and feelings. While for educators this can not only be a platform for discussion but also a means of feedback from colleagues, families and children to add new insights in their own teaching approaches and make changes that provide avenues for advocacy. At the heart of critical conversations is critical thinking and reflection. According to Hooks (2010), this vital in child development liberation. She proposes that critical thinking from its establishment in young children encourages them to reflect on their own identity and how it impacts their experiences and interactions. A resilient child is formed. They grow into youth and adulthood being able to harness great skills in addressing the inequalities of racism, whereby creating a new generation of critical thinkers and activists. Through critical conversations, implicit biases can be addressed and the use of racialised terms and theory in education for teaching and learning fully incorporated. This method does not just confront racism but also tackles long-term institutional manifestations (Escayg, 2019).

A third method of implementing anti-racist pedagogy in the early years is through community engagement for democracy. Involving parents/guardians and the wider community within ECEC are important in any child's development. The community around the child has been a long-standing focus that is often associated with Bronfenbrenner's ecological systems theory (1979). This theory points towards the importance of context and the environment in shaping human development. Many early years educators apply the levels of this system to babies, infants and young children in terms of their interaction and influences on them at various levels/systems in operation (Haynes *et al.*, 2022). However, when viewing this applied theory with an anti-racist lens one of the challenges is managing fairness for all as collaboration with families and communities highlight many diverse agendas. The context and environment shift over time for any human development (both educators and children), therefore to balance community engagement through activities, time and history are sensitive elements (Bronfenbrenner, 1979; Clark, 2020). Community engagement should therefore include aspects of democracy whereby all feel invited and share in expertise and traditions and the past racial trauma are reflected on and restorative. The challenges of community engagement in the early years within English settings have been researched extensively, and although bring many positive aspects, the challenge of sustainability and relevance are often accounted for (Boyd, 2018; Brown and Rogers, 2015; Murray, 2022a). Implementing an anti-racist pedagogical stance in community engagement through democracy requires a form of active participation by early years educators and the communities they serve. Indeed, children are involved in decision making, and their families and society also contribute ideas; this empowers all. One of the greatest challenges in implementing anti-racist pedagogy with a community democratic focus is that policies and budget are often limited. In England alone it has been suggested that early years entitlement falls short of the cost of delivery by up to 9% in 2024 (Local Government Association, 2023). This will impact the reach of community engagement with families that are struggling. Notwithstanding the legacy of the 2020 Covid-19 pandemic where the influence on health and development in the early years will only be fully known in future years (La Valle *et al.*, 2022). Democracy in community engagement for anti-racist pedagogy needs systematic and monetarily commitments to promote long-term social change that includes the excluded. Accountability and transparency for early years leaders, educators and other key decision-makers form a fundamental aspect of this type of anti-racist pedagogy. As such community engagement as a form of democracy demonstrates accountability in processes and outcomes, and as appropriate this is accessible to all members of the community around the child.

There are some good examples of anti-racist pedagogy in literature and contemporary research. In work undertaken by Tager (2022, p. 10), she highlights that anti-racism requires educator materials to always be reviewed, examined, and revised for teachers to be established as lifelong learners and children to so reflect this process. She also strongly promotes the inclusion of visual arts, dance and theatre to capture the stories and lives of the children and their communities. Maitra and Miler (2005) in their clinical considerations point towards the need for cultural relativism in practice. They include case study examples of talking with children about their opinions as part of an anti-racist approach with 5-year-olds that enabled them to process trauma. Although not named as anti-racist pedagogy, one higher educational provider facilitated early childhood students' engagement in critical conversations and observations within ECEC settings (Murray, 2022b). The use of children's artefacts as tools for questioning enabled the establishment of a contextualised co-researcher exploratory environment. Through harnessing creative questioning, the process of language development, a form of critical consciousness was started. Such early childhood anti-racist pedagogy demonstrates the practice and embedding of theory that is linked to racial rights and responsibilities for young children. Anti-racist pedagogy safe spaces in ECEC refers to the environment where children, their families and educators feel able to engage in discussions on race, racism, and social justice. In such a supportive and encouraging environment the mechanisms for resolution and restitution is respectfully achievable. Souto-Manning (2013) explains that within such safe environments staff can revolutionise their own positioning in the workplace, create career progression and incorporate reflection spaces for others (be that teachers and administrators). This has meant that conversations about race and racial identity are not emotionally draining but rather restorative and welcomed by ECEC practitioners. Unlike tokenistic gestures, such as running a one-off cultural event (which many educational institutions do as part of decolonisation activities), critical conversations have been formed in safe spaces for continual growth, representation and participatory decision making in the early years workforce. Finally, Smidt (2020) in her writings recounts a period where sustained campaigns from children, parents and teachers resulted in the overturning of an unjust deportation decision. The unified community front meant that at the outcome all 'were equally praised and pilloried' (Smidt, 2020, p. 87). They now regularly meet in their alliance and for addressing systemic barriers as well as celebrating local advancements.

Transformative anti-racist activism

To be free is to be without constraints. Those that seek racial equality often require a liberation from oppression (Freire, 1970; Hooks, 2010) and in contemporary movements call for reparations (Spriprakash, 2022). However, in early year settings in England it can be difficult to conceptualise and enact long lasting anti-racist pedagogy. Indeed, many who claim to have anti-racist pedagogical strategies in nurseries and early childhood settings often only have actioned short-lived cultural activities (Escayg, 2019; MacNevin and Berman, 2017; Seltzer and O'Brien, 2024). For those subjected to racialised experiences, anti-racism is not only a declaration of changes by key early years stakeholders but rather a shaped identity that must daily demonstrate commitment to a better state of being. Hence to those on the periphery, true equality is a compulsion by all to continuous improvement. Anti-racist pedagogy would benefit from adopting a long-term view to racial activism, advocacy and restoration. Activism must play a more crucial role in shaping early years settings that deeply appreciate advocating for change by giving voice to marginalised children and their families, alongside practitioners. When so many intersecting protected characteristics operate in legal requirements for early years providers (Equality Act, 2010; DfE, 2023) it can be easy to treat matters of EDI as a targeted list of actions. However, it has taken time to institutionalise racism, and it is an ongoing commitment to dismantle it. Therefore, simply put, anti-racist activism is learning, listening, applying theory and amplifying marginalised voices, whereas transformative anti-racist activism unceasingly raises awareness, consistently campaigns for change and persistently harnesses critical thought. Transformative anti-racism by its nature repels complacency on matters of race in the early years community. It is restorative in its application within ECEC, and thus transformative anti-racist activism nourishes the belonging of babies, young children and their community. Therefore, a model of transformative anti-racist activism for early years settings is encapsulated in Figure 2.1.

Racism is discrimination that influences the lives of babies, young children, families, and staff working in early childhood settings. As part of a transformative anti-racist approach, early years institutions must be committed to not tolerating racism in any form. Therefore, consistent financial and time resources should be dedicated to opposing racism and seeking a community of belonging. Within that are key markers that characterise the embodiment of anti-racism,

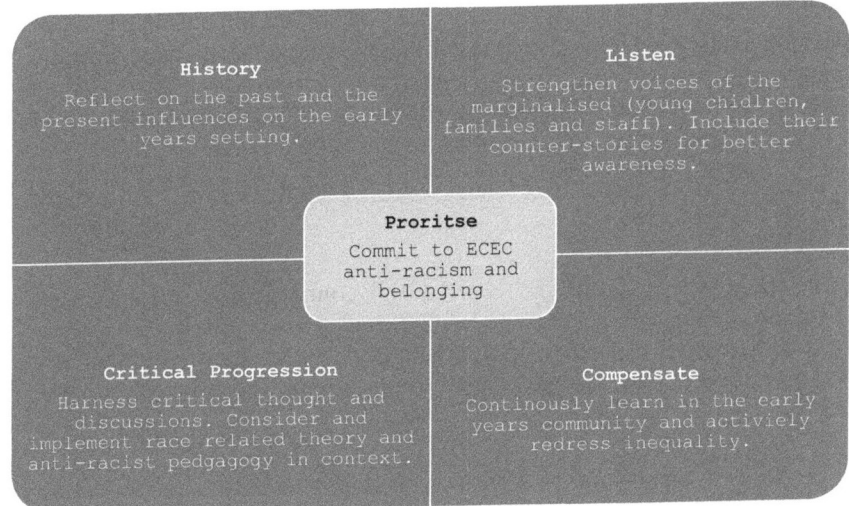

Figure 2.1 Ongoing transformation elements for anti-racist activism within early childhood education and care spaces.

Such as considering history and current events that might be locally, nationally and internationally influential on the marginalised. Leadership in early childhood settings would do well to genuinely listen to the voices different to their own. Doing so requires all to develop critical thinking and being skills, from the youngest to the oldest. For critical consciousness to take hold in ECEC there must also be the application of anti-racist theory and practice in context, notably not just activities for change as discussed earlier in this chapter. Finally, transformative anti-racist activism is a continuous campaign of racial education, resistance and redress. The elements in Figure 2.1 do not always need to operate as singular stages or as part of a linear process. They are key elements that might occur simultaneously for continuous improvement. The elements enable early years settings to integrate long-term transformation through relational responsibility. This mean working 'with' early years babies, young children, families and staff and not 'to' or 'for' them. The result is early years spaces where a change way of thinking and working is part of the being of an institution, with anti-racism as a core element of its being to belong (See Tables 2.1 and 2.2).

Conclusion

Racism in early years spaces is challenging to identify and systemically tackle. In contemporary times drawing attention to measures of 'race and anti-discrimination' in legislation and policy (Equality Act 2010; DfE 2023) has neglected the nature of anti-racist activism in ECEC. This chapter has presented the core terms associated with race, racism and anti-racist pedagogy in ECEC. It has argued for a sustained and tolerant integration of method, practice and theory in pedagogy. This is most evident in culturally responsive teaching, cultivating critical conversations and facilitating ongoing community engagement through democracy. Therefore, transformative anti-racist activism as proposed in this chapter is critical agency that continuously listens, reviews, examines, revises and restores in early year settings.

> **Activity**
>
> Although this chapter has charted the contradictory and contested nature of race and racism in early childhood settings, often practitioners and researchers seek 'top tips' for change. There are many contemporary models and guides that can be used to support anti-racism in ECEC. For example:
>
> - Are you starting anti-racist work with children and local communities?
>
> Check out: 'The tiney guide to becoming an inclusive, anti-racist early educator' by Henry-Allain and Lloyd-Rose (2021). Website: https://www.tiney.co/blog/becoming-an-inclusive-anti-racist-early-educator/

Reflection questions and possible developments

Table 2.1 Early years institution and staff

Consider	Develop
Do all ECEC staff have a knowledge of the meaning of race, racism and anti-racist pedagogy?	✓ Establish regular opportunities for staff training and conversations about the race, racism and anti-racism. ✓ Develop staff confidence in speaking about race and racism. ✓ Explore and apply pedagogical theories and philosophies of influence.
Is there information about the ethnicity and diversity within the organisation?	✓ Regularly compile and examine the data associated with race. Be sure to collaborate with others when reviewing and revising data driven actions. ✓ Listen and reflect on the stories and counter-stories within the ECEC institution and wider community.

(Continued)

Table 2.1 (Continued)

Consider	Develop
How can the organisation demonstrate transformative anti-racist activism?	✓ All staff and the institution establish a commitment to anti-racism. ✓ Consistently self-reflect. ✓ Protect money and time for sustainable race related pedagogy and activities. ✓ Establish a network for organisational critical conversations on race and anti-racism.

Table 2.2 Children, families and the wider community

Consider	Develop
Do all children and families have access and feel a sense of belonging to the ECEC environment?	✓ Form sustainable networks and relationships through conversations and ECEC activities. ✓ Observe the physical spaces where children are. Ensure there is representation of the diversity of the children and families in the ECEC physical and teaching environment. ✓ Draw on the resources of local businesses and charities to facilitate a sense of local community, tolerance and compassion.
How are critical thinking skills cultivated in young children?	✓ Embed a culture of questioning and learning between the child and the ECEC practitioner. ✓ Creatively integrate race related research opportunities in the ECEC environment. ✓ As appropriate, draw on the Mosaic approach when listening and learning from children.
How can children, families and the wider community become transformative anti-racist activists?	✓ Meet the basic needs of children and families and/or 'green light'/signpost to services that can. Build on aspects of transparency, trust and compassion. ✓ Co-construct forums and/or advocacy groups among the ECEC community to empower children and their families. ✓ Regularly celebrate success and special occasions with children, families and the local community. Memorialise cultural representations and celebrations so that it is accessible to all. Consider using photographs and technology to cultivate growth and activism.

References

Akala. (2019), *Natives: Race and Class in the Ruins of Empire*. London: Two Roads.

Arndt, S. (2018), Early childhood teacher cultural otherness and belonging. *Contemporary Issues in Early Childhood*, *19*(4), pp. 392–403.

Ang, L. (2010), Critical perspectives on cultural diversity in early childhood: Building an inclusive curriculum and provision. *Early Years*, *30*(1), pp. 41–52.

Barron, I. (2014), Finding a voice: A figured worlds approach to theorising young children's identities. *Journal of Early Childhood Research*, *12*(3), pp. 251–263.

Batty, D., Parveen, N. and Thomas, T. (2021), Hundreds of schools in England sign up for anti-racist curriculum. *The Guardian*, 26 March. Available at https://www.theguardian.com/education/2021/mar/26/schools-england-anti-racist-curriculum (Accessed January 4, 2024).

Borsheim-Black, C. (2015), "It's pretty much white": Challenges and opportunities of an antiracist approach to literature instruction in a multilayered white context. *Research in the Teaching of English*, *49*(4), pp. 407–429.

Boyd, D. (2018), Early childhood education for sustainability and the legacies of two pioneering giants. *Early Year: Journal of International Research and Development*, *38*(2), pp. 227–239.

Boyle, R. C. (2022), We are not 'mixed', we are 'all': Understanding the educational experiences of mixed ethnicity children to enhance learner agency. *Education 3–13*, *50*(4), pp. 471–482.

Bradbury, A. and Swailes, R. (eds). (2022), *Early Childhood Theories Today*. London: Learning Matters.

Bradford, H. (2012), *Appropriate Environments for Children Under Three*. Abingdon: Routledge.

Bronfenbrenner, U. (1979), *The Ecology of Human Development: Experiment by Nature and Design*. Massachusetts: Harvard University Press.

Brown, C. and Roger, S. (2015), Knowledge creation as an approach to facilitating evidence informed practice: examining ways to measure the success of using this method with early years practitioners in Camden (London). *Journal of Educational Change*, *16*, pp. 79–99.

Brown, S., Souto-Manning, M. and Laman, T. T. (2010), Seeing the strange in the familiar: Unpacking racialized practices in early childhood settings. *Race, Ethnicity and Education*, *13*(4), pp. 513–532.

Cambridge Assessment. (2013), *What Is Literacy? An Investigation into Definition of English as a Subject and the Relationship between English Literacy and 'Being Literate'*. Cambridge: University of Cambridge.

Capita. (2020), Insight: Reflecting on equality, diversity, and inclusion in the early years. *Entrust: Inspiring Futures*. Available at https://www.entrust-ed.co.uk/insights/reflecting-equality-diversity-and-inclusion-early-years (Accessed January 4, 2024).

Clark, A. (2022), *Slow Knowledge and the Unhurried Child: Time for Slow Pedagogies in Early Childhood Education*. London: Routledge.

Clark, R. M. (2020), *Childhood in Society for the Early Years*. 4th Ed. London: Learning Matters.

Clarke, V. and Watson, D. (2014), Examining whiteness in a children's centre. *Contemporary Issues in Early Childhood*, *15*(1), pp. 69–80.

Conteh, J. (2011), Empowering learners from 3–11 through language diversity and bilingualism. In J. Moyles, J. Georgeson and J. Payler (eds.), *Beginning Teaching, Beginning Learning: In Early Years and Primary Education* (pp. 215–225). Maidenhead: Open University Press.

Coard, B. (1971), *How the West Indian Child Is Made Educationally Subnormal in the British School System*. Kingston, Jamacia: McDermott Publishing.

Costa, A. and Sebastian-Gilles, N. (2014), How does the bilingual experience sculpt the brain? *Nature Reviews Neuroscience*, *15*(5), pp. 336–345.

Cumbria County Council. (2024), *Embedding Cultures and Diversity within an Early Years Setting and Supporting Children with Learning English as an Additional Language*. Available at https://www.cumbria.gov.uk/eLibrary/Content/Internet//537/955/6075/6263/6314/42965143226.pdf (Accessed February 3, 2024).

D'Arcy, K. (2017), Using counter-stories to challenge stock stories about Traveller families. *Race, Ethnicity and Education*, 20(5), pp. 636–649.

Devarakonda, C. (2016), *Diversity and Inclusion in Early Childhood: An Introduction*. London: SAGE.

DfE. (2023), Early years foundation stage statutory framework. *Department for Education*. Available at https://www.gov.uk/government/publications/early-years-foundation-stage-framework--2 (Accessed January 4, 2024).

Dwivedi, K. N. (ed) (2005), *Meeting the Needs of Ethnic Minority Children*. London: Jessica Kingsley Publishers.

Eardley, N. and Gilder, L. (2024), Budget: Do councils spend too much on diversity schemes? *British Broadcasting Corporation (BBC)*, 6 March. Available at https://www.bbc.co.uk/news/uk-politics-68482172 (Accessed March 10, 2024).

Escayg, K. A. (2019), Exploring anti-racism in early childhood education: Teacher identity and classroom practices. *Bridging Research and Practice*, May/June. pp. 11–13.

Equality Act. (2010), London: TSO.

Freire, P. (1970), *Pedagogy of the Oppressed*. New York: Seabury Press.

Gillborn, D. (2006), Critical race theory and education: racism and ant-racism in educational theory and praxis. *Discourse: Studies in the Cultural Politics of Education*, 27(1), pp. 11–32.

Gillborn, D. (2008), *Racism and Education: Coincidence or Conspiracy?* London: Routledge.

Goswami, U. (2011), What cognitive neuroscience really tells educators about learning and development. In J. Moyles, J. Georgeson and J. Payler (eds.), *Beginning Teaching, Beginning Learning: In Early Years and Primary Education*. Maidenhead: Open University Press, pp. 21–31.

Hall, K., Murphy, P. and Soler, J. (eds). (2008), *Pedagogy and Practice: Culture and Identities*. London: SAGE Publications Ltd.

Hayes, N., O'Toole, L. and Halpenny, A. M. (2022), *Introducing Bronfenbrenner: A Guide for Practitioners and Students in Early Years Education*. London: Routledge.

Henry-Allain, L. and Lloyd-Rose, M. (2021), The tiney guide to becoming an inclusive, anti-racist early educator. *Tiney*. Available at: https://www.tiney.co/guides/ (Accessed March 10, 2024).

Hooks, B. (2010), *Teaching Critical Thinking: Practical Wisdom*. New York: Routledge.

Kellett, J. (2011), Accessing children's voice and experiences. In J. Moyles, J. Georgeson and J. Payler (eds.), *Beginning Teaching, Beginning Learning: In Early Years and Primary Education* (pp. 226–238). Maidenhead: Open University Press.

Johnson, B. (2019), The parents who say their kids are being indoctrinated by UK schools. *Sky News*, 19 May. Available at: https://news.sky.com/story/the-parents-who-say-their-kids-are-being-indoctrinated-by-uk-schools-11720871 (Accessed February 3, 2024).

Ladson-Billings, G. (1998), Just what is critical race theory and what's it doing in a nice field like education? *International Journal of Qualitative Studies in Education*, 11(1), pp. 7–24.

Ladson-Billings, G. and Tate, W. F. (1995), Towards a critical race theory of education. *Teachers College Record (1970)*, 97(1), pp. 47–68.

Lane, J. (2008), *Young Children and Racial Justice: Taking Action for Racial Equality in the Early Years—Understanding the Past, Thinking about the Present, Planning for the Future*. London: National Children's Bureau.

La Valle, I., Lewis, J., Crawford, C., Paull, G., Lloyd, E., Ott, E., Mann, G., Drayton, E., Cattoretti, G., Hall, A. and Willis, E. (2022), *Implications of COVID for Early Childhood Education and Care in England*. London: Centre for Evidence and Implementation.

Leonardo, Z. (2018), Dis-orientating western knowledge: Coloniality, curriculum and crisis. *Cambridge Anthropology*, *36*(2), pp. 7–20.

Letterbox Library. (2024), *A children's booksellers celebrating equality & diversity*. Available at https://www.letterboxlibrary.com/acatalog/Early-Years-0-5yrs.html (Accessed February 3, 2024).

Local Government Association. (2023), *Early Education and Childcare: Changes and Challenges for the Future*. Available at: https://www.local.gov.uk/publications/early-education-and-childcare-changes-and-challenges-future (Accessed February 3, 2024).

Lumsden, E. (2023a), Curriculum that promotes equality and challenges racism and sexism. In L. Grenier and C. Vollans (eds.), *Putting the EYFS into Practice*. London: Sage Publications.

Lumsden, E. (2023b), *MANDELA Model for Early Childhood Education and Care (ECEC) – Mandela Model Workbook*. Available at https://tapestry.info/the-mandela-model-workbook-2.html (Accessed March 10, 2024).

MacNevin, M. and Berman, R. (2017), The black baby doll doesn't fit the disconnect between early childhood diversity policy, early childhood educator practice, and children's play. *Early Child Development and Care*, *187*(5–6), pp. 827–839.

Macpherson, W. (1999), *The Stephen Lawrence Inquiry: Report of an Inquiry by Sir William Macpherson of Cluny*. London: TSO.

Maitra and Miler. (2005), Children, families and therapists: Clinical considerations and ethnic minority cultures. In K. N. Dwivedi (ed.), *Meeting the Needs of Ethnic Minority Children* (pp. 108–129). London: Jessica Kingsley Publishers.

Matebekwane, K. A. (2022), Counter-storytelling: A form of resistance and a tool to reimagine more inclusive early childhood education spaces. *Education*, *28*(1b), pp. 116–125.

Murray, J. (2022a), All things being equal. Editorial. *International Journal of Early Years Education*, *30*(2), pp. 127–129.

Murray, J. (2022b), Any questions? Young children questioning their early childhood education settings. *European Early Childhood Research Journal*, *30*(1), pp. 108–130.

Nelson, F. (2020), Kemi Badenoch: The problem with critical race theory. *The Spectator*. Available at: https://www.spectator.co.uk/article/kemi-badenoch-the-problem-with-critical-race-theory/ (Accessed January 4, 2024).

Race Relations Act. (1965), London: HMSO.

Race Relations Act. (1976), London: HMSO.

Race Relations (Amendment) Act. (2000), London: TSO.

Riddell, S. (2009), Social justice, equality and inclusion in Scottish education. *Discourse: Studies in the Cultural Politics of Education*, *30*(3), pp. 282–296.

Rodman, G. B. (2020), What we (still) need to learn: Stuart Hall and the struggle against racism. *New Formations*, *102*, pp. 78–91.

Rufo, C. F. (2023), *Critical Race Theory Briefing Book*. Available at https://christopherrufo.com/p/crt-briefing-book (Accessed January 4, 2024).

Saul, R. (2021), Racism on the playground: Notes from parenthood. *Multicultural Perspectives*, *23*(4), pp. 248–258.

Seltzer, M. C. and O'Brien, L. M. (2024), Fostering racial literacy in early childhood contexts. *Early Childhood Educational Journal*, *52*, pp. 181–189.

Siraj-Blatchford, S. and Clarke, P. (2000), *Supporting Identity, Diversity and Language in the Early Years*. Buckingham: Open University Press.

Smidt, S. (2020), *Creating an Anti-Racist Culture in the Early Years: An Essential Guide for Practitioners*. Abingdon: Routledge.

Smith, D. (2021), How did Republicans turn critical race theory into a winning electoral issue? Explainer. *The Guardian*. Available at https://www.theguardian.com/us-news/2021/nov/03/republicans-critical-race-theory-winning-electoral-issue (Accessed February 8, 2024).

Souto-Manning, M. (2013), *Multicultural Teaching in Early Childhood Classroom*. Washington D.C: Teachers College Press.

Spriprakash, A. (2022), Reparations: Theorising just futures of education. *Discourse: Studies in the Cultural Politics of Education*, *44*(5), pp. 782–795.

Tager, M. (2022), *Anti-racist Pedagogy in the Early Childhood Classroom*. London: Lexington Books.

Tedam, P. (2012), The MANDELA model of practice learning. *The Journal of Practice Teaching and Learning*, *11*(2), pp. 60–76.

Tedam, P. and Cane, T. (2022), "We started talking about race and racism after George Floyd": Insights from research into practitioner preparedness for anti-racist social work practice in England. *Critical and Radical Social Work*, *10*(2), pp. 260–279.

Tembo, S. (2021), Black educators in (white) settings: Making racial identity visible in early childhood education and care in England, UK. *Journal of Early Childhood Research*, *19*(1), pp. 70–83.

Tudge, J. R. H., Navarro, J. L., Mercon-Vargas, E. A. and Payir, A. (2021), The promise and practice of early childhood educare in the writings of Urie Bronfenbrenner. *Early Child Development and Care*, *191*(7–8), pp. 1079–1088.

Waxman, O. B. (2022), Anti-'critical race theory' laws are working. Teachers are thinking twice about how they talk about race. *TIME*. 30 June. Available at https://time.com/6192708/critical-race-theory-teachers-racism/ (Accessed January 13, 2024).

Thomas, E. (2012), Beyond the culture of exclusion, using critical race theory to examine the perceptions of British 'minority ethnic' and Eastern 'immigrant' young people in English schools. *Intercultural Education*, *23*(6), pp. 501–511.

Thomas, E. (2024), *Critical Race Qualitative Methods*. Research methods: Diversifying and decolonising research [online series]. London: Sage Publications.

Urbani, J. M., Collado, C., Manalo, A. and Gonzalez, N. (2022), Building the on-ramp to inclusion: Developing critical consciousness in future early childhood educators. *Issues in Teacher Education*, *31*(2), pp. 91–121.

Vincent, C. (2019), Cohesion, citizenship and coherence: Schools' responses to the British values policy. *British Journal of Sociology of Education*, *40*(1), pp. 17–32.

Wandsworth Borough Council. (2024), *EDI Audit Tool for PVIs and Early Year Settings*. Available at https://earlyyears.wandsworth.gov.uk/Pages/Download/77d167b6-20c0-42ab-b565-2d982e650949/PageSectionDocuments (Accessed January 15, 2024).

Warmington, P. (2020), Critical race theory in England: Impact and opposition. *Identities*, *27*(1), pp. 20–27.

Warmington, P., Gillborn, D., Rollock, N. and Demask, S. (2018), "They can't handle the race agenda": Stakeholders' reflections on race and education policy, 1993–2013. *Educational Review*, *70*(4), pp. 409–426.

Williams, S. (2020), *Anti Racist Ally*. London: Harper Collins Publishers Ltd.

Wolgast, M. and Wolgast, S. M. (2024), Exclusionary and exploitative racism: Empirical analyses of two facets of contemporary racial ideologies. *Nordic Journal of Migration Research*, *14*(1), pp. 1–19.

3 Religion, Belonging and Childhood in the Primary Classroom

Matthew Vince

Introduction

Simran (aged 14) and Vraj (aged 11) talk about what it means to be a British Hindu. Simran discusses her hobbies, music and photography, while Vraj reveals that his favourite hobby is taekwondo. In the next scene, Vraj is smiling stood in front of a delicious cuisine and declares that 'this food looks tasty', followed by a voiceover from Simran shares that they are vegetarian and that it is a 'big part of being Hindu'. Simran explains how they believe that God is in everything, including animals, so it is important to respect all living things. Following this, Vraj happily expresses how being vegetarian is fun because all the dishes are so tasty and 'the spices are nice'. To a backdrop of animals and nature, Simran then links being vegetarian to their belief that God exists in everything and a respect for all living things (My Life My Religion, BBC Teach, 2020).

I draw attention to this video clip 'My Life My Religion' episode titled 'Meeting as two young British Hindus' (BBC Teach, 2020), and I recommend that you, the reader, watch it as it encapsulates the message of this chapter: that children should be encouraged to tell stories about the religious and spiritual aspects of their lives and have opportunity to explore these in their school contexts. When talking about who they are, Simran and Vraj begin by telling us about their hobbies. Their faith is introduced through food, specifically the 'fun' delicacies that Vraj is preparing. It is through these everyday experiences that central beliefs and practices of Hinduism are introduced: namely God, karma and the cycle of rebirth, and not the other way round. For Simran, Vraj and many others, these mundane, everyday social activities are part of what gives meaning being a 'British Hindu', and, in turn, the mundane and everyday are shaped by belonging to this community. As the teachers emphasise, the 'jigsaw' of their identities as 'British Hindus' is also created with other aspects of living in Britain today, whether they be budding photographers or trainee taekwondo masters (My Life My Religion, BBC Teach, 2020).

The 'My Life My Religion' (BBC Teach 2020) series is still groundbreaking in its giving voice to children of various faiths to talk about their religion. It is commonly used in Religious Education (RE) classrooms across Britain at both primary and secondary level because, historically, teaching resources have scarcely engaged with the voices of those who belong to a faith (CoRE, 2018). Such 'de-contextualised' representations of religion have long been criticised within RE (Benoit, 2021; Hayward, 2006; Vince, 2023), and the incorporation of everyday religious perspectives is a priority in the new vision of RE outlined by CoRE (2018). Likewise, initiatives such as the Discovering Muslims in Britain project (Vince, 2023) have sought to provide teachers with the disciplinary tools and teaching resources to incorporate these voices in the classroom.

Accordingly, the aim of this chapter is to acknowledge children's exploration of their sense of belonging to the religious and spiritual within the primary classroom. In particular, we consider how telling stories, and living them, is a powerful tool at the heart of this exploration, revealing how children are making sense of themselves, their beliefs and how they belong to these wider communities, religious or otherwise. Moreover, while these narratives may be messy, inconsistent or seemingly incoherent in relation to the 'facts' of religious traditions, it is vital to remember that this reflects children's own reflective, playful 'figuring out' of what these meanings mean to them. To do so, we begin with a brief survey of the disciplinary and policy foundations underpinning this discussion, highlighting the marginalisation of children and (their) religious identities in education, and from this forward narrative notions of 'childhood' and 'religion' that allow us to explore senses of belonging meaningfully in primary settings. From this, we explore some areas where children's religious narratives may be expressed in and around the primary school. By doing so, we can better reflect on and appreciate the importance of sharing and living these narratives of belief and belonging in school contexts.

Before we begin, it is widely acknowledged that religion and spirituality are incredibly contested terms. While there is some discussion engaging with this contestation in the present chapter, it is beyond its scope to determine a concrete definition. Broadly, the term 'religion and spirituality' is used throughout to encompass children's worldviews that may or may not be 'otherworldly' in orientation, building upon the Commission on Religious Education's (CORE, 2018) notion of 'worldviews' in RE. Importantly, and to stress, this catch-all definition, while woolly and contentious, also applies to children with nonreligious worldviews and traditions.

Childhood and religion

Awareness of the importance of religion and worldviews to the identities of children has long been overlooked (Hemming and Madge, 2012; Hemming, 2015; Scourfield *et al.*, 2013). In many ways, this lacuna stems from a tendency for both children and religion to be marginalised within scholarship (Shillitoe and Benoit, 2021). Furthermore, both of these spheres of scholarship have recently been shaped by sociological developments that highlight the socially constructed nature of these categories, emphasising how each are created by social actors (people) living their lives in particular social contexts.

This sociological turn toward religion, childhood and the primary classroom is the vantage taken in this chapter, which, in turn, shapes how we understand the nature of these concepts. Hence, the reader should bear this in mind as we proceed with our discussion.

Narratives of childhood

As alluded to, sociological approaches to childhood have ushered in a new 'sociology of childhood' (Prout and James, 2015). This 'new age' emerges from criticisms of developmental notions of childhood that are predominantly grounded in biology and psychology. As Prout and James (2015) note, these developmental notions, enshrined in the likes of Piaget, create a concept of childhood that is direct toward becoming adult. By understanding childhood as 'becoming', rather than 'being' in and of itself, two central critiques are raised. First, as something that is always 'becoming', the sense of being a child in and of itself is therefore diminished, important only in terms of how far 'becoming' childhood is (Alanen, 2017). In turn, this leads to 'childhood' being conceptualised in relation to achieving a series of established milestones: Frustrations with this are no doubt relatable to readers in the education space. A second effect of this is that children as a category of social actor are then rarely considered, as 'childhood' itself is understood as a temporary state of 'becoming'. Again, this is relevant where foundational thinkers like Bourdieu, who underpin much of educational scholarship, struggle to conceptualise children for themselves within their broader theoretical frameworks and go some way to highlight why children continue to be marginalised in developing scholarship, policy and practice. Furthermore, biological and psychologically grounded notions of childhood belie the socially constructed nature of childhood—that the idea of what it is to be a child is given meaning not by immutable natural processes but actually by our current historical and social contexts. When one looks at changing understandings of childhood throughout history, or how different cultures view children, this brings the shortcomings of purely developmental approaches into sharp relief. Together, these critiques highlight a dissatisfaction with the capacity of children to be considered children in their own way and from their own understanding.

Accordingly, the new sociology of childhood grounds the notion of childhood in our shared meaning and understanding of what it means to be a child. We can find this meaning by examining public discourse, enshrined in policy documents and educational directives, and by talking with people. Moreover, acknowledging that children are social actors in themselves means that we can therefore afford agency and a sense of self to children to create their own meaning about what it means to be them, a child living in the world today. It also means we can, and should, be asking children about what they think about this and things affecting them! Specifically, recent shifts toward child-centred methodologies have shed light on the narratives and 'hidden' priorities that children use to construct their identities (Wall, 2022). The recovery of narratives in this case is significant because it gives voice to children on the social and political stage, allowing them to tell their own stories, and for these to be taken seriously as social constructions of what it means to be a child in the world today.

Taking seriously children's narratives about themselves is emboldening discussions of children's rights (Wall, 2022). A growing popularity of 'child-friendly' approaches in local government has this aim to allow children to speak for themselves at its core. UNICEF's (2018) Child-friendly Cities and Communities initiative champions 'effective, representative, and inclusive child-participation' at all levels of social decision-making. Adopting this approach has led Cardiff to be named the UK's first 'child friendly city', through initiatives such as involving young people in urban planning and design, along with a social action grant scheme specifically for young people, supporting projects that aim to promote gender equality (Child Friendly Cardiff, 2023). Likewise, Torbay Council (2021) are adopting a child-friendly language policy in all their work with children, in an effort to enable young people to understand for themselves what work local authorities are doing to support them.

Coming back to the present discussion, we move forward with this understanding that children are 'beings' in themselves, create meaning about who they are by reflecting on their own experiences and give voice to this through the narratives that they share. This emphasis on narrative is symbolic of the capacity of sociological approaches to empower by giving voice. It also dovetails well with our approach to religion, which similarly centres on socially constructed meanings and narratives of religion-as-lived.

Narratives of religion

It is safe to say that 'religion' and 'spirituality' are hotly contested terms, defined and redefined not only in relation to different religious traditions but also when viewed through different disciplinary lenses (Benoit *et al.*, 2020). Our common imaginary tends to reflect a 'world religions paradigm', popularised by Ninian Smart in the 1960s, which has, and continues to, inform RE syllabi and teaching since this time (Cooling *et al.*, 2020). The world religions paradigm is conceptualising religion by a set of 'essential' characteristics, such as key beliefs and practices, sources of wisdom and authority, and holy days and celebrations, typically focussing on the 'big six' world religions: Christianity, Islam and Judaism as western traditions, and Hinduism, Sikhism and Buddhism as eastern traditions (Vencatsamy, 2024).

Given its links to RE syllabi, Benoit (2021, p. 314) notes that primary teachers tend to construct religions through this essentialised prism, which leads to 'reified and objectified' representations in the classroom. The world religions paradigm's tendency to reproduce essentialised constructions of religion results in traditions viewed as monolithic, homogenous and towering edifices of codified beliefs: about God, the afterlife, the spiritual and 'otherworldly', conducted in special places of worship. Reducing religion to these distinctly religious arenas exacerbates a supposed divide with secular society, which itself has been subject to increasing critique (Possamai, 2017), erroneously positioning religion as competing 'irrational' belief systems against dominant rational secular worldviews (Beniot et al., 2022). Moreover, scholars have highlighted colonial discourses embedded within its foundation, with a framework of Protestant Christianity serving as the 'model religion' within which other traditions are forced to fit (Masuzawa, 2005). Hence, there have been long-standing critiques of the 'de-contextualised' approach to religion in the world religions paradigm (Hayward, 2006), reproduced by RE, that fails to account for the lived experience and manifestations of religion that continues to give meaning to billions of people's lives today.

Difficulties in capturing the diversity of religion, and overcoming the foregoing critiques, are further reflected in recent policy debates. The Commission on Religious Education (CoRE, 2018) consistently and (refreshingly) openly acknowledges the difficulty in defining the term, and, by extension, the subject. The new proposal is a move toward 'religion and worldviews', investigating 'a person's way of understanding, experiencing and responding to the world ... influence and be influenced by their beliefs, values, behaviours, experiences, identities and commitments' (CoRE, p. 4). A distinction is made between an 'institutional' and 'personal' worldview, the former representing shared understandings by groups while the latter represents individual accounts (CoRE, p. 4). In addition, there is also the acknowledgement that looking at religion through other disciplinary lenses is needed in order to properly convey its complexity. Of note here are the sociological (religion in society) and historical (religion through time) disciplinary lenses, that, with them, aim to explore lived, contextualised accounts of religion in the classroom.

The foregoing discussion sets the scene for an understanding of religion that too is socially constructed, given meaning by people and expressed by them through their personal narratives. A 'lived religion' approach champions this perspective, and so formulates how we should approach religion in the present chapter. McGuire (2008, p. 98) succinctly summarises how 'lived religion' conceptualises religion as,

> constituted by the practices people use to remember, share, enact, adapt, create and combine the stories out of which they live ... [brought] into being through the often-mundane practices people use to transform these meaningful interpretations into everyday action.

Adopting this 'lived' lens means we look for religion not (only) in theology, doctrine or scripture but in the narratives, practices and embodied experiences that lie at the heart of people's everyday existence (Ammerman, 2016; McGuire, 2008). From this, what is religious adopts a much more fluid, flexible and contextual form, responding to, incorporating and melding with everyday British life. This kind of identity-formation is bricologic; emphasising how people pick and choose aspects of, in our case, religious narratives to form their identity, alongside the other aspects of their social identity (Ammerman, 2016). What makes these 'religious' narratives distinct is that they tend to be 'other-worldly' in orientation (Mellor and Shilling, 2014, p. 12). Moreover, 'lived religion' encourages us to look beyond the traditional sites of religion (i.e., places of worship) to the street itself (Bender *et al.*, 2013).

The reader should be aware that viewing religion through this lens is somewhat controversial. For some, social construction takes the epistemic weight out of the meaning of religious traditions, and particularly the weight of divine authority. Instead, by focussing on narrative religious meaning is reduced it to 'what said goes' (Archer *et al.*, 2004). For others, 'lived religion' overemphasises the fluidity that belonging to a religious tradition itself offers and downplays moments of challenge that modern, secular society may usher (Altglas, 2014). McLoughlin (2007), for example, highlights how many Muslims do talk and act in a way that recognises the centrality of text (the Qur'an) in terms of meaning making surrounding what it means to be a Muslim. Notions of the Ummah (brotherhood) and visible symbols of belonging are also important for many Muslims (Shah, 2018). Likewise, my previous research (Vince, 2018) has revealed the importance of belonging to a religious tradition for Muslims who work as RE teachers, navigating the secular professional standards of their role.

So, much like the methodological shifts in approaching childhood, we can see a turn toward giving voice to religious people and their experience through narrative. In the primary classroom, understanding this disciplinary and policy foundation attunes us to why this aspect of children's lives may be missed.

Religion, belonging and childhood

Perhaps the most influential picture of religious belonging in our contemporary picture is Davie's (2001) articulation of 'believing without belonging'. In an attempt to rectify the persistent paradox of growing secularisation, evidenced by declining church attendance or the public importance of religion, with enduring religious identification among the British public, Davie (2001) posits that it is not religious affiliation that is in decline, but that how people are religious has changed. Specifically, people seem to be less engaged with the codified, 'official' practices of religious traditions, often its most symbolic elements, and rather belong on a more individual level, embodying their commitment in their everyday lives and actions (Davie, 2001). Rather, we see that religious believers engage 'vicariously' through an active minority who engage in these practices 'on their behalf', belonging through an implicit approval of their devotional activities (Davie, 2001). This recognition brings our attention to the symbolic and 'hidden' ways children may believe and belong in school settings.

Specifically, Smith (2005) shows how children's sense of religious belonging considers both their personal perspective and their wider community in distinct yet overlapping ways. On the one hand, children expressed knowledge of the 'facts' of a religious tradition: its institutions, practices, beliefs, and values, which had been transmitted to them by adults, whether through family or teaching (i.e., RE). In particular, children emphasised the 'dos' and 'don'ts' of their tradition. However, they also shared their own understanding of belonging to a religious tradition, enshrined in their own thoughts, feelings, and meanings behind the beliefs, practices, and values they were engaged in. Importantly, the latter often involved a creative and subjective element, reflecting how children are active in creating what religious belonging means to them (see also Hemming, 2016). Accordingly, the picture of religion shared by children may not reflect the 'official' picture as captured in our religious imaginary.

Likewise, Day (2009) highlights that young people's sense of religious belonging is enshrined in their social relationships, acting as spaces in which their meaning, happiness and moral frameworks can be explored. Typically, engaging with a religious community in turn encourages and reinforces these social expectations for individuals. However, Day (2009) argues that these relationships 'in themselves' were found by young people to encapsulate the heart of spiritual and religious meaning, beliefs, morals and values by conducting themselves in particular ways, such as showing love. As such, young people were found to be more likely to 'believe without belonging', engaging in formal religious practice, as their religious practice was fulfilled through these social relationships.

By providing spaces for self-exploration and social relationships, we can see how primary schools are particularly important in relation to children's religious identities. Hemming (2016) has drawn attention the fact that schools are vital in the formation of children's complex social identities, which incorporates their religious identities. This reminds us that religious identities are not constructed in a vacuum but in conjunction with other social factors, influences and identities that one holds (Hemming, 2016). Research has highlighted the importance of school to valuing children's 'clear sense' of religious self (Harmon, 2018), their 'Belonging, Being and Becoming' (Meehan, 2011) and creating spaces of self-exploration of religious ideas (Ipgrave, 1999). However, RE can also reify dominant discursive constructions and 'othering' narratives surrounding religious belonging (Benoit, 2021). Moreover, the recent disruption prompted by Covid has further highlighted the role school plays in developing children's identities, particularly fostering a sense of 'feeling a part of something bigger that yourself' (Buchanan et al., 2023, p. 1087) as vital for the wellbeing of children. As such, primary schools are a significant site of children's religious and spiritual development, as part of their holistic development as young people.

> **Reflection**
>
> **Messy narratives**
>
> Consider the following narrative:
>
> *Girl:* Sundays, it's the most boring time of the week.
> *Interviewer:* Why is it boring?
> *Girl:* I go to church ... the priest goes on ... we don't even know what he is talking about most of the time.
> (Christian girl, School 2, Smith, 2005, p. 18)
>
> - What classroom activities and moments might elicit the kinds of responses in this dialogue?
> - What might the narrative tell us about the girl's sense of religious belonging?
> - What challenges may there be when encountering notions of identity and religion through children's narratives?

However, anxieties can emerge when different stories and meanings of people's spirituality, religion and identity suffuse the classroom space. During your reading, the foregoing narrative may have elicited some unease, associating aspects of something as 'serious' as religion as boring, for example. Admitting to 'not having a clue' may lead one to question a child's capacity to create meaning appropriately in relation to their ideas, or that these ideas may need correcting. Particularly within the context of RE lessons, this issue emerges when it comes to ensuring that children understand the 'right' answer, often in relation to some form of looming examination, despite the aforementioned pedagogical importance of self-reflection and exploration in the subject.

This issue of power is worth raising as it elicits issues of authority within the school space, asking who gets to speak for different religious traditions. Ipgrave (1999) has highlighted the dissonance for school children where their understanding contradicts the 'textbook' answer as presented in teaching materials or enforced by exams. Typically, these materials are found to privilege deeper and more symbolic accounts and eschew mundane, eclectic or embodied explanations. Consequently, Ipgrave (1999) remarks how Muslim children were frequently corrected in their understanding of their beliefs and practices if they didn't fit the mould.

Rather than attempt to 'correct', we should acknowledge that messy narratives are at the heart of children's understanding and experience. This kind of messy narrative play is vital for children's self-development, reflecting children's propensity to play, try and figure out different ways of navigating their social, cultural and religious worlds (Wall, 2010, pp. 82–83). Conversely, adults can tend to try and 'tidy up' these narratives (Beazley *et al.*, 2009).

Rather than seeing these answers as wrong, we should seek to understand where that meaning comes from (Ipgrave, 1999). This messiness is reflective of children drawing from the array of narratives that surround them, for fascinating results. As such, although there can be complications and tensions, we must avoid the urge to 'correct' these messy narratives.

Moreover, it is important to remember that this meaning-making can go both ways. It may not be that always the religious and spiritual always takes precedence, or always comes from this source. Rather, being in school for so long, we should expect narratives of school life to inform how children understand and shape their own sense of being religious.

> **Reflection**
>
> **Contested meaning**
> Ipgrave (1999, p. 19) offers a particularly poignant example of contested meanings in the classroom:
>
> > In one lesson, a teacher asked about the symbolism of the Muslim open-handed prayer gesture. A Muslim boy replied that it was so an angel could be supported on each hand. This explanation was ignored, however, and the class were taught that the gesture represented 'openness to God'.
>
> - Reflecting on this situation, how may the teacher have handled this differently to not ignore the boy's narrative?
> - What challenges or pressures may you feel in this situation?

Opportunities to live these narratives in school

So far, we have discussed religion primarily in terms of narrative. We have emphasised how these narratives allow children to consider and create meaning regarding some of the most fundamental questions, who they are and what it means to belong to their communities, through exploration of their beliefs and values. As part of this, we must try and embrace the discomforting messiness of such accounts, recognising both 'official' religious narratives and the mundane or eclectic meanings that children may share about what their religious or spiritual belonging means to them. However, an emphasis on telling stories about something can create a sense that that something exists 'out there' and not 'here and now'.

As such, we must keenly remember that religious belonging is also something that is lived, implying that it is something done by humans with bodies, here in the world, through action, behaviour and practice. Think back to Simran and Vraj, who introduce their Hindu commitment through food and hobbies, not a statement of the main tenants of Hinduism. Overlooking the lived experience of religious and spiritual belonging fails to capture much of its reality. Hence, although we have highlighted moments of classroom practice and behaviour previously, now we turn our attention to how children can be encouraged to live these narratives in school.

Mellor and Shilling (2014) stress that understanding religion and belonging purely at an epistemological level is a mistake, the 'cognitive fallacy' of studying religion. They posit, for example, that the overdetermination of secularisation in the modern world is, in part, due to an undue preoccupation with the rationalisation of religious belief, ignoring the embodied spiritual, cultural and social location of religion that makes it continue to 'make sense' in millions of people's lives. Rather, Mellor and Shilling (2014, p. 11) remind us that religion is 'grounded in contrasting embodied experiences and cognitive orientations'.

From this, Mellor and Shilling (2014) emphasise the importance of being able to craft your religious self across these cognitive and embodied perspectives. As they (2014, p. 4) put it, creating a religious habitus (or self) requires 'the reflexive crafting of a mode of being that locates human action, feeling and thought at the embodied intersection of worldly and other-worldly realities'. This intersection means that otherworldly orientations can shape and reshape worldly existence, and vice versa, intwined in an interrelated network of crafted meanings by individuals. Hence, the act of being and belonging in the world is a vital part of crafting, or 'instaurating', a religious identity.

A consequence of such a notion of religious identity is that we should therefore expect to see this happening in everyday life! Religion as lived in this way goes beyond just telling stories for, and about, its meaning and who you are, but also 'living these'. From this vantage, part of the function of the rituals and practices symbolic for many of belonging to a religious or spiritual community are there to remind one of the beliefs, values and teachings so that they become habitual, embodied throughout their everyday behaviour (Mellor and Shilling, 2014). At the same time, we also see that religious and spiritual commitments are made to work in the context of people's everyday social lives, becoming entwined with the needs of their work, or hobbies and social activities that they also enjoy. As a result, religious and spiritual embodiment can be 'hidden in plain sight', embodied by infusing everyday action with a religious or spiritual ethos (Cadge and Konieczny, 2014).

As such, facilitating opportunities for children to explore their embodied religious and spiritual belonging can take two forms. First, schools can be attentive to the particular religious or spiritual needs of children and support them where possible. Often these cover the most visible aspects of religious and spiritual traditions, and there is much guidance out there on accessible school uniforms, school dinners and spaces for prayer (see for example the Muslim Council of Britain's (2022) guidance on setting up a prayer room in school). Slightly overlooked might be the impact of different religious calendars on the school year on children, where the school calendar is organised broadly on a Christian calendar. Different festivals, such as Holi, or periods of holy time, such as Ramadan, can mean different expectations and experiences on children that reach into school life. Fasting, for example, may affect a child's ability to concentrate, which is particularly pertinent during exam time. Hence, awareness of the temporal dimension of religious and spiritual belonging can make a significant impact on children's sense of belonging in school.

Second, there is this 'hidden' dimension where children can infuse their everyday action with a religious or spiritual ethos. I suggest that this overlaps considerably with the telling of narratives through play, where doing so reveals these hidden moments of children trying to embody their religious and spiritual meaning-making in their everyday school lives. Play has long been known to be significant in children's development, championing children's agency in the construction of knowledge about the world and themselves within it (Hughes, 2010; Kreig et al., 2023). Ridgely (2012, pp. 244–245) highlights how children use play to 'respond to and reinterpret' religious and spiritual narratives as part of this wider world-building process, sorting what works and doesn't work in their social contexts. Dramatic play also encourages children to engage with narrative by nurturing their ability to adopt different characters (Panagoitaki et al., 2014).

Bringing this together, we should therefore expect to witness children to be 'playing' with notions of their religious and spiritual selves in order to figure out what it means to them and how it fits with their everyday life as a child in their school. By play here I do not mean exclusively religious-orientated play, such as Godly play, but rather, much like in the foregoing case of exploring narratives, providing opportunities for children to embody their spiritual and religious belonging in different contexts. Kreig et al. (2023) delineate two kinds of play for this kind of exploration: free play and guided play, the latter of which involves subtle scaffolding by the teacher in the form of prompting questions to stimulate reflection. This kind of embodied exploration can readily be achieved in the primary classroom where play is commonplace, guided by our attention to the religious and spiritual, bringing these 'hidden' meanings to the foreground through prompting children to reflect on why or how their activities may reflect their belonging to particular traditions or beliefs.

There are some interesting parallels to other aspects of school here, especially the 'hidden curriculum' that aims to inculcate certain beliefs and values in children. In addition, it is not being attentive just to proactive action, but also the degree to which children embody prohibitions common to many religious traditions. 'Being good' can also overlap, between being a good child and good observant, but take on different guises in different moments, or look the same but be being achieved for different reasons. Asking children how and why these may be similar and different may bring this to light.

Some may baulk at the idea of play being associated with something as serious, or potentially controversial, as religion. However, contrary to downplaying the import of religious belonging here, the notion of playing with religion and spirituality as an important part of children's wider sense of figuring things out, crafting their own selves and actively engaging their own communities on their own terms reflects how vital this sense of play can be. Moreover, while for some this may produce moments of tension in settings with a distinct religious ethos, we must remember this is not a confessional activity. Instead, such play can encourage children's agency in understanding their faith, and that of others faiths and perspectives, in turn cultivating belonging to their local and wider social community, which is plural and multifaith. Again, this keeps at its core the broader communities that children belong to and navigate in the world.

In conclusion, shining a light on how religion is 'made real' through children's embodied action and behaviour allows us to remain attentive to, and create opportunities for, children to create religious and spiritual selves that incorporate their school contexts.

Reflection

Reflecting on play

The previous section has considered the importance of play for children embodied religious and spiritual exploration.

Take some time to think about the kinds of play that occur in your classroom. Draw a scene from this imaginary.

Then, annotate the drawing with the following:

- How may this reflect religious and spiritual belonging?
- How might you guide and prompt children to bring these 'hidden' meanings to the foreground?
- What challenges might you feel in this situation?

Concluding reflections

It is hoped that through the discussion of this chapter the reader will feel emboldened to enable children to explore their religion and spiritual belonging in the classroom. We have emphasised notions of childhood, religion and belonging that are socially constructed, privileging children's agency in the understanding of themselves, their beliefs and values and the world around them. From this child-centred perspective, religious and spiritual belonging can be developed through narrative and embodied play, both of which encourage children to reflect on these aspects of their lives. The role of the teacher, then, is to facilitate opportunities for active reflection, understanding and embodied play so children can explore what these things mean and belong to these communities on their own terms.

Importantly, it is hoped that the chapter also contends some potential anxieties around engaging with the religious and spiritual in the classroom outside of RE. It is hoped that it is clear that this is not a confessional activity, nor requires religious or spiritual commitment in its traditional sense. Nor is associating play with the religious and spiritual downplaying its significance. It also does not locate itself purely within the 'official' sites of religion within school contexts, the RE lesson, assembly or possibly prayer spaces. Rather, the aim is to cultivate a sensibility that is attentive to the importance of children actively engaging with their religious and spiritual belonging on a daily basis, rather than being a passive part of their growing up.

References

Alanen, L. (2017), Childhood studies and the challenge of ontology. *Childhood*, 24(2), pp. 147–150.

Altglas, V. (2014), *From Yoga to Kabbalah: Religious Exoticism and the Logics of Bricolage*. Oxford: Oxford University Press.

Ammerman, N. (2016), Lived religion as an emerging field: An assessment of its contours and frontiers. *Nordic Journal of Religion and Society*, 29(2), pp. 83–99.

Archer, M., Collier, A. and Porpora, D. (2004), *Transcendence: Critical Realism and God*. London: Routledge.

Beazley, H., Bessell, S., Ennew, J. and Waterson, R. (2009), The right to be properly researched: Research with children in a messy, real world. *Children's Geographies*, 7(4), pp. 365–378.

BBC Teach. (2020), My life, my religion: Hinduism. *BBC*. Available at https://www.bbc.co.uk/teach/class-clips-video/religious-studies-ks2-my-life-my-religion-hinduism-meeting-two-british-hindus/zkghf4j (Accessed February 18, 2024).

Bender, C., Cadge, W., Levitt, P. and Smilde, D. (eds.). (2013), *Religion on the Edge: De-centering and Re-centering the Sociology of Religion*. Oxford: Oxford University Press.

Benoit, C. (2021), 'I'm just British—normal British': Exploring teachers' and pupils' conceptualisations of religion(s) and religious belonging. *Journal of Contemporary Religion*, 36(2), pp. 311–328.

Benoit, C., Hutchings, T. and Shillitoe, R. (2020), *Worldview: A Multidisciplinary Report*, Religious Education Council. Available at https://religiouseducationcouncil.org.uk/rec/wp-content/uploads/2020/10/20-19438-REC-Worldview-Report-A4-v2.pdf (Accessed February 18, 2024).

Benoit, C., Hutchings, T. and Shillitoe, R. (2022), 'Religion and worldviews: The way forward? Considerations from the study of religion, non-religion and classroom practice, *Journal of the British Association for the Study of Religion*, 2(1), pp. 8–28.

Buchanan, D., Hargreaves, E. and Quick, L. (2023), Schools closed during the pandemic: revelations about the well-being of 'lower-attaining' primary school children, *Education*, 51(7), pp. 1077–1090.

Cadge, W. and Konieczny, M. (2014), Hidden in plain sight: The significance of religion and spirituality in secular organizations. *Sociology of Religion*, 75(4), pp. 551–563.

Child Friendly Cardiff. (2023), *Plan UK Social Action Grants— Cardiff Young Changemakers*, Cardiff. Available at https://www.childfriendlycardiff.co.uk/2023/10/plan-uk-social-action-grants-cardiff-young-changemakers/ (Accessed February 18, 2024).

Commission on Religious Education (CORE). (2018), *Religion and Worldviews: A Way Forward*. London: Religious Education Council. Available at https://www.commissiononre.org.uk/wp-content/uploads/2018/09/Final-Report-of-theCommission-on-RE.pdf (Accessed February 18, 2024).

Cooling, T., Bowie, B. and Panjwani, F. (2020), *Worldviews in Religious Education*. Theos Think Tank. Available at https://www.theosthinktank.co.uk/cmsfiles/Worldview-in-Religious-Education---FINAL-PDF-merged.pdf (Accessed February 18, 2024).

Day, A. (2009), 'Believing in belonging: An ethnography of young people's constructions of belief'. *Culture and Religion*, 10(3), pp. 263–278.

Davie, G. (2001), *Religion in Modern Europe: A Memory Mutates*. Oxford: Oxford University Press.

Goldburg P. (2008), Teaching religion in Australian schools. *Numen*, 55(2/3), pp. 241–271.

Harmon, M (2018), *'I am a Catholic Buddhist': The Voice of Children on Religion and Religious Education in an Irish Catholic Primary School Classroom*. Doctor of Education thesis. Dublin: Dublin City University.

Hayward, M. (2006), Curriculum Christianity. *British Journal of Religious Education*, 28(2), pp. 153–171.

Hemming, P. (2015), *Religion in the Primary School*. London: Routledge.

Hemming, P. (2016), Childhood, youth, and religious identity: Mapping the terrain. In *Identities and Subjectivities*. Singapore: Springer, pp. 51–68.

Hemming, P. and Madge, N. (2012), Researching children, youth and religion: Identity, complexity and agency. *Childhood*, 19(1), pp. 38–51.

Hughes, F. (2010), *Children, Play, and Development*, 4th Ed. London: SAGE.

Huth, K., Brown, R. and Usher, W. (2021), The use of story to teach religious education in the early years of primary school: a systematic review of the literature. *Journal of Religious Education*, 69(2), pp. 253–272.

Ipgrave, J. (1999), Issues in the delivery of religious education to Muslim pupils: perspectives from the classroom. *British Journal of Religious Education*, 21(3), pp. 146–157.

Kreig, J., Tewathahákwa, J. and Froats, K. (2023), *Children's Learning through Play*, Loyalist College. Available at https://ecampusontario.pressbooks.pub/childrenslearningthroughplay/ (Accessed February 18, 2024).

Laminack, L. (2016), Story matters. *The Reading Teacher*, 7(2), pp. 250–253.

Masuzawa, T. (2005), *The Invention of World Religions*. Chicago: Chicago University Press.

McLoughlin, S. (2007), Islam(s) in context: Orientalism and the anthropology of Muslim societies and cultures. *Journal of Beliefs & Values*, 28(3), pp. 273–296.

McGuire, M. (2008), *Lived religion: Faith and Practice in Everyday Life*. Oxford: Oxford University Press.

Meehan, C. (2011), Belonging, being, and becoming: The importance of understanding beliefs and practices in the teaching of religious education in the early years. *Journal of Religious Education*, 59(3), pp. 36–49.

Mellor, P. and Shilling, C. (2014), *Sociology of the Sacred: Religion, Embodiment and Social Change*. London: SAGE.

Muslim Council of Britain. (2022), *The Muslim Council of Britain's Guidelines for Staff in Secondary Schools Muslims and Reflection Spaces: Prayer Room Guidelines*, Muslim Council of Britain. Available at https://mcb.org.uk/wp-content/uploads/2022/11/MCB_PrayerGuide2022_20.06.pdf (Accessed February 18, 2023).

Panagoitaki, A., Trouli, K., Linardakis, M. and Grammatikopoulous, V. (2014), *Influence of Dramatic Play in the Development of Playfulness in Early Childhood*. International Conference on Education 2014, Szombathely: Savaria University Press. Available at https://www.researchgate.net/profile/Aspasia-Panagoitaki/publication/340264873_Influence_of_dramatic_play_in_the_development_of_playfulness_in_early_childhood/links/5e80b894a6fdcc139c1259b8/Influence-of-dramatic-play-in-the-development-of-playfulness-in-early-childhood.pdf (Accessed February 18, 2024).

Possamai, A. (2017), Post-secularism in multiple modernities. *Journal of Sociology*, 53(4), pp. 822–835.

Prout, A. and James, A. (2015), A new paradigm for the sociology of childhood? In A. James and A. Prout (eds.), *Constructing and Reconstructing Childhood*. London: Routledge, pp. 7–32.

Reed E., Freathy, R., Cornwall, S. and Davis, A. (2013), Narrative theology in religious education. *British Journal of Religious Education*, 35(3), pp. 297–312.

Ridgely, S. (2012), 'Children and religion. *Religion Compass*, 6(1), pp. 236–248.

Scourfield, J., Gilliat-Ray, S., Khan, A. and Otri, S. (2013), *Muslim Childhood: Religious Nurture in a European Context*. Oxford: Oxford Academic Press.

Shah, S. (2018), "I Am a Muslim First ...": Challenges of Muslimness and the UK state schools. *Leadership and Policy in Schools*, 18(3), pp. 1–16.

Shillitoe, R. and Benoit, C. (2021), Towards a new research agenda. In C. Starkey and E. Tomalin (eds.), *The Routledge Handbook of Religion, Gender and Society* (pp. 261–274). London: Routledge.

Smith, G. (2005), *Children's Perspectives on Believing and Belonging*. London: Joseph Rowntree Foundation.

Torbay Council. (2021), *Children and Young People's Plan*, Torquay. Available at https://www.torbay.gov.uk/media/15799/torbay-children-and-young-peoples-plan-updated-19-february-2021.pdf (Accessed February 18, 2024).

UNICEF. (2018), *Child Friendly Cities and Communities Handbook*. UNICEF. Available at https://www.childfriendlycities.org/reports/child-friendly-cities-and-communities-handbook (Accessed February 18, 2024).

Vencatsamy, B. (2024), The world religions paradigm: Why context matters in religious studies. *Critical Research on Religion*, 12(1), pp. 12–25.

Vince, M. (2018), *Muslim Identities in Contemporary Britain: The case of Muslim Religious Education Teachers*. Doctor of Philosophy thesis, Cardiff: Cardiff University.

Vince, M., Bryant, M. and Gilliat-Ray, S. (2020), *Discovering Muslims in Britain: For Key Stage 3*. Cardiff: Cardiff University. Available at https://www.cardiff.ac.uk/research/explore/find-a-project/view/2412788-discovering-muslims-in-britain-for-key-stage-3 (Accessed February 20, 2024).

Vince, M. (2023), What does it mean to be a Muslim in Britain? Talking about identity in the classroom. *RE Today*, Birmingham. Available at https://retodaymagazine.online/article/what-does-it-mean-to-be-a-muslim-in-britain-talking-about-identity-in-the-classroom/ (Accessed February 22, 2024).

Wall, J. (2010), *Ethics in Light of Childhood*. Georgetown: Georgetown University Press.

Wall, J. (2022), From childhood studies to childism: Reconstructing the scholarly and social imaginations. *Children's Geographies*, 2(3), pp. 257–270.

4 Unmasking Toxic Masculinity in Early Years and Primary Schools

Exploring the Impact on Children's Socialisation and Development

Alison Milner

Introduction

Toxic masculinity is a phenomenon that is becoming increasingly prevalent today. It is characterised by traits such as aggression, dominance and emotional suppression and is often associated with negative outcomes such as violence, substance abuse and mental health problems. Although toxic masculinity has been widely studied in adults, its impact on children's development and socialisation is less understood. The aim is to explore toxic masculinity in early years and primary schools, with a particular focus on its impact on children's socialisation and development. This chapter will explore toxic masculinity, providing examples of how it manifests in primary schools, discuss the impact of toxic masculinity on children's socialisation and development and examine the role of primary schools in perpetuating or mitigating toxic masculinity. Importantly, this chapter will give suggestions and guidance on how practitioners can minimise the impact of toxic masculinity in the learning environment. Incorporating a range of activities suggested in this chapter, early years practitioners and primary school teachers can support children's holistic socialisation in their pedagogy.

Knowledgeable practice-based solutions are always beneficial when raising awareness of a particular issue in education. As educators, gaining a deeper understanding about toxic masculinity in early childhood and primary education settings can only be a positive development. Identifying the educational implications of children's socialisation for their own wellbeing and sense of belonging in society is imperative for everyone to feel welcome and safe. Highlighting how primary schools can begin to reduce the harmful impacts of toxic masculinity, children's understanding of gender norms can be embedded into pedagogical practices—meaning that by effectively reviewing ways that early years practitioners and primary teachers address toxic masculinity in early years settings and primary schools, children will understand their worth.

DOI: 10.4324/9781032716190-6

Social implications of toxic masculinity

The diverse problem of toxic masculinity influences children on an individual, community and societal level. It is anticipated that educators, policymakers and other stakeholders who are dedicated to encouraging healthy gender norms and offering inclusive, secure learning environments for all children would find benefit in the insights and strategies discussed.

Unfortunately, the prevalence of toxic masculinity in contemporary society needs to be addressed. Socialising children in early years and primary school education to challenge toxic masculinity can only be a positive move towards a more equal accepting society. The forthcoming discussions will incorporate definitions and examples of toxic masculinity to provide a backdrop as an acknowledgement of the importance of early years and primary school education. Terms of reference, behaviours and associated practices in early years and primary schools that potentially exacerbate or relieve the situation will be explored. Solutions that challenge some of the identified behaviours will be examined as an alternative approach to neutralise the gendered stereotypes promoted in society. The Good Childhood Report published by the Children's Society (2023) highlighted the impact of traditional gendered norms. Children who experience less pervasive traditional gendered stereotypes relate to feelings of unhappiness (The Children's Society, 2023). For children to gain a comprehensive understanding of their sense of belonging in their family unit, education and society they need to experience positive gender relationships. Without positive intervention in educational settings, children can often struggle to create a sense of self. Self-expression together with the maintenance of positive role models in children's lives supports socialisation. However, as is often the case, the presentation of ideas acts as a guide to potentially minimise the negativity surrounding the promotion of positive gender norms. The identifying monikers of boys and girls will be used to differentiate between the genders. These labels encompass all, whether male or female, to simplify the existing rhetoric in the literature and educational practices. The terms are merely to illustrate the differences and similarities rather than alienate individuals in society when discussing toxic masculinity.

In the late 20th century, the term 'toxic masculinity' was coined by men's movements (Harrington, 2021). Today, it is used in therapeutic and social policy settings to move away from negative connotations associated with gender roles such as misogyny, homophobia and men's violence (Parent, Gobble and Rochlen, 2019). The idea behind this term was to offer an alternative to the concept of toxic masculinity as a hegemonic analysis (Harrington, 2021). By looking into the historical hierarchies inherent within the United Kingdom (UK), we can begin to understand some of the marginalising narratives associated with masculinity. However, while toxic masculinity is a useful concept, some experts argue against adopting it as an analytical concept. The emotionally distant relationships that often existed between fathers and sons in the past were problematic and still are, but they can be repaired (Ford, 2019). Early years practitioners and primary school teachers can intervene and begin educating the whole family to address some of the discrepancies surrounding the negative behaviours, language and education that reinforced toxic masculinity in the past. Gendered approaches from educators can also influence the pedagogical focus in the learning environment highlighting the discourses associated with the acceptance of social codes (Duckworth, Farrell and Rigby 2016). Early years practitioners and primary school teachers are required to model the expected roles at any given time; currently, there is a need to address the inadequacies of agentic societal acceptance. Experts suggest ways to nurture boys to become supporters rather than perpetrators. For instance, some advocate for improving family and societal relationships between males and females in the narrative surrounding toxic masculinity (Ford, 2019; Farrell, 2016). Others have an interactive approach to raising boys, providing insights into how to raise confident, happy and kind boys from a parent's perspective (Biddulph, 2014). The education system is failing to help boys become emotionally confident adults. Therefore, early years and primary schools should adopt a pedagogy that prioritises nurturing, supporting and guiding children through life. Environmental factors and relationships play a significant role in shaping individuals (Wingrave, 2018).

Children perceive gender differences in tasks and features as early as two years old, and these disparities immediately start to influence children's behaviour (Berenbaum *et al.*, 2008; Skipper and Fox, 2022). '(G)irls and boys behave differently because their brains are wired differently,' claims Sax (2005), who also suggests that biology and the brain explain everything (p. 28). This biological argument refutes Schmitz's (2010) assertions regarding brain plasticity, which hold that malleability affects the changes during a child's development and learning. How a child is raised has an impact on the connections and circumstances with the myriad of experiences unaccounted for during early childhood and primary school education. The neural pathways in the brain alter with everyday life due to all our experiences in a substantial way. According to Schmitz (2010), our experiences have a significant impact on the brain, which in turn influences how the brain develops later in life and shapes the neural pathways. Male and female neural networks are unexpected if experiences are fundamentally different for girls and boys (Millet, 1971). Importantly, brain plasticity demonstrates why early years education can supportively build children's positive neuropathways to develop their sense of belonging in society from an early age.

The presence of male and female early years practitioners and teachers represents individuals in society. Unseen barriers often remain in place that prevent the fair appointment and representation of males and females in educational roles in the UK. Individuals in society and parents are more than happy with the presence of a male primary school teacher. What does appear to be slightly less acceptable is the appointment of a male early years practitioner. Unfortunately, this is in part due to many contemporary incidents where male early years practitioners have abused their positions in settings. When compared to educational settings in many European countries, the appointment and presence of male early years practitioners are more accepted in their roles to support young children (Moosa and Bhana, 2023). Recent global studies about these phenomena concluded that fewer than 3% of early years practitioners are men (Xu, Warin and Robb, 2020). Briefly, ignoring the obvious issue, a cross-section of society within an early years setting models the socialisation of our children. Without exposure to a range of practitioners, male and female, children will not get the appropriate socialisation required to ensure they are well-rounded citizens. The acknowledgement of toxic masculinity traverses the various experiences situated uniquely in the educational arena. Therefore, open communication about how to mitigate the wider sociological experience that impacts children is a definitive movement in the right direction.

Individually, boys should be encouraged to express a variety of emotions, not just anger, from an early age. By experiencing different emotions in various situations, children can learn to understand themselves and their reactions better. This understanding can help them to express their emotions honestly without feeling ashamed or embarrassed, even if their actions are not positively received. It is important for parents and educators to reject outdated ideas about hypermasculinity and instead emphasise the importance of treating women with respect, as well as the dangers of striving for a 'perfect physique'.

The role of social media in toxic masculinity

The increasing media presence at play within the toxic masculinity arena demonstrates the awareness early years practitioners and teachers in primary schools need to have when working with young, impressionable children. Demonstrating a working knowledge of the messages portrayed in the media should also be transparently communicated to children when used to develop teaching resources to aid interaction and learning. Since many young children are exposed to the vagaries of television programmes as part of their daily lives, using popular or relevant characters can motivate and enthuse children's learning. Therefore, using readily available storylines or character plots can promote children's engagement. However, being careful to reduce the negative plots or narratives that exacerbate the promotion of toxic masculinity is important. Instead, promoting a positive, all-inclusive plot or narrative to work within children's schemas can be incredibly beneficial in the pedagogy.

Toxic masculinity has become increasingly used in social media and society to define the behaviours, attitudes and expectations targeted at boys. The impact of such targeted language and attitude can detrimentally effect boys and girls in early years and primary education settings. Children's socialisation and subsequent development are determined from an early age (King *et al.*, 2021).

The role of early years and primary settings perpetuates many of the learned behaviours that form individual identities for adults (Scottish Government, 2012). Importantly, educating children today impacts society's future citizens; therefore, to ensure that the practices, behaviours and actions are positive for individuals, impactful changes are required to equalise and reduce toxic masculinity today (Coles *et al.*, 2016). To minimise the impact of toxic masculinity and its effects on children in early years education, these basic actions could be incorporated into practice. We need to address the problem of toxic masculinity in the media as part of media literacy. It has been said that rather than encouraging more negative preconceptions about what it means to be a young person, popular shows like *Love Island* should spread more positive messages. Children are exposed to various media influences even to early years and primary schools. Therefore, teaching about gender stereotypes through education including early years and primary schools will allow them to be free to be who they are without having to conform to rigid gender norms. The reduction of toxic masculinity promotes a healthier environment for everyone to live in harmony (Childrens Society, 2020).

Healthy activities to minimise toxic masculinity

Positive, supportive activities to introduce gender neutral learning should be encouraged within the theoretical practice of teaching. Challenging gender stereotypes has become a persuasive way to engage all in society (Skipper and Fox, 2022). Whether you are an educator or not, behaviour has a profound effect on all people. The socialisation we receive from early life influences our behaviour choices, including how we respond to our surroundings. Importantly, developing ways to engage practitioners in educational settings to model resilient, positive habits increases how individuals navigate both the present and the future of all. Ford (2019) argues that aggression and dominance are not inherent traits for boys, instead suggesting that toxic masculinity can often limit male emotional expression, which perpetuates harmful behaviours to self and others, which can lead to harming individual wellbeing (Ford, 2019). Toxic masculinity harms girls' and boys' behaviours, which can lead to a restricted emotional range that is required for self-reflection and self-knowledge. The knowledge of self-experienced children will inhibit their opportunity to become by challenging predominant masculine ways (Farrell, 2016). Ford (2019) emphasises that the patriarchy harms not only women but also men. The restriction of their emotional range stifles vulnerability and perpetuates harmful stereotypes. Therefore, being able to express a full range of emotions when experiencing life adds to the ability to socially engage with other people. Not only does this change posit a shift in societal norms and expectations, but it also brings about a change in attitude towards all in society. Challenging toxic masculinity opens a dialogue about mutual respect between men and women, boys and girls, for equality in the world (Ford, 2019).

How can behaviours, attitudes and practices in early years and primary schools mitigate the impact of toxic masculinity?

Reducing noticeable behaviours associated with the effects of toxic masculinity can help primary school teachers and early years practitioners improve their pedagogy. In early years and primary school settings, attitudes towards behaviour regulation can be negotiated with the aim of helping minimise the impact of toxic masculinity. In early years and primary school, children are learning how to manage the range of emotions they are experiencing. One way to manage this situation is to practice modelling interactions. Early years practitioners and primary school teachers can set an example of acceptable behaviour to stop children from developing dangerous and violent impulsive behaviours that might harm people around them.

Hostile attribution bias is a cognitive tendency where individuals interpret ambiguous social cues as intentionally hostile or threatening. In other words, they are more likely to perceive neutral or ambiguous actions as aggressive or harmful. Hostile attribution bias can lead to aggressive responses, as individuals may react defensively or aggressively even when the situation does not warrant it. While there tends to be a predisposition for men and boys to exhibit these behaviours, this is not solely the case. Now, let us explore how hostile attribution bias can be linked to toxic masculinity. As we now know, toxic masculinity refers to cultural norms and expectations that promote harmful and rigid views of masculinity. Exaggeration of traits such as dominance, emotional suppression, aggression and the devaluation of femininity are often attributed to toxic masculinity. Unfortunately, when boys experience behaviours linked to the foregoing traits, the behavioural expectations are often normalised. This can lead to boys feeling pressured to enact these experiential norms, leading to behaviours that reinforce gender stereotypes that hinder emotional expression (Skipper and Fox, 2022).

Hostile attribution bias can be seen as a manifestation of toxic masculinity. Here is how they are connected. Aggressive behaviour is often encouraged by toxic masculinity, which establishes authority and preserves a sense of control. Due to this bias, people may react violently when they see dangers or difficulties, which result in a hypervigilant state. The possible anxiety experienced from the unease of the situation becomes an expression that is discouraged by toxic masculinity as being particularly vulnerable. These situations are then exacerbated as men may begin to repress their feelings and see the world negatively. People who are prone to hostile attribution bias often mistake neutral or ambiguous stimuli as hostile. Men who have been exposed to toxic masculinity during their childhood may be more likely to see other people as disrespectful or threatening. Aggressive tendencies experienced during childhood can emerge during adulthood, leading to destructive behaviours towards themselves and others (Skelton, 2001). Reactive aggressiveness, or spontaneous, emotionally driven reactions to perceived threats, can often be linked to hostile attribution bias, which can lead to reactive aggression being reinforced by toxic masculinity, often discouraging emotional responsiveness. The emphasis on dominance and power in toxic masculinity can lead to violent behaviours that can trigger violent responses in situations that are not dangerous. The combination of hostile attribution bias and toxic masculinity perpetuates harmful gender dynamics. Often men who follow these conventions could find it difficult to control their emotions, which could result in violent outbursts. Toxic masculinity and emotional intelligence should be addressed in violence prevention programmes to decrease aggressive behaviour. In conclusion, toxic masculinity and hostile attribution bias are linked, which perpetuates negative behavioural patterns. To encourage more positive masculinity displays and lessen aggressiveness, it is crucial to acknowledge and question these conventions.

What positive practices can promote boys' and girls' holistic development?

Here are some practical activities and strategies for early years practitioners and primary education teachers who may wish to try to support the movement towards minimising toxic masculinity. These include awareness of behaviours, language use, using the resources on offer in the learning environment as well as the displays for signposting information.

Language: Modelling appropriate communication in early years and primary schools

To address the potential for gender stereotypes, consider actions such as raising language awareness. The impact of words and phrases on boys and girls often extends beyond initial thoughts. Pay particular attention to the words that are spoken in the classroom. Language awareness should become a general approach within the learning environment. Early years practitioners and primary school teachers consider the use of language when introducing activities. Model the language you expect to be reflected in the children you are teaching. Endeavour to remove the repetition of stereotypes such as 'girls are not good at maths' or 'boys don't cry', demonstrating emotional awareness. Promote open discussions on these stereotypes when and if they are highlighted in the discussion between the children. The use of inclusive language can be introduced to ensure all children feel valued. With the adoption of slight changes, like saying 'children' instead of 'girls and boys' or 'parents and carers' or 'families' rather than Mums and Dads' can help to affirm the things we have in common rather than our differences. Language and understanding the power of language when addressing toxic masculinity signifies the importance of all narratives surrounding positive practices to minimise gender stereotypes.

> **Reflection**
>
> Think about how you interact with the children in your class.
>
> - Do I promote collaboration and respect?
> - How can I use language to emphasise the importance of group working when children are struggling to work together?
>
> Discuss respectful communication and active listening.

Fostering a supportive emotional learning environment?

Teach emotional intelligence and empathy to all around you, including the staff team. Modelling emotions enables children and adults to communicate and replicate authentic expressions. Emotional expression supports children in understanding their environment. The creation of a safe space for children to openly communicate their feelings is to be encouraged. Create a safe and supportive learning environment where children can express their thoughts and feelings comfortably. Preschool or nursery should be a safe environment to learn and explore—you can help children by affirming unconventional choices, reassuring them that it is okay to be different and encouraging a culture of acceptance. For example, a parent may question boys dressing up as princesses. As practitioners and primary school teachers, your role is to support the children in their choices. As professionals, early years practitioners and primary school teachers' role is to facilitate learning, to encourage children to feel comfortable, and 'to have a go'. Fostering open dialogue between the early years practitioners and primary school teachers with the children in their care enables a nonjudgemental environment. Encouraging all children to discuss their feelings in an open learning environment allows sharing thoughts nonjudgementally. Honest talks with the children can be incorporated into circle time in early years settings. Teach respect and empathy by incorporating lessons on empathy, kindness and understanding. Discuss stereotypes and challenge them. Encourage children to listen to and learn from each other's experiences. There are numerous opportunities for children in primary school to be encouraged to open up about their feelings. Whether on a one-to-one basis or in small group work, teachers can engage with children, asking them to reflect or talk about their weekend, holidays or how they are feeling daily.

Encourage children to have an open discussion about their feelings. Empathy-building activities can encourage children to discuss their feelings during activities that foster empathy (Kucirkova, 2019). Some examples of activities early years practitioners and primary school teachers may adopt are reading stories about empathy. Questioning the children to think about how the characters in the story may feel encourages alternative perspectives to be considered when addressing some sensitive issues. Opening conversations about feelings and adopting perspective-taking throughout the learning process will support children as they become adults. More engagement around perspective-taking children's experiences will help prepare them to think before they act. Here are some suggestions to start the process. Begin by selecting age-appropriate books to read that will help to develop an emphatic perspective. Children are often inspired by stories and characters that they can relate to. You want to select books that highlight behaviours or characteristics that will get the children thinking and talking about them. As children begin discussing the characters or perspectives to consider within the book(s), they create emotional language (Kucirkova, 2019). The early years practitioners and primary school teachers can then model the language created to support children relating to characters in the book to model their behaviours.

Introducing positive male role models promotes the importance of everyone's place in society, irrespective of gender. Draw attention to values like cooperation, kindness, and compassion. Similarly, give children real-life examples that counter stereotypes in your activities and topic work and external visitors. Invitations to a range of guest speakers can highlight the diverse range of people and their careers. Promoting equality by asking men who have careers as nurses, professors, artists, male dancers and stay-at-home Dads, for example, to share their experiences about their roles. Similarly, women have careers as firefighters, police officers, engineers and plumbers. Visit a range of workplaces that support a diverse workforce such as local sports clubs. Encouraging the boys and girls to join in with football, netball, hockey and a range of other sports together will also break down the expectations for gender-specific sports. To further highlight a range of diverse roles in society, discuss superheroes, reminding boys and girls that they are not just male characters in stories and films. Engaging in a range of activities such as learning a skill, for example, knitting or crocheting, cooking and baking demonstrates gender balance to minimise toxic masculinity.

> **Reflection**
>
> Think about how to foster an atmosphere where all children are at ease expressing their feelings.
>
> - Am I promoting emotional expression?
>
> Encourage boys to express their emotions without fear of rejection.

Normalising inclusion for all in the learning environment or setting

Another normal activity that regularly takes place in UK learning environments is decorating the walls. The straightforward actions connected with the poster displays around the learning environment can have a positive impact on celebrating diversity to minimise stereotypes. Artwork can be displayed to highlight key topics on the curriculum while displaying issues or challenges within society. Display inclusive artwork and posters by decorating classrooms with artwork posters that celebrate diversity, equality and kindness. Showing images of people from various backgrounds, cultures and abilities offers alternative images of people in the world, enabling children to connect with unfamiliar cultures and societies. To break down stereotypical connotations attached to different people's lives and livelihoods. Again, engagement with difference supports 'traditional' imagery related to toxic masculinity. Incorporation of all learning opportunities should be embraced as a way for children to recognise themselves in a global environment. The resource of displays can often be overlooked as a useful addition to the learning environment, that enables the children to feel a sense of belonging in their classroom. Displaying children's work can foster a keen sense of pride that their work has been selected to be shown to others in the school. Remember, presenting all children's work on the display boards cultivates an inclusive ethos within the learning environment.

> **Reflection**
>
> Reflect on the displays in the classroom.
>
> - Are my displays gender-inclusive?
> - Do they challenge stereotypes and provide diverse representations of both genders?
> - Do all children have a piece of work on display?

The promotion of inclusive resources for practice

Reading materials and the selection of books for children in the early years and primary school are a useful way to explore narratives around toxic masculinity that may challenge gender stereotypes. Practitioners and teachers could tell stories that portray a diverse variety of characters who challenge stereotypes. These stories can be extended by the children acting out the roles, working through some of the topics highlighted within the story to challenge stereotypes. Play around with the characters; female roles become male roles for example. The National Union of Teachers (NUT) collaborated with a few primary schools in 2013 to incorporate the curriculum to remove 'traditional' gender stereotypes. The project's goal was to provide primary schools with a selection of books that portrayed characters that challenged some of the established gender stereotypes of boys and girls in children's books (NUT, 2013). View stories and factual books in your classroom.

Are there examples of working women, caring fathers, active girls and creative boys? Are all the animals in the story male? The 'It's Child's Play' report from the NUT's Breaking the Mould project (2013) has suggested books with additional notes and ideas for discussion. Some of the activities that should be avoided in the learning environment are labelling a bookshelf 'Boys' Books', which might seem like an effective way to encourage reluctant boy readers. Unfortunately, this can be counterproductive, reminding boys of the stereotype that they are less interested in reading, and encouraging the idea that only certain interests are allowed. Instead, present alternative reading materials that include diverse genders, cultures and abilities for all children to enjoy.

The introduction or continued use of diverse learning materials can allow children to challenge any preconceived ideas they have developed from their family(ies). Provide a wide range of learning materials, including books, toys and art supplies, that represent diverse genders, cultures and abilities that offer alternatives. Avoiding stereotypical gendered toys and books again offers options that appeal to all children.

> **Reflection**
>
> Observe the children who use the various spaces and equipment.
>
> - Do certain areas get dominated by certain groups, or by one gender or the other?
> - Are there changes or adjustments you could make to encourage children to feel equally free to use the home corner, the reading corner, the bikes, the Legos and outdoor space?

How to promote an anti-bullying learning environment

Addressing bullying and aggressive behaviours in early years and primary school settings is vital to creating a safe and supportive environment for all children and professionals. There should always be consistent policies and practices, including clear and consistent anti-bullying policies that outline expectations, consequences and reporting procedures. The minimisation of toxic masculinity unfortunately should be addressed throughout educational settings to support children and professionals alike. Teachers and early years practitioners must be aware of the policies to ensure they are enforced to foster a culture of respect and accountability for all. Even though the children in early years settings are younger, there should be a provision for age-appropriate educational guidance about bullying, empathy and respectful behaviour. Social gatherings such as circle time in early years or assemblies in primary school remain a useful space to address some of the topics in a shared discussion. In classroom discussions, older children can develop an awareness of unacceptable behaviours and promote understanding of positive conduct around the school.

Continued professional development should support early years practitioners and primary school teachers to identify and deal with bullying. These workshop sessions can provide appropriate language use and communication and intervention techniques that work. Engage the children to foster a supportive learning environment where they feel safe. This can be through the introduction of anti-bullying clubs, student councils or peer mentorship initiatives. Ask parents and guardians to be involved in the promotion of anti-bullying by hosting workshops. Give parents and guardians information and direction on how to spot bullying symptoms in their children and how to help them. Efficient monitoring and assessment enable all those involved to evaluate the success of anti-bullying initiatives regularly. Governors and senior leaders should be involved in tracking developments and making necessary adjustment plans. Offering a bullying prevention–based approach can manage prejudice in the learning environment. This will address any bullying motivated by bias based on a person's race, ethnicity, gender, religion or other characteristics. To encourage diversity and inclusivity throughout the school community, it is important to keep in mind that stopping and dealing with bullying calls for a comprehensive strategy involving parents, teachers, students and the entire school community. Early years and primary schools may establish a secure and encouraging environments for all children by promoting a positive culture and fulfilling evidence-based practices.

Where there are cases of bullying, conflict resolution can be used to stop aggressive behaviour and teach conflict resolution techniques to both parties involved. The role of conflict resolution can encourage empathy, compromise and communication, again addressing toxic masculinity. Conflict resolution, however, is only successful when both parties are willing to make amends. Children can begin to understand that their behaviours are not acceptable in the learning environment or anywhere else for that matter; the support of early years practitioners, primary school teachers and parents/guardians is vital. An integrated approach to the behaviours exhibited by the children involved further demonstrates a supportive mechanism around the problem behaviours, hopefully offering an improved positive outlook moving forward. Anti-bullying campaigns establish initiatives against bullying that emphasise courtesy, compassion and speaking up against unacceptable behaviour (Kucirkova, 2019). Remember that preventing and addressing bullying requires a comprehensive approach involving children, early years practitioners, primary school teachers including parents and the entire school community. By fostering a positive culture and implementing evidence-based strategies, nurseries and primary schools can create a safe, supportive environment for all children.

> **Reflection**
>
> Consider your response to remarks or actions related to a child's gender: Think before you speak and behave.
>
> - Should I respond to gender stereotypes?
> - Do I unintentionally support stereotypes, or do I constantly challenge them?

Inclusive environment in practice

Remember, all activities to minimise toxic masculinity should be integrated into the curriculum consistently. Through promoting positive masculinity and breaking down harmful stereotypes, early years practitioners and primary school teachers can foster a more inclusive and supportive learning environment for all children. Creating gender-neutral learning spaces for early years and primary-age children is essential to foster an inclusive and supportive environment. Here are some practical steps and considerations to potentially incorporate into your practice. Where possible allow flexible seating arrangements. Arrange desks and seating in a way that allows for flexibility. Avoid fixed rows, and encourage collaborative groupings. When children are seated together, they can engage with different people from alternative backgrounds, and experiences will become more diverse. Use a mix of individual desks, tables, cushions and floor seating to accommodate different learning preferences. This will work particularly well in early years settings, as children can choose where to sit, forming friendships to develop their agency. The incorporation of neutral colour schemes can help reduce any overly gendered colours, for example pink for girls, blue for boys. Instead, using calming tones like greens, yellows, and greys can aid the creation of a soothing atmosphere. Remember that creating a gender-neutral learning space is an ongoing process. Involve parents and guardians by communicating the importance of gender-neutral spaces. Share resources and strategies to create an inclusive home environment as well and regularly assess and adapt your classroom and learning space practices to ensure all children feel valued and respected.

> **Reflection**
>
> Ensure that all students have a voice during discussions.
>
> - Am I inclusive in classroom discussions?
> - How can I avoid favouring one gender over another?

Conclusion

The introduction of educational practices to minimise toxic masculinity has been discussed. Any definitions have supported the context that encapsulates the early years and primary school settings' practices as a way of observing pedagogical development to minimise toxic masculinity. Solutions have been offered to challenge some of the identified behaviours to neutralise the gendered stereotypes promoted in society. Instead, promote equality, kindness and inclusion, for children to experience minimal toxic masculinity, which is often found in wider society. Children can gain a deeper self-knowledge, aside from traditional gender norms. Positive reinforcement in educational development found in daily pedagogy will generate good relationships for children to explore and express themselves. Consideration has been given to some of the many positive actions early years practitioners and primary school teachers can employ in their practice to minimise toxic masculinity. By removing many negative connotations attached to the persistent repressive behaviours of children's historical experiences of education, children can have less restrictive expectations, enjoying a happier life. Remember, children who experience less pervasive traditional gendered stereotypes relate to feelings of unhappiness (The Children's Society, 2023). As professionals with a societal responsibility, we aim to ensure all children can be who they want to be without being remonstrated for their behaviours, actions and gender.

References

Berenbaum, S.A., Martin, C.L. and Ruble, D.N. (2008), Gender development. In W. Damon and R. Lerner (eds.), *Advances in Child and Adolescent Development*, pp. 647–696. Virginia: Wiley.

Biddulph, S. (2014), *Raising boys: Why Boys Are Different—and How to Help Them Become Happy and Well-balanced Men* (3rd Ed.). Berkeley: Ten Speed Press.

Coles, E., Cheyne, H., Rankin, J. and Daniel, B. (2016), Getting it right for every child: A national policy framework to promote children's well-being in Scotland, United Kingdom. *Milbank Q*, 94(2), pp. 334–365. https://doi.org/10.1111/1468-0009.12195

Duckworth, V., Farrell, F. and Rigby, P. (2016), 'Ways of 'being': Alternative critical dialogic perspectives on gendered identity in education, training and work'. *Education and Training*, 58(3). https://doi.org/10.1108/ET-01-2016-0003

Farrell, F. (2016), 'Learning to listen': boys' gender narratives—implications for theory and practice, *Education and Training*, 58(3), pp. 283–297. http://dx.doi.org/10.1108/ET-06-2015-0046

Ford, C. (2019), *Boys Will Be Boys: Power, Patriarchy and Toxic Masculinity*. London: Simon and Schuster.

Harrington, C. (2021), What is 'Toxic Masculinity' and why does it matter? *Men and Masculinities*, 24(2), pp. 345–352. https://doi.org/10.1177/1097184X20943254

King, T.L., Scovelle, A.J., Meehl, A., Milner, A.J. and Priest, N. (2021), Gender stereotypes and biases in early childhood: A systematic review. *Australasian Journal of Early Childhood*. https://doi.org/10.1177_1836939121999849

Kucirkova, N. (2019), How could children's storybooks promote empathy? A conceptual framework based on developmental psychology and literary theory. *Frontier in Psychology*, 10, pp. 121. https://doi.org/10.3389/fpsyg.2019.00121

Millet, K. (1971), *Sexual Politics*, New York: Avon Books.
Moosa, S. and Bhana, D. (2023), Men who teach early childhood education: Mediating masculinity, authority and sexuality. *Teaching and Teacher Education*, 122, 103959.
National Union of Teachers. (2013), *Breaking the Mould*. https://neu.org.uk/advice/classroom/teaching-resources/breaking-mould (Accessed March 20, 2024).
Parent, M.C., Gobble, T.D. and Rochlen, A. (2019), Social media behavior, Toxic masculinity, and depression. *Psychology of Men and Masculinity*, **20**(3), pp. 277–287. https://doi.org/10.1037/men0000156
Sax, L. (2005) Why Gender Matters: What Parents and Teachers Need to Know about the Emerging Science of Sex Differences. New York: Doubleday.
Schmitz, S. (2010), Sex, gender and the brain: biological determinism versus socio-cultural constructivism. In I. Klinge and C. Wiesemann (Eds.), *Gender and Sex in Biomedicine: Theories, Methodologies, Results* (Göttingen, Germany: Universitätsverlag Göttingen), pp. 57–76.
Scottish Government. (2012), *A Guide to Getting It Right for Every Child*. Edinburgh, United Kingdom: Scottish Government.
Skelton, C. (2001), *Schooling the Boys: Masculinities and Primary Education*, Maidenhead: Open University Press.
Skipper, Y. and Fox, C. (2022), Boys will be boys: Young people's perceptions and experiences of gender within education. *Pastoral Care in Education*, **40**(4), pp. 391–409, https://doi.org/10.1080/02643944.2021.1977986
The Childrens Society. (2020), Time to banish toxic masculinity. https://www.childrenssociety.org.uk/what-we-do/blogs/how-toxic-masculinity-affects-young-people (Accessed March 6, 2024).
The Children's Society. (2023), *The Good Childhood Report 2023*. The Children's Society, London.
Wingrave, M. (2018), Perceptions of gender in early years. *Gender and Education*, **30**(5), pp. 587–606, https://doi.org/10.1080/09540253.2016.1258457
Xu, Y., Warin, J. and Robb, M. (2020). Beyond gender binaries: Pedagogies and practices in early childhood education and care (ECEC). *Early Years*, **40**(1), pp. 1–4. https://doi.org/10.1080/09575146.2020.1728077

Part II
Social interaction; social beings and relationships

5 Supporting Children's Sense of Belonging and Feelings of Mattering Through Relationship-Rich Pedagogies

Eleonora Teszenyi

Introduction

A substantial body of literature suggests that children, like all humans, have an innate desire to be needed, to feel important and to matter to others, which injects meaning into their lives (Rosenberg and McCullough, 1981; Marshall *et al.*, 2010). There is also compelling evidence to suggest that a sense of belonging is crucial to children's participation in the activities of their groups and communities (Allen *et al.*, 2023; Sykes and Teszenyi, 2018; Vang and Nishina, 2022). Children who feel they belong and matter to others are happier, better adjusted, more engaged at school and more motivated to learn (Allen and Boyle, 2023; Alink *et al.*, 2023; Korpershoek *et al.*, 2020). Belonging is how children and young people feel towards their group and communities, whereas children interpret how much they matter within their communities from how others behave towards them. Mattering is defined as a 'psychological tendency to perceive the self as significant to others' (Marshall *et al.*, 2010, p. 367) or 'individuals' self-construal of their significance or import to specific others' (Marshall *et al.*, 2010, p. 368).

In educational contexts, the sense of belonging and mattering are intrinsically connected to relational pedagogies, poised to provide relationship-rich education (Gowing, 2019). Practitioners in early years settings and teachers in schools play a significant role in establishing a social and emotional environment that affords children with a sense of belonging and mattering. They can achieve this by genuine listening, sensitive positive relationships and respectful interactions through which children's voices are heard and their views taken seriously in matters that are important to them. Harnessing the potential of slowing down (Clark, 2023) and the visceral qualities of interpersonal interactions, such as attunement, intuition (Sipman *et al.*, 2019) and empathy (Segal, 2011) can all be in service of helping children feel that they matter and they belong.

In the first two sections of this chapter, belonging and mattering are discussed through highlighting seminal pieces of work to provide the foundations for the subsequent sections that evidence their psychological, social and educational benefits. The second half of the chapter turns to practical ideas that teachers and practitioners can implement in their everyday practice to nurture children's sense of belonging and mattering, key to establishing a

DOI: 10.4324/9781032716190-8

cohesive community of learners. Here, slowing down, attunement and pedagogic tact are discussed along with intersubjective action for its intuitive sensitivity and responsiveness to children. The pedagogic strategies outlined are demonstrated by examples from empirical research in five short vignettes.

Sense of belonging

In his seminal work, Maslow (1943) asserted that love and belonging are one of the fundamentals in the hierarchy of human needs. Most humans would strive for affectionate relationships and for a place in a group, which would suggest that belonging is important to the social lives of people. The plethora of literature around school belonging suggests that belonging is a multidimensional concept, so examining the many layers of how it is understood would helpfully underpin the implications for practice in later sections of the chapter.

Goodenow (1993) and Willms (2003) constructed a psychological understanding of school belonging, emphasising the personal significance of being accepted, included, respected, valued and supported by others in a school's social environment. Osterman (2000), however, approached belonging from a community perspective, highlighting the significance of the relationship a person has with a group as a whole. He associated belonging with a sense of acceptance and relatedness and used them as shorthand for a sense of community. More recently, Alink *et al.* (2023) has distinguished between the feeling of belongingness as a psychological concept, manifesting in positive relations, and belonging as a relational construct realised in active participation in one's community.

Interestingly, Allen and Boyle (2023) consider engagement and belonging as two complementary constructs and recognise that engagement contributes to the sense of belonging and vice versa. Although there does not appear to be a universal definition for school belonging, there does seem to be an agreement on its importance in contributing to positive outcomes for children. These are associated with mental health and wellbeing, academic achievement, social behaviour including social bonding between peers, such as friendships, and engagement and motivation to learn (Alink *et al.*, 2023). Allen and Boyle (2023) explain the interrelated nature of these positive outcomes like a chain of influences that goes from children forming relationships in order to fulfil the need to belong, to active participation in activities, the success of which then fuels motivation and positive behaviour, leading to improved performance and academic achievement.

As seen in this brief summary, in whichever way belonging is understood and interpreted, one thing remains clear: belonging matters, especially to vulnerable groups of children. The subsequent section provides some ideas of what practitioners can do to help children develop a sense of belonging to their group and school community.

Helping children develop a sense of belonging

In today's quickly changing world, a sense of belonging to communities offers stability for all generations, including the young. Sykes and Teszenyi (2018, p. 22) describe communities as living organisms and highlight their 'locatedness' that calls upon the loyalties and collective responsibilities of their members, who share lived experiences. The cultural experiences children share with adults and peers help them develop a sense of how they fit into their communities and how they are valued and respected as members (Rogoff, Dahl and Callanan, 2018). One would argue, then, that adults play a significant role in helping children come to understand the codes and ethic of care for their communities, which are reflected in sensitive, respectful, reciprocal, democratic relationships and behaviours—in other words, in taking 'response-abilities' for others (Ritchie, 2015, p. 47).

Following this sociocultural logic, teachers and practitioners unsurprisingly strive to establish inclusive environments in their settings, where all children feel they can take responsibility for and contribute to the lives of their communities. The significance of early education and knowledgeable, skilful adults cannot be underestimated in promoting learning, which fosters the attitudes of care for fellow human beings and helps understand the power of commitment to others.

Hence pedagogic approaches that are specifically designed to support socialisation processes present pathways in achieving and supporting a sense of belonging. The United Nations Convention of the Rights of the Child (UN, 1989) and the African Charter on the Rights and Welfare of the Child (African Union, 1999) provide helpful steering for rights-based pedagogies that encourage curriculum approaches and practices that go beyond upholding children's rights to protection and strive to realise their rights to provision and participation in their everyday lives and educational contexts. These are the only two international treaties that cover children's civil, political, economic, social and cultural rights, both reflecting sensitivity to their social, cultural and geopolitical situatedness.

Practitioners and teachers may helpfully think about belonging as two sides of the same coin in identifying practical implications of rights-based pedagogies. On one side is belonging as relating to people and places, and on the other is belonging as participation. Belonging in a 'children's rights' sense is a two-way and often (but not always) reciprocal process. On the one hand, children have the right to be protected, provided for and included, and on the other, they have the right to express their views, exercise their agency, care for others, take on responsibilities and be part of, and also separate from, their social environment. It is also useful to remember that belonging is organic; it evolves and expands as children come across new people, places and cultural practices and as they actively interpret and internalise what they experience.

There are fine examples of pedagogies worldwide that support children's sense of belonging and have synergies with rights-based pedagogies. One is the pedagogy of listening and relationships from Reggio Emilia in Italy, which anchors children's sense of belonging through the reciprocity of relationships, not only within each setting but also between settings and the local municipality (council). This opens up social spaces for making even the youngest of children visible and agentic in their immediate and wider communities.

Belonging is also one of the three pedagogic priorities for children's learning in the Early Years Learning Framework for Australia (Department of Education, Employment and Workplace Relations [DEEWR], 2022). Threaded through the document is a deeply rooted respect for their rich history as they claim that,

> Experiencing belonging-knowing where and with whom you belong-is integral to human existence. Children belong to diverse families, neighbourhoods, local and global communities. Belonging acknowledges children's interdependence with others and the basis of relationships in defining identities. In early childhood, and throughout life, trusting relationships and affirming experiences are crucial to a sense of belonging.
>
> (p. 6)

Similarly, one of the key strands of the early childhood curriculum in New Zealand, the Te Whāriki (New Zealand Ministry of Education, 2017) is 'belonging' (mana whenua), which is nurtured through 'the Māori views of the world, the natural environment', and 'the interconnectedness of people, place, time and things' (p. 31). The concept of belonging is also highlighted in the firmly rights-based Quality Framework for Early Childhood Play, Learning and Care in Wales (Welsh Government, 2023), where educators are encouraged to create a sense of 'cynefin', a sense of connection in and with the natural world. The word 'cynefin' translates as, 'the place where we feel we belong, where the people and landscape around us are familiar, and the sights and sounds are reassuringly recognisable' (Dylan and Beauchamp, 2022, p. 40).

Reflection

In this chapter section so far, foundational ideas relating to 'belonging' have been discussed, including acceptance, respect, inclusion, relatedness, sense of community, engagement, locatedness and connectedness. Putting yourself in the shoes of a child, ask yourself the following questions and think about how a child's answers to these questions affect the way you feel about and currently understand 'belonging'.

- Is there anyone who looks and dresses like me at home in my family and in my community outside school? Or can I find them in books, pictures or artifacts around the room?
- How will people remember my name?
- What is expected of me?
- How should I behave? How should I talk?
- What things in the room are familiar to me?
- What can I explore on my own or with others?
- Who can I talk to, especially if I am upset, need help or want to share something?

The concept of 'mattering'

As discussed so far, belonging is how children feel towards their group or community. The flipside of belonging is 'mattering', the 'psychological tendency to perceive the self as significant to others' (Marshall *et al.*, 2010, p. 367). To be needed and wanted or to be significant to others is a powerful human experience and injects meaning into people's lives. Children can glean how others feel towards them through social referencing: how they are seen by others, how others interact with them, how much they feel they are valued as a member of a group. It is widely believed that children need to feel they matter at home, in school and in their communities. For practitioners to be able to help children feel that they matter in practice, understanding the concept is a good place to start.

'Mattering' was first conceptualised in the 1980s by Moris Rosenberg as an integral component of one's self-concept (Rosenberg and McCullough, 1981): to be the focus of interest and feeling significant to others is paramount to humans across the lifespan. 'Mattering' could be best characterised by three psychosocial sources: awareness or attention, which refers to being noticed by others; importance, which relates to the one's perceived relevance to others or the feeling of being a concern of others; and dependence or reliance, which encapsulates the feeling that others can depend on us. Just as the sense of belonging yields positive outcomes, 'mattering' can also contribute to greater psychosocial wellbeing, improved self-esteem, greater resilience to stress and higher levels of satisfaction with one's life (Flett, 2022).

There are some interesting controversies in the study of mattering, one of which revolves around validating 'mattering' as a separate construct from 'belonging'. Dixon Rayle (2006) argues that 'mattering' occurs between two people, whereas 'belonging' is between the individual and a group. In relation to the direction of flow in 'mattering', Elliott (2009) asserts that due to the bidirectional nature of caring relationships, one form of mattering is when others show an individual that they care, and the individual can rely on them. The other is the inverse: The individual shows others that they can depend on him. This scholarly debate highlights an important extension to the original concept of 'mattering' by Rosenberg: It includes both the feeling of being valued by others and adding value to others' lives.

Some synergies can be noted here with the two sides of the sense of belonging discussed earlier (the feeling of belongingness versus belonging via participation), which heightens practitioners' and teachers' awareness of the perhaps two counterintuitive notions. One is that a child might have the feeling they matter, but their emotional investment towards their group is not reciprocated, bringing them up to the sharp realisation that there is a darker side to belonging. The other is that despite having a sense of belonging, they may still feel that they do not matter to their community, be it within or outside their school or setting. Children who feel they belong and matter to others are happier, better adjusted, more engaged at school and more motivated to learn (Allen and Boyle, 2023;

Alink et al., 2023; Korpershoek et al., 2020). Therefore, it is crucial that teachers and practitioners establish a nurturing environment and adopt pedagogic practices that foster belonging and 'mattering'. Foundational to these are positive relationships, child-respecting approaches and relationship-rich pedagogies, which are discussed in the subsequent section.

'Mattering' and 'belonging' underpinned by relationship-rich pedagogies

The Organisation for Economic Cooperation and Development (OECD) (2019) reports that around 30% of pupils do not feel a sense of belonging to their school. It, therefore, appears more important than ever to establish positive social and emotional environments that serve as the foundation for children and young people to develop a sense of belonging. Woven into the fabric of a supportive environment is a network of positive relationships, where relationality becomes the heartbeat of interactions with and between children.

Interpersonal relationships are core to human beings, and they shape who we are and how we are. The patterns of relationships evolve as individuals come together in a group, make emotional connections and learn about how each member of a community might act or react in particular situations. Relationships are bidirectional, each relationship influencing and being influenced by a network of relationships. They 'underpin the educational enterprise of schools' (Gowing, 2019, p. 74) and contribute to the overall climate of a school or setting. Emotionally literate relationships contribute to positive health and wellbeing outcomes and can have therapeutic and healing effects for children who find themselves in challenging circumstances (i.e., family breakdown or conflict).

Although relationships cannot single-handedly deliver a sense of belonging or mattering, they are key contributors and, therefore, a worthwhile focus of attention for practice. What practitioners can do is to create a caring, well-structured learning environment that facilitates the development of empathy and care and respect towards one another, carving out space and places for intimacy, friendships, shared play, peer support in the novice–expert dyads and so forth.

Adults themselves can actively contribute to the development of positive relationships by attuned listening, slowing down to pay attention to children's messages and meaning making and engaging in interactions that are conducive to community building such as collaborations, shared project, co-operation and joint problem solving.

Slowing down to listen—the importance of kairological time

Listening is the temporal aspect of the inseparable processes of teaching and learning and is part of actively participating in the life and learning of children. The process of listening is about deciphering not only what children say but also how they act, react and interact with each other and adults. The significance of adopting a pedagogy of listening (Rinaldi, 2021) is beyond doubt in the development of a sense of belonging and the feeling of mattering. In a classroom community, practitioners fulfil a fundamental role in pulling together into a coherent whole young children's experiences and relationships, and treating them as significant (Rinaldi, 2021). In the processes of listening, it is important for practitioners to be mindful of children who appear to be relegated to the margins because of the stronger voices in the group. It is their role to ensure that all children's voices are heard and taken seriously.

Attuned listening requires time, and it happens best when adults slow down and children are unhurried. How time is perceived and used by adults reveals attitudes, control, authority and where power is located. Time might be perceived as measured, and therefore a commodity to be spent most efficiently, or as fluid, which affords stretched teaching and learning experiences. How time is viewed by the adult will determine whether it might be a possession of children, or they might be possessed by it. This will consequently influence the climate in the setting, and reflect what and who is valued, what and who matters and how it is shown to children.

The origin of the word 'time' traces back to the Greek 'chronos' and 'kairos', delineating quantitative and qualitative time, respectively. Chronological time is linear and measurable, whereas kairological time is nonlinear and captures opportune timing, a temporal opening or favourable moment that needs to be seized before it passes (Cocker, 2015). The affordances of slow pedagogies (Clark, (2023) and stretching out time for children's learning experiences (Cuffaro, 1995) include stronger relationships, stronger community cohesion and therefore greater potential for a sense of belonging. However, 'prying open Chronos to create a present long enough to accommodate Kairos' (Stern, 2004, p. 27) is no easy task in today's 'fast schooling' climate (Clark, 2023, p. 8) where children are hurried along under the pressures of achieving the next goal.

The following vignette demonstrates how honouring children's genuine immersion in the flow of time enables practitioner to listen to children carefully, valuing their ideas in that moment fully.

VIGNETTE 1

Kata, the practitioner, is at the craft table with five children (4 to 6 years old), ready to fold paper boats from sheets of wallpaper samples a parent brough into nursery this morning.

Kata: "Now we 've got our papers, what kind of boat do you think we should make?"

Joel: "We caught an African catfish, because we put the right kind of bait on the hook. Then we took it to the farm and cooked it and we ate it."

Kata:	"What does an African catfish taste like?"
Joel:	"It's salty".
Kata:	"I think you must be right, Joel, I am sure it is not sweet tasting."
Sara:	"I had a chocolate swirl pastry for breakfast."
Kata:	"We had that at kindergarten yesterday. Did yours taste sweet, too?"
Sara:	"Yes."
Kata:	"Where did you buy your chocolate swirls?"
Sara:	"At the chemists."
May:	"No, silly. (laughing) At the bakery."
Attila:	"In the cake shop."
Kata:	"Yes, I buy mine at the bakery."
Leslie comes along and says:	"Well, I am going to just sit down here."
Kata:	"Come along and sit with us, Leslie. We were about to start making paper boats, but we got distracted and started chatting. Have you ever eaten catfish, by the way? Joel and his grandad caught one and cooked it."

(Teszenyi, 2023)

The role of the adult here was to remain open to children's interests and prior experiences that they together built new understandings on. The stretch of kairos time afforded an unpredicted turn in the conversation. Neither the children nor the practitioner was imprisoned by time. Kairos time was given to the children as opposed to chronos time held onto by the adult. Kata was happy to slow down, and by shifting the locus of power, she gave control to the children. The practitioner created an opportunity for group bonding through this kind of merging and fusing temporal experience, where curriculum pressures for testing children's knowledge were replaced by genuine interest in the children's individual contributions.

This is only one example of ethical child-respecting interpersonal relationships enacted by the means of listening. It gives clear messages to the members of a classroom community: that they are valued as people and their contributions add value to the life their community. Slowing down to listen can create a climate that is poised to support a sense of belonging. This can be further supported by visceral qualities, and some of these will be discussed next.

The ethics of attunement, pedagogic tact and empathy

Attunement is born out of kairos time as it connects temporality with resonance expressed in interconnection with and attention to others. Emphatic attunement refers to 'the capacity to think and feel oneself into the inner life of another person' (Lipari, 2014, p. 207). In educational contexts, the visceral qualities of intuition and attunement serve adults well in being able to read situations and make decisions in the moment (van Manen, 2015). An example of this is captured in the following vignette.

VIGNETTE 2

A circle of differently sized stepping stones is set up in the middle of the room for children to play with. A group of four children is going round the circle, hopping from one stone to the other. Aron rhythmically bends his knees every time he steps onto the next stone. From previous conversations with the parents, Zara, the practitioner, knows that Aron goes to folk dance classes with his parents. This knowledge helps her recognise the discrete movements that resemble dance moves in his play, so on impulse, she prepares to respond. After creating some space on the rug, Zara turns to Aron: "I have cleared some space for you if you want to dance with a partner." Aron's eyes light up, so Zara assumes her instinct were right. Aron moves over to the rug to dance to the folk music Zara is just switching on. This leads to a group dance, short individual performances from Aron, then turns into group singing as more children join in.

(Teszenyi, 2023)

Zara's attunement, fuelled by in-depth knowledge of Aron and his family's culture, enabled her to see Aron interact with his environment via his cultural tools. It enabled Zara to respond in a socially and culturally supportive way through an action that was pedagogically thoughtful in that moment. The message was clear: Aron's contribution to the life of the group was recognised and valued, and Zara created an opportunity for it to act as a psycho-social 'glue' is his play with his peers.

Now let's continue the story of Zara and Aron.

VIGNETTE 3

Soon after, the children move back to the stepping stones and instead of stepping from one to the other, they start to run through them. Children who appear more confident in their physical abilities start to push past those who still need help with balancing. To avoid the situation getting out of hand, Zara, tactfully and seamlessly, takes her flute to the stepping stones and plays a rhythm. This draws children's attention, and she speaks to them: "Let see who can step in time with the rhythm I am playing." The children start to giggle and have a go.

Here we can see Zara skilfully acting with pedagogic tact that prevents the situation getting out of hand as children choose to evade the agreed code of conduct in their pursuit of fun and enjoyment. Sipman *et al.* (2019, p. 1186) claim that pedagogic tact is an enactment of intuition and define it as a 'teacher's ability to instantly and adequately act upon the complexity of classroom situations… that require immediate action'. Pedagogically tactful action only happens in kairos time, at a critical or opportune moment sensed intuitively by the practitioner. It has consequences for the 'climate' of a classroom mentioned earlier and also impacts on how children feel about their communities. Chaos can breed disruptive behaviour and vice versa, which can create anxiety for some children and injure community cohesion. This situation in the vignette could have been dealt with differently: by asserting authority and power to maintain order. This is the flipside of pedagogic tact, prohibiting the improvisational characteristic necessary for pedagogic tact in the immediacy of the kairotic moment.

Collaborative and socially constructed learning in schools and early years settings are hotbeds for sharing a sense of belonging and learning empathy through children developing trust in adults and their peers. Segal (2011) suggests that empathy includes 'the act of perceiving, understanding, experiencing and responding to the emotional state and ideas of another person' (p. 267). Picture this:

VIGNETTE 4

A group of mixed-age (3 to 6 years) children in Hungary are in the cloakroom of their nursery, getting ready to go outside. In the hustle and bustle of children getting their jumpers and coats on, and changing into their outdoor shoes, no one notices that young Anika (3 years and 4 months old) is struggling to button up her cardigan. Her peers' excited voices recede as they gradually leave the cloakroom. Anika's eyes are filling with tears, and she looks towards the door through which the others have disappeared out of sight. Six-year-old Sasha is last out of the classroom, grabs her shoes and coat, quickly gets dressed and is about to leave the cloakroom when she stops by Anika. "It's the buttons, isn't it?", she says. Anika nods and the pool of tears roll down her cheeks. Without a word, Sasha fetches some tissue from the room, wipes Anika's tears and says comfortingly: "It's ok, you'll be able to do them up soon. I'll wait for you." She then buttons up the cardigan, says that Anika looks pretty, takes hold of her hand when fully dressed, and they go outside together."

(Teszenyi, 2023)

The scenario demonstrates the value of the interpersonal nature of peer support in helping children feel they matter. Physical touch, the embodied act of tender care between these two children and the intimacy of the support Sasha provides to Anika reflects a climate of respect that sensitive adults can nurture by creating a social-emotional environment that affords acceptance of both giving and receiving support.

Symmetrical interactions, such as those in the previous vignette, happen between people who are similar in age and status. When school adults are involved, their interactions with children are asymmetrical and they hold within a difference in status, or indeed power. However, the possible power imbalance between an adult and a child can be put to good use when it is used to model desirable behaviours and interactions from which children can take their cues. It would seem that attunement and empathic listening integrate well with a particular kind of interaction Teszenyi (2023) refers to as 'intersubjective-action'. In these interactions, a great deal can be learnt about power and being empowered, which could be harnessed for the development of the sense of mattering and belonging.

Meaning for everyone through intersubjective action

The proximity and enduring forms of interactions between people (subjects) prompt reciprocity and involve energy exchanges in both directions. If occurring with regularity over a period of time, they can either be disruptive or generative (Bronfenbrenner and Morris, 2006). Adult–child interactions are one of the most salient aspects of the teaching and learning processes in an educational context, even more so in early childhood as they capture both the social and instructional aspects of practice. Adults can interact with children in a variety of ways depending on their philosophy, the values they hold and their image of the child. For example, 'transaction' occurs when the adult is intent on directly teaching children because they believe to be the ones who drive children's learning. 'Intrapersonal actions' between practitioners and children are driven by the adults' own agenda, by an inward-looking view of what is important to the adult rather than the child in any given learning situation. Over time, this can be disruptive to the cohesion of a learning community and may make children feel they do not matter. The most powerful generative interactions are 'intersubjective actions' as they keep the child in the centre of their learning, include sensitivity and responsiveness towards children's collective engagement in the activities of their communities (Teszenyi, 2023).

Like in the 'African catfish' scenario earlier, in the following vignette, the practitioner is slowing down to listen and showing genuine interest in what children are saying, and her contributions sustain children's spontaneous conversation and shared meaning making.

VIGNETTE 5

It is lunchtime; five children and Juli, the practitioner, are sitting at the dinner table. On the menu is pork slices, mashed potato and apple compote. The children are relaxed, quietly chatting away.

Robi:	"How do I eat this compote?"
Juli:	"Well, you could eat the apple pieces using your fork and then drink the juice since it is served in a glass."
Ami:	"It has got a thing called cloves in it. We had some in Germany".
Petra:	"What's that?" (looking at the practitioner)
Juli:	"Yes, it is a spice, and you can get it in many countries."
Petra:	"It tickles my tongue. I can taste how it smells."
Gina:	"I have been to Italy."
Robi:	"And we often go to Austria."
Ami:	"In the summer we went to Mexico. We had to go in an aeroplane because it's so far away."
Petra (whispers):	"I have never been on an aeroplane."
Robi:	"My mummy says we are not going in an aeroplane because it's not good for the environment."
Juli (speaking directly to Petra):	"I think I know what you mean… I can taste the smell of the cloves, too."
Gina:	"What did you say?" (as she turns her head between the practitioner and Petra)
Juli:	"Petra said that the cloves in her compote tickles her tongue and…" (interrupted)
Robi:	"Once I bit into a whole onion and it stung my tongue like a bee. And my eyes!"
Gina:	(laughing along with the other children): "Why into an onion not an apple?"

(Teszenyi, 2023)

The leisurely atmosphere over lunch allows the focus of communicative exchanges to meander from spices to travel destinations. Juli senses the significance of the sophisticated connection between the taste and smell of cloves to Petra and mirrors her words back to her in acknowledgement, with which she draws the quietly speaking child into the group conversation. The relaxed lunch offers a staging for children to act as they would in out-of-nursery contexts, where, although significant learning happens, situations are not deliberately created for teaching. Children's 'home' ways are welcomed and respected, in this way adding value to the life of their nursery community (Fleer, 2010).

In these examples, the relational and attuned nature of the interactions between adults and children, underpinned by intersubjective sensitivities, emphatic sensibility and pedagogic wisdom, can offer ways to help children develop a sense of belonging and the feeling that they truly matter, both to their peers and the adults in their setting's community. But they are only tiny pieces of the larger picture of 'mattering' and 'belonging'.

Conclusion

To shift the pedagogical approach in the direction of relationship-rich pedagogies that nurture a sense of belonging and mattering requires collective and collaborative effort in a system that is built on measuring individual achievement in many parts of the world. It is much better for children if educational institutions and communities are organised through collective reciprocity, trust, respect and connectedness. Good teaching improves learning, and good practitioners achieve positive outcomes with highly motivated and engaged learners. Children who have affirming experiences develop an understanding of themselves as significant, respected and valued. They learn about relationships through their lived experiences and gradually develop a sense of themselves as contributing members of their community who matter.

References

African Union. (1999), *African Charter on the Rights and Welfare of the Child*. Available at https://www.acerwc.africa/en/page/about-the-charter (Accessed February 2, 2024).

Alink, K., Denessen, E., Veerman, G. and Severiens, S. (2023), Exploring the concept of school belonging: A study with expert ratings. In *Cogent Education*, 10(2), pp. 2235979. https://doi.org/10.1080/2331186X.2023.2235979

Allen, K.-A. and Boyle, C. (2023) School belonging and student engagement: The critical overlaps, similarities, and implications for student outcomes. In Reschley, S.L. and Christenson, C.L. (eds.), *Handbook of Research on Student Engagement*. Switzerland: Springer Link.

Allen, K.-A., Boyle, C., Wong, D., Johnson, R.G. and May, F. (2023), School belonging as an essential component of positive psychology in schools. In A. Giraldez-Hayes and J. Burke (eds.), *Applied Positive School Psychology*. London: Routledge, pp. 159–172.

Bronfenbrenner, U. and Morris, P.A. (2006), The bioecological model of human development. In W. Damon and M.R. Lerner (eds.), *Handbook of Child Psychology* (6th ed., pp. 793–828). New York: John Wiley & Sons.

Clark, A. (2023), *Slow Knowledge and the Unhurried Child*. Abingdon: Routledge.

Cocker, E. (2015), Kairos time: The performativity of timing and timeliness ... or between biding one's time and knowing when to act. *Semantic Scholar*. Available at https://api.semanticscholar.org/CorpusID:55887857 (Accessed February 16, 2024).

Cuffaro, H.K. (1995), *Experimenting with the World: John Dewey and the Early Childhood Classroom*. New York: Teachers College Press.

Department of Education, Employment and Workplace Relations for the Council of Australian Governments. (2022), *Being, Belonging and Becoming: The Early Years Learning Framework for Australia*, Canberra, Commonwealth of Australia. Available at: https://www.acecqa.gov.au/sites/default/files/2023-01/EYLF-2022-V2.0.pdf (Accessed on February 2, 2024).

Dixon Rayle, A. (2006), Mattering to others: Implications for the counselling relationship. *Journal of Counselling and Development*, *84*, pp. 483–487.

Dylan, A. and Beauchamp, G. (2022), A loss of "cynefin"—losing our place, losing our home, losing our self. *Wales Journal of Education*, *24*(1). https://doi.org/10.16922/wje.24.1.2

Elliott, G.C. (2009), *Family Matters: The Importance to Family in Adolescence*. Hoboken, NJ: Wiley-Blackwell.

Fleer, M. (2010), *Early Learning and Development: Cultural-Historical Concepts in Play*. Australia: Cambridge University Press.

Flett, G.L. (2022), An introduction, review and conceptual analysis of mattering as an essential construct and essential way of life. *Journal of Psychoeducational Assessment*, *40*(1), pp. 3–36.

Goodenow, C. (1993), The psychological sense of school membership among adolescents: Scale development and educational correlates. *Psychology in the Schools*, *30*(1), pp. 79–90.

Gowing, A. (2019), Peer-peer relationships: A key factor in enhancing school connectedness and belonging. *Educational and Child Psychology*, *36*(2), pp. 64–77.

Korpershoek, H., Canrinus, E.T., Fokkens-Bruinsma, M. and de Boer, H. (2020), The relationships between school belonging and students' motivational, social-emotional, behavioural, and academic outcomes in secondary education: A meta-analytic review, *Research Papers in Education*, *35*(6), pp. 641–680. Available at https://doi.org/10.1080/02671522.2019.1615116

Lipari, L. (2014), *Listening, Thinking, Being: Toward an Ethics of Attunement* (Illustrated ed.). Pennsylvania: Penn State University Press.

Marshall, S.K., Liu, Y., Wu, A., Berzonsky, M. and Adams, G.R. (2010), Perceived mattering to parents and friends for university students: A longitudinal study. *Journal of Adolescence*, *33*, pp. 367–375. Available at https://doi.org/10.1016/j.adolescence.2009.09.003

Maslow, A.H. (1943), A theory of human motivation. *Psychological Review*, *50*(4), pp. 370–396.

Ministry of Education. (2017), *Te Whāriki: He whāriki Mātauranga mō ngā Mokopuna o Aotearoa/Early Childhood Curriculum*. Wellington, New Zealand: Learning Media.

Organisation for Economic Cooperation and Development (OECD). (2019), *PISA 2018 Results (Volume III): What School Life Means for Students' Lives*. Paris: OECD Publishing.

Osterman, K.F. (2000), Students' need for belonging in the school community. *Review of Educational Research*, *70*(3), pp. 323–367.

Rinaldi, C. (2021), *In dialogue with Reggio Emilia: Listening, Researching and Learning*, (2nd ed.). Abingdon: Routledge.

Ritchie, J. (2015), Social, cultural and ecological justice in the age of the Anthropocene: A New Zealand early childhood care and education perspective. *Journal of Pedagogy*, *6*(2), pp. 41–56.

Rogoff, B., Dahl, A. and Callanan, M. (2018), The importance of understanding children's lived experience. *Developmental Review*, *50*(A) pp. 5–15.

Rosenberg, M. and McCullough, B. (1981), Mattering: Inferred significance and mental health among adolescents. *Research in Community and Mental Health*, *2*, pp. 163–182.

Segal, E. (2011), Social empathy: A model built on empathy, contextual understanding, and social responsibility that promotes social justice. *Journal of Social Service Research*, *37*(3), pp. 266–277.

Sipman, G., Thölke, J., Martens, R. and Mckenney, S. (2019) The role of intuition in pedagogical tact: Educator views. *British Educational Research Journal*, *45*(6), pp. 1186–1202. https://doi.org/10.1002/berj.3557

Stern, D.N. (2004), *The Present Moment in Psychotherapy and Everyday Life* (1st ed.). New York: W. W. Norton & Company.

Sykes, G. and Teszenyi, E. (2018), Introduction. In G. Sykes and E. Teszenyi (eds.), *Young Children and Their Communities: Understanding Collective Social Responsibility* (pp. 1–6). Abingdon: Routledge.

Teszenyi, E. (2023), *Features of Multi-Age Practice and Adult-Child Interactions: An Exploratory Study from Hungary*, PhD Thesis, The Open University.

United Nations General Assembly. (1989), *Convention on the Rights of the Child, Document A/RES/44/2*. New York, United Nations.

van Manen, M. (2015), *Pedagogical Tact: Knowing What to Do When You Don't Know What to Do* (1st ed.). Ontario: Routledge.

Vang, T.M. and Nishina, A. (2022), Fostering school belonging and students' well-being through a positive school interethnic climate in diverse high schools. *The Journal of School Health*, *92*(4), pp. 387–395. Available at https://doi.org/10.1111/josh.13141

Welsh Government. (2023), *A Quality Framework for Early Childhood Play, Learning and Care in Wales*. Available at https://hwb.gov.wales/curriculum-for-wales/early-childhood-play-learning-and-care-in-wales/ (Accessed February 4, 2024).

Willms, J.D. (2003), *Student Engagement at School: A Sense of Belonging and Participation: Results from PISA 2000*. Available at http://www.oecd.org/education/school/programmeforinternationalstudentassessmentpisa/33689437.pdf (Accessed February 2, 2024).

6 (LGBT+) and Different Family Structures

What Is a Family?

Helen Hughes and Cathie Burgess

Introduction: The family

'Family' is a complex concept, loaded with expectations, value judgements and perceptions that can be tricky for educators to negotiate. There is widespread acknowledgement that practitioners should work closely with family members to provide a consistent and joined-up approach and that this should underpin all aspects of a child's wellbeing (Cunningham and Cunningham, 2012). This is enshrined in legislation such as the Children Acts (1989 and 2004), the Children and Families Act (2014) and the Children and Social Work Act (2017). However, little guidance is given to help to unpick the myriad of knotty, often mysterious family structures and nuances that can shape a child's home life.

Bernardes (1985) notes that there is a tendency to use the term 'family' without considering the ideology behind it. This results in a general acceptance of traditional notions of 'family', often conforming to the evolutionary perspective of Francesconi, Ghiglino and Perry's (2010) intergenerational model or the culturally pervasive, heterosexual 'nuclear' family (Murdock, 1950). In fact, Wharton (2005, p. 101) notes that 'family is perhaps the most taken for granted of all social institutions'. However, sociologists such as Thorne and Yalom (1982) have challenged this norm with the argument that humans are able to form families in a way that is more socially constructed than biological or evolutionary in nature. This can be seen through the formation of step, reconstituted and blended families where adults, unrelated by blood, may take on parental responsibilities for children not their own. This is also evident for children who are looked after, or care-experienced. A 'heteronormative' view has been challenged through the revised Sex Relationship Education as part of the National Curriculum in 2021 which, for the first time, opens this aspect of the curriculum to the different sexualities, genders and relationships of learners in contemporary England and Wales, but simply revising the curriculum fails to take into account the legacy that decades of 'othering' has created and the barriers this presents to families within the school community.

Adult sexuality and family structures

Homosexuality, both within the UK and the wider global population, has been historically demonised, either by definition as a criminal act (Human Dignity Trust, 2024) or as a form of 'recognised disorder' under the World Health Organisation (2019). However, LGBTQ individuals, and indeed parents, both support and influence the LGBTQ rights movement, which seeks equality of opportunity and recognition of the unique situations of LGBTQ people. Various legislation changes in the UK have supported the rights of same-sex couples, enabling more family structures to emerge within the LGBTQ+ community, but cultural changes can take time to be reflected through institutions and structural systems such as education. While there is widespread recognition of the needs of specific children and young people in the LGBTQ+ community (Stonewall, 2017; Meanley et al., 2021; Aubrey and Riley, 2023), little acknowledgement is given to the influence of wider family who may be LGBTQ+.

One of the biggest challenges facing those wishing to promote a culture of inclusion for children of LGBTQ+ families is identifying who these children are in the first place. Such data may not be evident during the school admissions process and largely relies on self-declaration. In fact, on some data collection forms, gender binaries and assumptions can serve to alienate parents and carers from the outset. Some questions are simply not relevant and would actually breach data protection principles were they to be asked, as it could be argued that schools do not have a right to be aware of family structures or parental sexuality (or gender identity). So, it can be very difficult to include this within the demographic profile of children attending any setting. Furthermore, disapproving school cultures of 1970s and 1980s may actually discourage parents and carers from revealing their sexual orientation, gender identities or family situation (Sallis, 1988).

The decriminalisation of male homosexuality through the Sexual Offences Act of 1967 did not simply alter established heterosexual bias in public opinion, and indeed the Local Government Act 1988 still prevented the local authority, and in turn practitioners, from protecting those who were victims of homophobic bullying and promoting tolerance and acceptance within the curriculum and wider school community. Public health fears around human immunodeficiency virus (HIV) and acquired immunodeficiency syndrome (AIDS) exacerbated homophobia with propaganda suggesting that sexual acts between homosexual people were dangerous (Altman, 1998). It was not until the 1990s that LGBTQ+ issues were included in the political agenda and opinion began to shift towards acceptance. This has resulted in greater numbers of the UK population aged 16 years and over identifying as lesbian, gay or bisexual. The prevalence and more widespread acceptance of these lifestyles and sexual orientations were further supported and encouraged through the inclusion of discrete categories protecting these characteristics by the Equality Act (2010).

These changes represented huge steps forward for LGBTQ people, but despite the progress made over the last four decades, Rigg and Pryor (2006) argue that governmental policy has rarely caught up with family trends. As a result, LGBTQ families are often viewed as a homogeneous entity with a lack of acknowledgement of the enormous diversity that exists within this group. This approach can lead to tokenism, which further fails to consider the demographically diverse nature of gender, education, income, race and pathways to becoming parents, which are as individual and complex as for any other family. As Thompson (2020) suggests, it is important to acknowledge the various influences on an individual within a group rather than to define them by their group characteristics. While in education this is widely implemented within the disability rights movement with individual education plans, child-centred support and person-first language, this level of recognition and support does not appear to be evident for LGBTQ+ individuals or children from LGBTQ+ families (Heck, Poteat and Goodenow (2016)). As Kandola and Fullerton (1998) note, it is important to consider each individual holistically with not only sensitivity to a particular characteristic, but a deeper understanding of the many factors and characteristics that affect their day-to-day lived experiences. In short, practitioners wishing to truly uphold and promote human rights need to adopt a humanistic view if they are to be successful.

Different types of LGB family

Just as all people sharing LGBTQ+ characteristics are not the same, neither are the family structures around them. Emlen (1995) notes that in many societies, the nuclear family has become an outdated institution as more diverse structures emerge, including coresident adults who may or may not have the responsibility for children. Families and family structure have become increasingly varied and fragmented, and that this is evident in a postmodern society with a diverse, changing legal and social climate (Sharma, 2013). Same-sex parents may have emerged as the result of a breakdown of a previous heterosexual relationship (Young and Massey, 2022) or because of adoption, artificial insemination, sperm donation or other methods of assisted reproduction.

Stepparents and reconstituted families

In 2002, the Adoption and Children Act allowed full and equal parental rights for same-sex parents. This included adoption of partners' children from previous heterosexual relationships as well as joint adoption of children from care. This law affording full parental rights to same-sex stepparents may have supported children in finding stability in the new family unit. Nonetheless, children in stepfamilies can report problems adjusting to their new family structure. Bradshaw (2016) suggests that some children, particularly those in the older age groups, may have difficulty recognising the authority and parental rights of a stepparent. This may also occur in blended families where stepsiblings are also brought into the family unit. Stepparents, likewise, can have difficulty accepting their new partner's children. Kin selection theory claims that parents tend to favour biological children from an evolutionary standpoint (Mazrekaj, de Witte and Cabus, 2020). This can result in difficulties establishing relationships within the family, and obviously this instability can have a detrimental effect on children. Hawthorne *et al.* (2003) agree that it can be very difficult for older children to warm to and accept a stepparent. This can be even harder when that stepparent is a member of the same sex as their existing household parent. The 'coming out' of a biological parent as being gay may initiate reactions such as disbelief and shock, as well as blame and resentment of the new partner, but conversely the child may become closer to their parent and demonstrate feelings of love and acceptance as the relationship is strengthened between them (Young and Massey, 2022).

With this in mind, it could be that where concerns about wellbeing have been raised, it is the initial breakdown of the family that has created feelings of instability (Mazrekaj, de Witte and Cabus, 2020). Lau (2012) suggests that same-sex relationships have a higher rate of dissolution than heterosexual relationships.

As the Civil Partnership Act did not come into force for LGB couples until 2004, it could be argued that, in not reinforcing the legal and moral status of the relationship, higher rates of dissolution among same-sex couples such as those reported by Lau (2012) were inevitable. The Marriage (Same-Sex Couples) Act finally came into force in 2013, allowing same-sex couples to marry in the same way as mixed sex couples, viewing the union as an equal marriage rather than 'separate but equal' and providing recognition of marital status in countries where civil partnerships are not recognised. That said, Bradshaw (2016) suggests that contrary to popular beliefs and claims, there is no direct relationship between family breakdown and children's wellbeing at an international level, with many children in stepfamilies who exhibit similar outcomes to those living in two-parent households. In fact, Bradshaw (2016) claims many Nordic countries report high proportions of children who have experienced family breakdown and correspondingly higher rates of child wellbeing. Moreover, while lone parenthood yields statistically lower outcomes, this may be attributable to lower household income as opposed to parental situations alone.

If this is the case and children experiencing parental relationship breakdown within the UK display less predictors of wellbeing, it is important to look outside of the family and acknowledge external variables, to consider what else may be affecting that child's life. This is supported by Bronfenbrenner's (1979) ecological systems theory, which recognises the contexts of the child's life in terms of the microsystem, including school, family and friends; the meso- and exosystems to take in local governments, extended family, media, health and social care systems; and the macrosystem, which provides cultural norms and values as well as legal and political structures. By taking this more holistic view, practitioners can strive to provide support for children who may be affected by family breakdown and signpost affected family members (including stepfamily) to appropriate support. Working within the macrosystem, those in education can serve to create a culture of inclusivity by discussing issues around LGBTQ+ rights, promoting respect for all individuals and challenging discriminatory behaviour.

Split parents can present many challenges to educators in terms of how to include relevant parties in the child's progress, particularly where a split has been acrimonious or custody is shared between parents who are not co-operative in co-parenting. This is just as much of an issue where the divided couple are heterosexual as same-sex; however, same-sex couples can present a more complicated family dynamic to navigate, if the practitioner is unfamiliar with the people involved and their role in the child's life. Encouraging families to be open and honest and to build trust can create meaningful dialogue between practitioners and the family (including children) and can reduce the chances of adults becoming aggrieved and the child facing turmoil.

Of course, prior relationships are not the only route into becoming a parent for LGBTQ+ people. Young and Massey (2022) argues that this is the most common among older parents and it is also the only type of pathway where the couple (or individual if referring to a lone parent) may not have considered their LGBTQ+ status before planning to become a parent.

Family and adoption

Adoption refers to the process of taking in a child who was born to parents (or a parent) not related to the adoptive parent(s). As has been examined previously, this may involve a stepparent legally adopting their partners' child, but it can also be a means of becoming a parent when neither adult is able to conceive. As Young and Massey (2022) claim, many factors lead people to consider parenting. These include the need to bond emotionally, personal fulfilment, giving and receiving love, not being alone in old age and continuing the family line. However, LGBTQ+ people may face unique challenges in becoming parents and the National Academies of Sciences, Engineering and Medicine (2020) claim that LGB people are less likely than heterosexual individuals to want to have children or become parents. Tate, Patterson and Levy (2019) concur, suggesting that data shows that bisexual individuals show a similar trend, although studies of parenting desire among transgender and intersex people are not yet established.

In part, diminished desire for parenthood may be attributed to cultural myths around the need for children to be raised in a home with both genders (Allen, 2013). Likewise, concerns around children's mental health, self-confidence and identity may colour expectations of parenthood (Young and Massey, 2022). D'Augelli, Hershberger and Pilkington (1998) highlight troubled relationships that LBGTQ+ youth have previously experienced with their own parents due to coming out, which may in turn create guilt, shame and a feeling of unworthiness. However, it may also be that the adoption process can be incredibly complex for any couple (Department for Education, 2021). Also, in accordance with the paramountcy principle of the Children Act (2004), the welfare of the child is supremely important and therefore families are founded for children rather than a child for a family. This can mean long waiting times, sometimes multiple visits from and to professionals and matching panels and, in some cases, disappointment.

The rights of same-sex couples to adopt children were not recognised in the UK until 2002. Until that time, some agencies would approve one of the couple for adoption as a single parent, but both members would not be included as having parental rights. Now, regardless of civil or marital status, same-sex couples just need to show that they are living together in an enduring relationship (First 4 Adoption, 2024). This enduring relationship is particularly important to provide the stability that a child will need when entering a family not their own, but it is also essential for the couple to support one another through this process as it can be a long, complicated and often emotional journey.

When adopting children out of the care system, there are several legal steps that must be taken before a permanency planning meeting takes place and a family finding process is instigated. There are then checks and procedures that will occur, including looking at other potential parents and checking the child's wider family, to establish which would be the best outcome for the child. Care experienced children are statistically at higher risk of lower educational outcomes including absenteeism; 16% of adopted children were found to have had contact with the criminal justice system and over a third needed support for mental health (Adoption UK, 2019).

Older children who are adopted may bring to the family a history that includes behaviours stemming from adverse childhood experiences, which further put stress on the family unit, sometimes involving significant or extreme challenges including violence (Adoption UK, 2019).

> Parents who adopt older children or children with difficult histories or behaviours might need special attention paid to their relationships (e.g. in the form of therapy or support groups aimed at helping them to proactively and constructively handle stress and minimize its impact on their intimate relationship).
>
> (Goldberg and Garcia, 2015, p. 399)

With this in mind, it is vital that practitioners are aware of services available to support any adoptive parents. It may be necessary to work with a child through interventions to support social emotional and mental health wellbeing. Timely and accurate recording in terms of observations, assessments and referrals are needed to ensure that children get sufficient support to meet the challenges both within and outside education.

Family and surrogacy

According to NHS (2024), there are a range of ways that LGBT+ individuals may become parents. These include donor insemination, intrauterine insemination, surrogacy, fostering or adoption and co-parenting. The first three options in this list are considered surrogacy, where the baby will be born to a gestational surrogate, someone who has agreed to carry and give birth to the baby for the intended parents. Unlike adoption, which involves written consent of the birth parent after the baby is born, the contract to address to become a surrogate is completed before the embryo is placed.

Several laws have been enacted supporting the rights of LGBTQ people to become parents through surrogacy including the Human Fertilisation and Embryology Act (2008) for female same-sex couples. This law allows two women to be registered on a child's birth certificate for the first time. Couples who were civil partners or who conceived at a UK fertility clinic could now be recognised as their children's joint legal parents from birth. However, this relies on the child's biological (or birth) mother being one of these women.

Under UK law, regardless of where the child is born, the surrogate will be the child's legal mother and, if she is married, her spouse will be the legal second parent (or father, depending on gender). This can make for confusion and difficulty for intended parents who would then need to apply for adoption or a parental order to recognise their legal status as parents. This necessitated a further change to legislation, and at this point, male same-sex couples were also accorded the right to apply for a parental order to give a child through surrogacy a UK birth certificate recording two men as their legal parents (NGA Law, 2023).

While a slightly more complex process, parental orders also allowed for same-sex parents to go through UK surrogacy matching organisations to organise surrogacy. This is critical as it is illegal in the UK to advertise that you are either willing to be a surrogate or are looking for a surrogate. This includes third parties acting on behalf of surrogates and for any payments to be made outside of agreed reasonable expenses, which are normally overseen by the surrogacy agency. The process of surrogacy involves an investment of time; surrogates and intended parents to get to know each other properly, discuss the process, concerns and outcomes and develop trust before entering into a surrogacy agreement (Department of Health and Social Care, 2024). To this end, the provision for same-sex parents through surrogacy to claim the same rights to time off work and pay as parents giving birth or adopting a child through the Children and Families Act (2014) has been welcomed by the LGB intended parents.

In terms of education, it may not be clear whether a child has come to a relationship through surrogacy or from a previous relationship, or even adoption, but this does not mean that it is not useful to be aware of this. For example, for some children, the question of their own identity may be raised by lessons around personal, social and health education. It is advantageous for same-sex parents to have addressed this with their child before it suddenly becomes a question asked one day in class.

Generally, outcomes for children born through surrogacy are good, and Brilliant Beginnings (2024) argue that it is the quality of the relationships within a family that is important for children rather than the gender of parents. The National Academy of Sciences, Engineering and Medicine (2020) reported, from a small convenience sample, that typically a child growing up in a household with same-sex parents will experience less pressure to adhere to gender roles, particularly in households headed by lesbians. They also claim that, once grown, children from same-sex families suggest that they have higher rates of wellbeing when the social climate is supportive of LGBTQ people and that this is regardless of their own sexuality.

Family and lone parenting

As has been discussed, family breakdown may lead to a child being raised in a single-parent family, and this parent may be any gender or sexual orientation. Also, lone parents may also use surrogacy to have a child. The Human Fertilisation and Embryology Act 2008 (Remedial) Order (2018) enabled single parents through surrogacy (including single gay men) to apply for a parental order to become their child's sole legal parent.

Recent statistics show that '23% of UK families are headed by a single parent (of whom some 90% are women), compared with an EU average of 13%' (Apthorpe, 2022). Yet the problems facing single parents in the UK are many. The Children's Commissioner for England (2022) points out that single-parent families, post pandemic, are facing huge financial hardship due to cost of living rises and low household income. Often a lone working parent will also have constraints on working hours due to childcare, and this can also financially hamper the family.

The cost of starting a family via surrogacy can be particularly prohibitive for lone parents, although some may choose to go to other countries where legislation and costs are different (St James's Place, 2023). Surrogacy costs are also high, and while parents are not paying the surrogate a fee, their expenses and medical procedures must be covered financially. For this reason, many children who are in a single-parent family (whether heterosexual or same-sex) will have experienced some kind of family breakdown that, as an adverse childhood experience, may impact their wellbeing.

Lone LGBTQ+ people may find it difficult to talk to practitioners about their lives. When same-sex couples first contact the school, it may not be apparent to practitioners that a lone parent is LGBTQ+. It is important here that the culture of the school enables the parent to build trust with the practitioner. This should be underpinned by professional practice, detailed and inclusive policies and a warm approach where the parent is made welcome. As with same-sex couples who have arrived at parenthood through surrogacy or through previous relationship breakdowns, the family history may never be something that is willingly shared so it is important to avoid making assumptions, and this should be supported through the practice of establishing introductions that include checking the person's preferred pronoun, hearing their own description of their relationship to the child and listening attentively and without judgement to what is being said by the parent or carer.

Outcomes for children of single-parent families are generally understood to be lower than those of two-parent households, regardless of the parents' gender or sexual orientation (Bradshaw, 2016). This is echoed more recently by the Children's Commissioner for England (2022), who highlights the need for more support for lone parents in the UK and better financial parity across regions.

Family and transgender parenting

Transgender includes everyone who experiences some degree of gender variance (MacBlain, Dunn and Luke, 2017). Collett (2022) suggests that it is incredibly difficult to estimate the number of trans adults in a particular population, suggesting that the adult trans population in the UK is between 200,000 and 500,000 people of whom between 24% and 49% are believed to be parents. While the legal status of a parent does not change after transitioning, the law fails to address the changing of a person's identity within the family, which can have a direct impact on terminology used and, in some cases, gender identity that may be recorded with schools, places of education and other childcare services.

The Gender Recognition Act (2004) allowed transgender adults to apply to formally change their birth certificates to record the gender that they identify as rather than their biological birth status. However, NGA Law (2024) suggests that this is not yet fully inclusive as this process is long and drawn out and does not include nonbinary identities. It is also not legal (yet) for a transitioned parent to be able to change their revised name or ascribed binary gender on their child's birth certificate (Collett, 2022). This can result in 'deadnaming', where professionals may use the parents' name that they had before changing their identity, or in a lack of recognition of their parental status.

Some transgender individuals may have retained the means to carry and give birth to children from a previous female gender while others transitioning from males may have frozen sperm to retain the ability to have biological children through surrogacy. This means that they may have come to parenthood either as a child's biological parent or an adoptive parent. Educational practitioners may have little or no specific training to help them to understand or gain experience of working with adults who are transgender or experiencing gender dysphoria. Outdated, intolerant attitudes among other parents may serve to undermine the welcoming and inclusive environment that the educational establishment has sought to create, and for this reason, parents and carers should be made aware of school policies around bullying, acceptable behaviour and anti-discrimination. Opportunities to celebrate diversity can help to establish a friendly, accepting and warm culture for all (Saggu, 2022).

LGBTQ+ people come to parenthood through a range of means, and Tate, Patterson and Levy (2019) argue that outcomes for children are largely unaffected, with most demonstrating the same kind of variance in wellbeing as those children raised by heterosexual parents. Allen (2013) however calls into question the methodology of many studies looking to ascertain children's wellbeing in same-sex parented households, suggesting that small sample sizes and lack of control for variables lead to unreliable data. Allen (2013) recommends that studies need to address statistical and empirical data from which to draw inferences. The problem with this assumption, again, is that it is reductionist in assuming that any cause-and-effect relationship can be established with something as deep and complex as human lives, and this quest for rigour could undermine any study's validity. Nonetheless, Allen (2013) does raise interesting points about the extraneous factors that can affect outcomes for children. These include previous breakdown of parental relationships, the gender of the child relative to that of the parents, disability, race and family size. When outcomes are determined by any number or combination of these factors, it is evident that practitioners need to view any family as a holistic unit, unique with its own challenges, history, connections and strengths. Perhaps what matters more than anything else is the child's experience within it.

Children's views on family

Morrow (2018) suggests that children's perspectives on family differ according to age. Younger children refer to aspects such as marriage, location and children or siblings as important factors while older children can perceive family in terms of more abstract concepts such as quality of relationships, interactions and wider extended family structures that can transcend location. This aligns with Piaget's stage theory, which suggests that children up to the age of around 11 years rely on concrete experiences to understand and make sense of the world around them, rather than those in the formal operational stage who are more able to hypothesise and conceptualise experiences beyond their own experience (Boampang, 2023). Furthermore, research into children's view on family showed that children across a range of ages placed much higher emphasis on the presence of loving, nurturing adults than the make-up of the family structure. Meanley *et al.* (2021) stress the importance of family relationships, warmth and acceptance on adolescents' self-esteem, pointing out that often this has a direct impact on academic achievement, health outcomes and social exclusion as a precursor to risk-taking behaviour.

When one discusses family, even with a focus on parents and carers, it is important not to ignore the influence of siblings. As Morrow (2018) claims, cohabiting siblings and to some extent stepsiblings are the people that children are most likely to spend time with during their childhood. As they grow into adulthood, these relationships can become the longest continuous relationships that they will experience. Grafsky (2018) explores this further in relation to the idea of children and young people coming out as LGBTQ+ to siblings, sometimes before other family members. This closeness can have outcomes for children in LGBTQ+ families both in terms of providing a support network through shared experience and because some children may have LGBTQ+ siblings rather than parents. Siblings can often take a share in providing care for younger siblings (Boampang, 2023); such children may have experiences of discrimination and bullying (Stacey and Biblarz, 2001). However, the Stonewall (2017) report reflected on changes experienced by LGBT pupils in Britain over the past 10 years, with bullying due to sexual orientation falling by around a third. With an increasing number of schools reporting that this bullying is less tolerated, they concede that there is still some way to go towards the truly accepting culture that is necessary to establish equality.

The Children's Commissioner for England (2022) notes that,

> Irrespective of ethnicity, gender or age, the most frequently used word to describe family was love. And they all recognise that family has a protective effect. It insulates us from life's adversity, and every child should have the benefits of it.
>
> (Children's Commissioner for England, 2022)

To this end, this chapter has demonstrated the differences, challenges and unique context of LGBTQ+ families. They are as diverse as the children in the classroom, but a true family has love at its centre, and it is our duty to preserve this for the children through a curriculum that not only recognises it but celebrates it.

Representation through resources, culture and curriculum

Despite a general incline in LGBTQ+ populations across the USA (National Academies of Sciences, Engineering and Medicine, 2020), and a similar trend in the UK, it is recorded that sexual and gender diverse populations are increasingly racially and ethnically diverse, younger and more female. However, this data is largely limited to measures of sexual preference with demographics such as transgender, nonbinary and intersex communities going largely unrepresented within datasets (National Academies of Sciences, Engineering and Medicine, 2020). This may be due to underreporting in general, but it also highlights the need to recognise a wider range of identities within research, data collection and policymaking.

GLSEN (2019) use the analogy of the curriculum as both a window, reflecting the child's identity back to them, and a mirror, allowing them to explore the identities and lives of others. This means that providing positive representation of LGBTQ people, and in particular parenting and families, can reaffirm the child's view of their own family and themselves as well as educating others and challenging taken for granted assumptions. This relates to Rogers' theory around congruence (Smith, 2014). Congruence is the extent to which a person's life and existence overlaps with what they believe it should be. For children, who are questioning the world around them, many conversations, exposure to new experiences or media can cause incongruence, where they may lack confidence that they are their 'ideal self'. Conversely, as Saggu (2022) argues,

> When young people experience representation of all diversity through an inclusive education, they are more likely to develop a stronger sense of self, empathy, and confidence, thereby strengthening their social and emotional development.
>
> (Saggu, 2022)

Of course, it is rarely as simple as peppering resources with positive representations of LGBTQ+ people, although the Chartered College of Teaching (2022) does stress that this is also important; after all, 'we can't be what we can't see' (Chartered College of Teaching, 2022). Neither can this be addressed through a discrete course such as the new Relationships, Sex and Health Education (RSHE). This is because, although the potential is there to open dialogue, discuss genuine issues affecting those LGBTQ+ families and talk about relationships for the future, the delivery is usually through a heteronormative lens, often reduced to scientific biological facts about heterosexual intercourse and mixed-gender birthing, with a tokenistic nod to LGBTQ+ definitions. This was reflected in Stonewall's (2017) report where only 20% of pupils (with an even lower 10% in faith schools) claim that they have learnt about 'where to go for help and advice about same-sex relationships at school' (Stonewall, 2017, p. 22).

Olteanu (2017) proposed an addendum to Schon's 'Reflection-in-action' and 'Reflection-on action' with a prequel, reflection for action. This term encompasses the conceptualisation of what could and should happen because of planning. In short, as professionals, it is not always necessary to enact a plan to decide whether it is appropriate for the cohort that one is working with. This is something important to consider when working with children in any context and can help practitioners to reflect for anti-discriminatory practice in a variety of ways.

A study published by the Organisation for Economic Co-operation and Development (OECD) in 2023 looked at a specific intervention implemented across a range of schools in the Paris region of France, designed to promote acceptance and curiosity among pupils in regard to lesbian, gay, bisexual, transgender and intersex (LGBTI) issues and lives. It was revealed that even just a short-term intervention (in this case two hours), when children were allowed to talk openly about LGBTI issues, could have far reaching effects. Furthermore, such conversations could reveal to children a diversity among their student group that they had previously not considered, revealing to them conformity bias and in turn encouraging them to challenge taken-for-granted assumptions about what they consider to be the 'norm'. The sessions allowed for dissent in opinion, with open discussion about homophobic and transphobic views. Findings suggested that, even when negative group dynamics emerged, they were not powerful enough to counter the positive effects of the intervention towards respect and tolerance (OECD, 2023).

What this shows is that it does not take long, nor a complex, lengthy programme, to hold high quality, meaningful LGBTQ+ conversations, but that to do so, may take training, understanding and the ability to tackle knotty questions from stakeholders and parents, who may not recognise the legal and moral importance of LGBTQ+ rights. This, however, is no excuse, simple changes can make a huge difference in the lives of children, young people and their families.

Esteem, outcome: Pride

Patterson (1992) examined research around sexual identity, personal development and social relationships in children of gay and lesbian parents. Her research concluded no significant difference in the outcomes for these children than peers raised by heterosexual relationships. That said, Mazrekaj, de Witte and Cabus (2020) note the limitations in comparisons between educational outcomes of children of same-sex parents against those of heterosexual parents. Specifically, there is an over-reliance on small, selective samples, often opportunity or purposive sampling, which obviously can skew data provided. However, using longitudinal data from the Netherlands, they noted that,

> Children raised by same-sex parents from birth outperform children raised by different-sex parents on standardized test scores at the end of primary education by about .14 standard deviations.
> (Mazrekaj, de Witte and Cabus, 2020, p. 831)

This was not true where children who started to live with same-sex couples later, with these children scoring slightly, albeit not significantly, lower than children who live with different-sex parents. As discussed earlier in this chapter, this could be attributed to familial breakdown or turmoil surrounding the disruption of a reconstituting family rather than the sexuality of the parent themselves.

Despite optimistic outcomes from Stonewall's 2017 and 2022 reports, findings acknowledge that more needs to be done to support those from the LGBTQ+ community in school and this includes the way that educators nurture a sense of inclusion. Regarding LGBT+ young people, The Chartered College of Teaching (2022) found that they are three times more likely to self-harm and twice as likely to contemplate suicide whilst Aubrey and Riley (2023) claim that LGBT pupils experience poor levels of mental health and have little confidence that their concerns will be addressed by their place of education. They also claim that this is worse for trans pupils who also report higher rates of bullying. With much of a child or young person's sense of identity based on their family, it is easy to extrapolate this to how they may interpret othering of their family members if they are also part of the LGBTQ+ community. The wellbeing of LGBTQ+ populations, family and social relationships have huge influence over lived experiences. Arguably 'teachers are among the most important non-family adults in the lives of youth' (National Academics of Sciences, Engineering and Medicine, 2020, p. 201).

Childhood is an important stage of the development of self-identity, and children develop a sense of self-worth from their social identities that allows them to gain a sense of belonging. LGBTQ children should be given the same freedom of thought and opinion as any other child. This is not only enshrined in developmental theories such as Maslow's hierarchy of needs, which asserts the importance of acceptance, love, belonging and security in order for a child to achieve their potential, but also in the United Nations Convention on the Rights of the Child (UNICEF, 2017), specifically articles 12 and 28. Children spend over 50% of their waking hours in school, during which time they should be taught about the diversity of gender identities and orientations, leading to acceptance and preventing discrimination, allowing the child to develop a holistic sense of self. This extends to their background, culture, family and beliefs and is a key driver to the Equality Act (2010)'s protected characteristics, which are also supported through equality, diversity and inclusion policies.

As Macblain, Dunn and Luke (2017) stress, early years settings and schools have not only a legal obligation to recognise and support a range of family structures and parental (or carer) gender identities without discrimination but a culturally significant role in redefining societal attitudes and norms for the future. However, as has been examined, some educators may exhibit a lack of confidence in working with and exploring LGBTQ+ issues. Diaz-Serrano and Meix-Llop (2016) report that some practitioners may be less happy to deal with single-sex parents rather than heterosexual parents, and discomfort can be further exhibited when working with transgender parents. This can include not being aware of preferred pronouns, lapsing into heteronormal language such as 'mother' or 'father' and in some cases the practitioner's own beliefs and religions (Aubrey and Riley, 2023). Nonetheless, to ensure that sense of belonging and fulfil the duty of care, Saggu (2022) argues that it is important that practitioners take issues that affect children and young people seriously and safeguard their health and wellbeing. To do this, practitioners should therefore adopt a three-pronged approach to safeguard children who are either themselves LGBTQ+ or who are part of the LGBTQ+ community through their relationships within their family. This approach includes:

1. Planning a safe and inclusive space, curriculum and culture within the school (achieved through policies, positive representation in resources, assessments and curricular tools).
2. Promoting rights, acceptance and understanding (using inclusive and person-first language, including avoiding gender binaries), embedding preferred pronouns into language and embedding LGBTQ+ relationships within.

3. Considering the representation of LGBTQ+ in the curriculum including sharing achievements in a variety of fields (including science, literature, history and humanities).
4. Addressing and challenging discrimination, name-calling and unacceptable behaviours immediately. Use the policies of your setting, and try to use restorative practice to enable children to learn empathy and understanding.

Acknowledging and teaching children about their rights in school can encourage engagement, respect and a feeling of safety within the school community (UNICEF, 2017). Children should not just feel 'tolerated' within the school community; they have a right to have their voice heard (UNICEF, 2017), be supported in their unique identity and family structures and have their characteristics and those of the people important to them mirrored and celebrated within the curriculum (GLSEN, 2019).

> **Reflection-for-action**
>
> Do your resources, (books, illustrations, case studies and questions) include gender-binaries? For example, are nonbinary, intersex and transgender people given meaningful representation within the curriculum and resources offered?
>
> When creating your next lesson, scheme of learning or programme of training, consider how you will acknowledge the different lived experiences of children in your class and encourage them to feel safe in their learning environment to discuss their family structure, parental or sibling gender and sexuality and how to also nurture this safety between peers.
>
> **Reflection-in-action**
>
> Think about the language you use in lessons. When referring to adults in the child's life, do you tend to use gendered terminology or gender-neutral language? Using inclusive language can encourage acceptance and belonging. This also helps children from other diverse family backgrounds. Using 'your grown ups' instead of naming a particular individual or their role can help children to feel that what you are saying is relevant to them.
>
> How confident are you in addressing school-related gender-based discrimination and having conversations around this? Try to make a point of addressing this in your next personal and professional development review or appraisal, especially if you feel you would benefit from training in this area.
>
> **Reflection-on-action**
>
> Think about your own family. To what extent do they affect your approach to teaching? How much do you know about your children's families and their unique challenges and strengths. How could you make this a priority when working with them?

References

Adoption UK. (2019), *Life Chances of Adopted Children Undermined by Battle for Government Support*. Available at https://www.adoptionuk.org/news/life-chances-of-adopted-children-undermined-by-battle-for-government-support (Accessed April 24, 2024).

Allen, D.W. (2013), High school graduation rates among children of same-sex households. *Review of Economics of the Household*, 11, pp. 635–658.

Altman, D. (1998), HIV homophobia and human rights. *Health and Human Rights Part 1: The Roots of Vulnerability*. 2(4), pp. 15–22.

Apthorpe, F. (2022), New report reveals true scale of family breakdown in the UK. Available at https://www.geldards.com/insights/new-report-reveals-true-scale-of-family-breakdown-in-the-uk/ (Accessed April 24, 2024).

Aubrey, K. and Riley, A. (2023), *Education Theories for a Changing World*. London: Sage Publications Limited.

Bernardes, J. (1985), 'Family ideology': Identification and exploration. *The Sociological Review*, 33(2), pp. 275–297.

Boampang, M. (2023), Diverse families. In V. Cooper and M. Tatlow-Golden (eds.), *An Introduction to Childhood and Youth Studies and Psychology* (pp. 75–89). Oxon: Routledge.

Bradshaw, J. (2016), Demography of childhood. In J. Bradshaw (ed.), *The Wellbeing of Children in the UK* (pp. 13–29). Bristol: Policy Press.

Brilliant Beginnings. (2024), Surrogacy for male same-sex parents. Available at https://brilliantbeginnings.co.uk/surrogacy-for-male-same-sex-parents/ (Accessed April 24, 2024).

Bronfenbrenner, U. (1979), *The Ecology of Human Development: Experiments by Nature and Design*. Massachusetts: Harvard University Press.

Chartered College of Teaching. (2022), LGBT+ inclusivity in schools. Available at https://chartered.college/2022/03/04/lgbt-inclusivity-in-schools/ (Accessed April 22, 2024).

Children Act. (1989), Chapter 41. London: The Stationery Office. Available at https://www.legislation.gov.uk/ukpga/1989/41/contents/enacted (Accessed April 20, 2024).

Children Act. (2004), *Chapter 31*. London: The Stationery Office. Available at https://www.legislation.gov.uk/ukpga/2004/31 (Accessed April 24, 2004).

Children and Families Act. (2014), *Chapter 6*. London: The Stationery Office. Available at https://www.legislation.gov.uk/ukpga/2014/6/contents/enacted (Accessed April 24, 2024).

Children and Social Work Act. (2017), *Chapter 16*. London: The Stationery Office. Available at https://www.legislation.gov.uk/ukpga/2017/16/contents/enacted (Accessed April 24, 2024).

Children's Commissioner for England. (2022), Children's Commissioner for England launches preliminary findings of the family review at Policy Exchange. Available at https://www.childrenscommissioner.gov.uk/news/childrens-commissioner-for-england-launches-preliminary-findings-of-the-family-review-at-policy-exchange/ (Accessed April 18, 2024).

Collett, R. (2022), Transgender parenthood: The current legal position. Available at https://www.flip.co.uk/transgender-parenthood-the-current-legal-position/

Cunningham, J. and Cunningham, S. (2012), *Social Policy and Social Work: An Introduction*. London: Sage Publications and Learning Matters.

D'Augelli, A.R., Hershberger, S.L., and Pilkington, N.W. (1998), Lesbian, gay, and bisexual youth and their families: Disclosure of sexual orientation and its consequences. *American Journal of Orthopsychiatry*, 68, pp. 361–371.

Department for Education. (2021), Adoption strategy: Achieving excellence everywhere. Available at https://assets.publishing.service.gov.uk/media/61001896d3bf7f044ee52330/_Adoption_strategy_.pdf (Accessed April 24, 2024).

Department of Health and Social Care. (2024), Guidance: The surrogacy pathway: surrogacy and the legal process for intended parents and surrogates in England and Wales. Available at https://www.gov.uk/government/publications/having-a-child-through-surrogacy/the-surrogacy-pathway-surrogacy-and-the-legal-process-for-intended-parents-and-surrogates-in-england-and-wales (Accessed April 24, 2024).

Diaz-Serrano, L. and Meix-Llop, E. (2016), Do schools discriminate against homosexual parents? Evidence from a randomised correspondence experiment. *Economics of Education Review*, 53, pp. 133–142.

Emlen, S.T. (1995), 'An evolutionary theory of the family, *Proceedings of the National Academy of Sciences of the United States of America*, 92(18), pp. 8092–8099.

Equality Act. (2010), Chapter 15. London: The Stationery Office. Available at https://www.legislation.gov.uk/ukpga/2010/15/contents/enacted (Accessed April 24, 2024).

First 4 Adoption. (2024), Lesbian, gay, bisexual or trans (LGBT+) and thinking about adoption? Available at https://www.first4adoption.org.uk/who-can-adopt-a-child/how-do-i-decide/thinking-about-adoption-lgbt/ (Accessed April 18, 2024).

Francesconi, M., Ghiglino, C. and Perry, M. (2010), On the origin of the family. *Centre for Economic Policy Research Paper no. 7629*. Available at https://ssrn.com/abstract=1539301 (Accessed January 7, 2023).

GLSEN. (2019), Developing LGBTQ-inclusive classroom resources. Available at https://www.glsen.org/sites/default/files/2019-11/GLSEN_LGBTQ_Inclusive_Curriculum_Resource_2019_0.pdf (Accessed April 26, 2024).

Goldberg, A. and Garcia, R. (2015), Predictors of relationship dissolution in lesbian, gay and heterosexual adoptive parents. *Journal of Family Psychology*, 29(3), pp. 394–404.

Grafsky, E.L. (2018), Deciding to come out to parents: Toward a model of sexual orientation disclosure decisions. *Family Process*, 57, pp. 783–799.

Hawthorne, J., Jessop, J., Pryor, J. and Richards, M. (2003), *Supporting Children through Family Change. A Review of Interventions and Services for Children of Divorcing and Separating Parents*. York: Joseph Rowntree Foundation.

Heck, N.C., Poteat, V.P. and Goodenow, C.S. (2016), Advances in research with LGBTQ youth in schools. *Psychology of Sexual Orientation and Gender Diversity*, 3(4), pp. 381–385.

Human Dignity Trust. (2024), A history of LGBT criminalisation. Available at https://www.humandignitytrust.org/lgbt-the-law/a-history-of-criminalisation/ (Accessed April 15, 2024).

Human Fertilisation and Embryology Act. (2008), *(Remedial) Order 2018, SI 2018/1413*. London: The Stationery Office. Available at https://www.legislation.gov.uk/uksi/2018/1413/contents/made (Accessed April 24, 2024).

Kandola, R. and Fullerton, J. (1998), Diversity in action: Managing the mosaic. (2nd ed.). London: Chartered Institute of Personnel and Development.

Lau, C. (2012), The stability of same-sex cohabitation, different-sex cohabitation and marriage. *Journal of Marriage and Family*, 74(5), pp. 973–988.

Local Government Act. (1988), Chapter 9. London: The Stationery Office. Available at https://www.legislation.gov.uk/ukpga/1988/9/contents/enacted (Accessed April 24, 2024)

Mazrekaj, D., De Witte, K. and Cabus, S. (2020), School outcomes of children raised by same-sex parents: Evidence from Administrative panel data. *American Sociological Review*, 85(5), pp. 830–856.

Macblain, S., Dunn, J. and Luke, I. (2017), *Contemporary Childhood*. London: Sage Publications.

Meanley, S., Flores, D., Listerud, L., Chang, C., Feinstein, B. and Watson, R. (2021), The interplay of familial warmth and LGBTQ+ specific family rejection on LGBTQ+ adolescents' self-esteem. *Journal of Adolescence*, 93, pp. 40–52.

Morrow, V. (2018), Children and their families. In H. Montgomery and M. Robb (eds.), *Children and Young People's Worlds* (2nd ed., pp. 267–282). Bristol: Policy Press.

Murdock, G.P. (1950), Family stability in non-European cultures. *The ANNALS of the American Academy of Political and Social Science*, 272(1), pp. 195–201.

National Academies of Sciences, Engineering, and Medicine. (2020), *Understanding the well-being of LGBTQI+ populations*. Washington, DC: The National Academies.

NGA Law. (2023), Surrogacy law for same-sex parents. Available at https://www.ngalaw.co.uk/knowledge-centre-repository/surrogacy-law-for-same-sex-parents/ (Accessed April 21, 2024).

NGA Law. (2024), Transgender parents conceiving children. Available at https://www.ngalaw.co.uk/knowledge-centre/transgender-parents-conceiving-children/ (Accessed April 21, 2024).

NHS. (2024), Ways to become a parent if you're LGBT+. Available at https://www.nhs.uk/pregnancy/having-a-baby-if-you-are-lgbt-plus/ways-to-become-a-parent-if-you-are-lgbt-plus/ (Accessed April 24, 2024).

Organisation for Economic Co-operation and Development. (2023), Policy briefing: Fighting homophobia and transphobia in schools. Available at https://www.oecd.org/els/soc/PolicyBrief-RCT-OECD-SOShomophobie-EN.pdf (Accessed April 18, 2024).

Olteanu, C. (2017), Reflection-for-action and the choice or design of examples in the teaching of mathematics. *Mathematics Education Research Journal*, 29, pp. 349–367.

Patterson, C. (1992), Children of lesbian and gay parents. *Child Development*, 63(5), pp. 1025–1042.

Recognition Act. (2004), *Chapter 7*. London: The Stationery Office. Available at https://www.legislation.gov.uk/ukpga/2004/7/contents/enacted (Accessed April 30, 2024)

Rigg, A. and Pryor, J. (2006), Children's perceptions of families: What do they really think? *Children & Society*, 21, pp. 17–30.

Saggu, A. (2022), Why Is LGBTQI+ inclusive education so important and what can be done? Available at https://www.sddirect.org.uk/blog-article/why-lgbtqi-inclusive-education-so-important-and-what-can-be-done (Accessed April 18, 2024).

Sallis, J. (1988), The listening school: Parents and the public. In M. Woodhead and A. McGrath (eds.), *Family, School and Society* (pp. 280–290). London: Hodder and Stoughton.

Sharma, R. (2013), The family and family structure classification redefined for current times. *Journal of Family Medicine and Primary Care*, 2(4), pp. 306–310.

Smith, M.K. (2014), Carl Rogers, core conditions and education. Available at https://infed.org/mobi/carl-rogers-core-conditions-and-education/ (Accessed April 23, 2024).

Stacey, J. and Biblarz, T. (2001), Does the sexual orientation of parents matter? *American Sociological Review*, 66(2), pp. 159–183.

St. James's Place. (2023), The hidden costs facing LGBTQ+ parents. Available at https://www.sjp.co.uk/individuals/news/the-hidden-costs-facing-lgbtq-parents (Accessed April 24, 2024).

Stonewall. (2017), School report: The experiences of lesbian, gay, bi and trans young people in Britain's schools in 2017. Available at https://www.stonewall.org.uk/system/files/the_school_report_2017.pdf (Accessed April 20, 2024).

Stonewall. (2022), Take Pride report: Public sentiment towards lesbian, gay, bi and trans people in the UK. Available at https://www.stonewall.org.uk/system/files/take_pride_-_june_2022.pdf (Accessed April 20, 2024).

Tate, D., Patterson, C. and Levy, A. (2019), Predictors of parenting intentions among childless lesbian, gay, and heterosexual adults. *Journal of Family Psychology*, 33(2), pp. 194–202.

Thompson. (2020), *Anti-Discriminatory Practice* (7th ed.). London: Bloomsbury Academic.

Thorne, B. and Yalom, M. (1982), *Rethinking the Family: Some Feminist Questions*. New York: Longman.

UNICEF. (2017), Rights respecting schools impact report. Available at https://www.unicef.org.uk/rights-respecting-schools/wp-content/uploads/sites/4/2018/05/Rights-Respecting-Schools_Impact-2017_180418_Final.pdf (Accessed April 19, 2024).

Wharton, A. (2005), *The Sociology of Gender: An Introduction to Theory and Research*. Oxford: Blackwell Publishing.

World Health Organisation. (2019), Moving one step closer to better health and rights for transgender people. Available at https://www.who.int/europe/news/item/17-05-2019-moving-one-step-closer-to-better-health-and-rights-for-transgender-people (Accessed July 19, 2024).

Young, S. and Massey, S. (2022), LGBTQ+ relationships and families. In D. Amory, S. Massey, J. Miller and A. Brown (eds.), *Introduction to LGBTQ+ Studies: A Cross Disciplinary Approach* (pp. 267–288). New York: State University of New York Press.

7 Fostering Belonging Through Compassionate Care in Education

Eunice Lumsden

Introduction

Children and young people encounter life differently. Their experiences in the family and wider communities, including school, influence their life journey. For some, these experiences have acted as barriers to learning. They can also affect their mental health, wellbeing, and behaviour in the classroom. For decades those working in health, social care and education have been addressing these issues. However, the compelling research evidence is beginning to influence policymakers to think differently. Scotland and Wales are examples of two nations of the UK pioneering societal approaches. They aim to ensure all know and understand the causes of trauma, the effects it can have and how the contributing factors can be addressed.

Educationalists have a long history of supporting children and young people who have experienced challenges in their lives. However, with ever-increasing societal changes, many are rethinking their approaches to the mental health and wellbeing of their pupils. Some have responded by focusing more on compassionate leadership and nurturing and trauma-informed approaches. This involves developing communities that foster belonging and relationships through a strengths approach. It also requires training and support that enables educators to develop their knowledge, understanding and skills of the wider global, community and family issues that permeate their setting and classrooms.

There are increasing literature, intervention methods, organisations, websites and consultants concerned with the health and wellbeing of children and young people in education. It is therefore not surprising that educators can be overwhelmed about how to address the challenges they are facing. Consequently, this chapter aims to support the reader to reflect on their knowledge, practice, approach to inclusivity, self-care and how their setting leads, or not, in these areas. The chapter provides an overview of some of the contemporary issues impacting the health and wellbeing of children and young people, including how the global pandemic of Covid-19 has facilitated new understanding.

There will be a focus on how experiences of trauma, abuse and adversity can affect development and behaviour. The terms and intervention methods currently in vogue will be considered as well as the importance of compassionate leadership that facilitates a whole setting response.

This chapter will look at self-care, but it is important to highlight at the start that these issues addressed may be personally challenging. Mental health and wellbeing issues are not just impacting children and young people; they affect us all. For some, it is their own experiences of trauma that may have led them to work in education. Whatever your reasons, experiences or role, it is important that you ensure you are a safe professional. Please seek support if any of the areas in this chapter raise issues for you and ensure you focus on your own wellbeing.

Contemporary factors impacting on the mental health and wellbeing of children and young people

Globally infants, children and young people are navigating environments that can negatively affect their development, mental health and wellbeing. These include the impact of social media, academic pressure, peer relationships, family environments including trauma and adversity, conflict, natural disasters and the increased challenges that the coronavirus disease Covid-19, declared in 2020, has brought. Consequently, those working in education increasingly need to understand the intersection between public health, social care and education.

More in-depth country-level information about young people's health, including the risk factors they face, can be accessed through the UNICEF (2023) online database. When global data is explored, challenges with mental health and wellbeing are a universal issue. Approximately one in seven young people experience mental disorders, and suicide is the fourth leading reason for death in the 15- to-19-year age bracket (UNICEF, 2021).

The challenges for children and young people have been exacerbated by the global pandemic. While there is no universal experience of Covid-19, evidence suggests that more than of 1.7 billion learners were affected (Reimers, 2022). The pandemic also illuminated the pre-existing inequity in education with vulnerable countries and communities being more adversely affected (Azevedo et al., 2022). In addition to the loss and interruption to education, Covid-19 also 'diminished the ability of families to support children and youth in their education' (Reimers, 2022, p. 2).

Others have reported children being unable to access outdoor play and participate in free play with their peers. There is also evidence that children and young people became increasingly socially isolated (de Araújo et al., 2020; Gill and Munro, 2020; Murray, 2021). Moreover, a review by the NSPCC (2022) in England highlighted that domestic violence and child abuse increased. They also found that there was a significant impact on the mental health and wellbeing of children and adult family members.

If the data for mental health in England is explored, four in ten children and over 50% of young people's mental health deteriorated between 2017 and 2021 (Newlove-Delgado *et al.*, 2022). They also found that:

- 18% of children aged from 7 to 16 years and 22.0% of young people aged from 17 to 24 years had a probable mental disorder.
- Children aged from 11 to 16 years with a probable mental health disorder were less likely to feel safe at school (61.2%) than those unlikely to have a mental health disorder (89.2%). They were also less likely to report enjoyment of learning or have a friend they could turn to for support.
- 1 in 8 (12.6%) children aged from 11 to 16 years who were social media users reported that they had been bullied online. This was more than 1 in 4 (29.4%) among those with a probable mental disorder.
- 1 in 9 (19.9%) children aged from 7 to 16 years lived in households that experienced a reduction in household income in the past year. This was more than 1 in 4 (28.6%) among children with a probable mental disorder.
- Among children aged from 7 to 22 years with a probable mental disorder, 14.8% reported living in a household that had experienced not being able to buy enough food or using a food bank in the past year compared to 2.1% of young people unlikely to have a mental disorder.

Newlove-Delgado *et al.* (2022, lines 9–39)

Further insights are provided in the Good Childhood report (The Children's Society, 2023), which found that low wellbeing was reported as an issue for 10% of children participating in their survey and 'almost a third were unhappy with at least one specific area of their lives' (The Children's Society, 2023, p. 4). This situation is exacerbated by the rising cost of living with one in five families facing serious financial difficulties, a situation which is impacting parents' mental health and causing sleep deprivation. This situation is worse for lone parents and those on a low income (Action for Children, 2023).

There is also evidence of disparities in accessing services for mental health. According to a review conducted by the Office of the Children's Commissioner for England, there are:

> 1.4 million children estimated to have a mental health disorder, less than half (48%) received at least 1 contact with CYPMHS [Children and Young Peoples Mental Health Services] and 34% received at least 2 contacts with CYPMHS.
>
> Children's Commissioner (2023, p. 8)

It is also pertinent to address the impact of technology and social media on children and young people. Research evidence suggests that as well as the benefits, excessive use can contribute to feelings of anxiety and depression (Robidoux *et al.*, 2019; Ventouris *et al.*, 2021). Cyberbullying brings with it a new range of concerns due to the anonymity of online platforms. Research by the Pew Centre in the USA found that 46% of young people aged 13–17 years experienced cyber bullying (Vogels, 2022). Data from England and Wales indicates that one in five children aged from 10 to 15 years have experienced online bullying (Office of National Statistics [ONS], 2020).

Trauma, child abuse, adverse childhood experiences

One of the important factors for educators and support staff who are navigating the complexities of learning in the context of societal, family and community issues is developing their knowledge and understanding of the lived experiences of some of their pupils. Traumatic experiences can happen at any age, though for some, the challenges they face in education began in early childhood. There is compelling evidence about the importance of this period, especially the first 1,001 critical days, for laying down the foundations of mental health and wellbeing (Center of the Developing Child, 2016, 2017; Royal Foundation Centre for Early Childhood, 2020, 2002; UNICEF, 2023). For some children, their parents' poor mental health and wellbeing, social circumstances and drug and alcohol addictions can lead to the children facing greater risks of harm including sexual, physical or emotional abuse or neglect and domestic violence (Center of the Developing Child, 2016; Shonkoff and Garner, 2012).

These experiences can impact brain development, mental health and wellbeing. However, how children and young people respond to abuse and adverse experiences depends on a range of factors including their age, the nature of the abuse or adverse experiences, the length of time it continued, the age it started, and the support provided. Protective factors such as supportive relationships, secure attachment and enabling a child to develop self-efficacy and control can also act as buffers to mediate their impact (Center of the Developing Child, 2016, 7; Royal College of Psychiatrists, 2023).

It is important the educators and support staff have a shared understanding of the language used (see "Terminology" box). For those wanting to extend their knowledge and understanding, further reading is identified at the end of the chapter.

Terminology	
Trauma	The three E's identified by the Substance Abuse and Mental Health Services Administration (SAMHSA) (2014) provide a helpful framework for understanding trauma: 1 Event(s): Some are single events, such as a car crash or the death of a parent, others classified as 'complex trauma' include prolonged exposure to the different types of child abuse, domestic abuse, displacement or war. 2 Experience(s): The way people experience traumatic events is different. It is influenced by how they psychologically and physically experience the event and how it makes them feel. Domestic violence, for example, is complex and can leave the victim feeling humiliated, responsible for their partner's actions and guilty. They may not always see what is happening to them or feel able to tell anyone because they fear the consequences. 3 Effect(s): The impact of trauma varies in severity, is specific to the individual and can impact on emotional, psychological and physical wellbeing across the life course. (See "Understanding Trauma-Informed Approaches" box)
Child abuse	This is an umbrella term for all the categories of abuse. These include physical and emotional abuse and neglect, sexual abuse and domestic violence. However, it is important to note that what constitutes child abuse is social constructed and evolves (Lumsden, 2018). How it is responded to varies internationally, and it is important that educators must understand what constitutes abuse and the policy and procedures of their organisation. For example, in England, Keeping Children Safe in Education provides guidance for education settings (Department of Education [DfE], 2023)
Adverse childhood experiences (ACEs)	This term emerged from the study in North America by Felitti *et al.* (1998). The term embraces toxic and traumatic experiences of some children that can 'cause chronic stress and can impact on their short-, medium- and long-term development' (Lumsden, 2018, p. 92). Ten adverse experiences were identified, including child abuse, domestic violence, a parent in prison, divorce and living with a parent who has a drug or alcohol addiction. It is important to note that ACEs should never be seen as deterministic, rather they need to be understood that these experiences in childhood can lead to poorer outcomes across the life course. It is also important to recognise that other adverse experiences impact children such as poverty.

Creating compassionate and trauma-informed environments

There is an ever-increasing focus on intervention methods that support emotional development, health and wellbeing in the classroom, including trauma-informed approaches. However, educational settings have always had an important role in supporting their pupils pastorally, as the complexities of children and young people's lives are not siloed; they bring them into the educational communities they are part of. The additional challenges settings face now stem from increasing concern about mental health and wellbeing and how these can impact behaviour. These concerns have led to an increased focus on understanding the causes and effects of traumatic experiences so that a compassionate approach to education can be strengthened. This requires high-quality, ongoing training for educators and support staff.

It is important to stress that any approach taken must be consistent, meaningful and sustainable. Compassion for others and ensuring that every child and young person is *seen, safe, secure* and *soothed* (Siegel and Payne Bryson, 2011; Lumsden, 2018) should be at their heart (see subsequent Reflection activity). As Potvin et al. (2022) and Spratt *et al.* (2006, p. 14) have purported, educational environments have 'the potential to either enhance or damage the mental wellbeing of both staff and pupils'. They go on to argue that leadership in schools has an important role in promoting mentally healthy environments. Underpinning this is the importance of compassionate leadership (Al-Ghabban, 2018; Riley, 2022). Sinek (2019) also reminds us that leadership is about caring for those you lead. It is about inspiring people to want to do things because they believe in the importance of what they are doing.

Reflection

Reflect on the 4 S's of *seen, safe, secure* and *soothed* in relation to the whole setting and your classroom or specific area of work.

1 *Seen*
  - How do the children and/or young people you work with know that you know who they are?
  - How do you value the contributions they make?
  - How do you give them feedback?
  - How do you support skill development?
2 *Safe*
  - How do you ensure that they feel safe?
  - How do you respond to conflict?
  - How do you know the children and/or young people feel safe?
  - How do you support them in managing their safety?

3 *Secure*
- How do you support children and/or young people develop a sense of worth?
- How do you address wellbeing?

4 *Soothed*
- How do you support children and/or young people to manage emotions?
- How do you support self-regulation?

Arguably, if an educational setting is to embed compassionate care in the classroom, those leading need to recognise that 'the walls that divide schools from the realities of life in the surrounding communities are porous' (Riley, 2022, p. 16). They need to appreciate their role in creating environments where staff and pupils feel they belong, valued and cared for (Riley, 2022; Cherry, 2021). However, Riley argues that understanding what it is like not to belong is also important. Drawing on OECD (2017, 2019) data, she heights that nearly one in three children who live in high- or middle-income countries do not feel they belong in school.

This leads to the question of what 'belonging' looks like in schools. For Riley (2022, p. 42), it is a dynamic term that recognises 'whatever the social context in which a school is located, what makes the difference is the quality of the daily experience, the relationships and the interactions.' Belonging also gives agency for teachings and pupils, and through this agency, and the conversations that evolve, change can happen (Sinek, 2019; Cherry, 2021; Riley, 2022).

Consequently, to create school environments that promote belonging and foster agency, compassion has an important place. Gilbert (2013, p. XXXV) contends that compassion involves sensitivity 'to the suffering of self and others, with a deep commitment to try to prevent and relieve it.' Drawing on this definition, Al-Ghabban (2018) argues that compassion has three intertwined elements:

1 Compassion for others
2 Receiving compassion
3 Self-compassion

However, these areas are not innate. It is important that training is provided and that a common understanding of what these mean in specific settings is co-constructed (Al-Ghabban, 2018; Potvin *et al.*, 2022).

The three factors identified by Al-Ghabban (2018) could be considered an essential starting point to facilitate spaces where conversations can be forged that connect those working in the school community. They provide an opportunity to develop a common focus to address the complex space where the public health, social care and education agendas, community and family life merge in the classroom. It is also the space where trauma-informed approaches aim to address the impact of the lived experiences of pupils on learning and the wider school community.

Given the relatively new focus in education on approaches that are trauma-informed, research is limited, and there is no consensus that they make a difference (Maynard et al., 2020). Their review of the literature in the USA found that there was no educational research that met the five categories of their inclusion requirements, including 'randomised or quasi-experimental study design' (Maynard et al., 2020, p. 2). However, evidence from studies into the number of ACEs that exist in communities is compelling (Bellis et al., 2014, 2016; Scottish Government, 2019), and two nations of the UK are proactively using the evidence to support a whole system approach that includes education (see Case Studies 1 and 2).

> **Understanding Trauma-Informed Approaches**
>
> Trauma-informed approaches find their roots in clinical practice and, over time, this approach has moved beyond therapeutic interventions to encompass a breadth of organisation and practice interventions aimed at alleviating the impact of trauma and/or preventing them from happening in the first place. The focus is on improving health and wellbeing, and more recently, these approaches have moved beyond the health and social care domains into education.
>
> There is currently no universal definition of what is meant by 'trauma-informed'. Rather, as Avery et al. (2021, p. 282) suggest, it comprises:
>
>> Four main premises: (1) that exposure to trauma is widespread and has pervasive impacts; (2) believing that healing from trauma is possible; (3) that relationships play a key role in the process of change; and (4) that safety is critical for healing and preventing further impact.
>
> The work of SAMHSA (2014) provides understanding about what trauma is (see "Terminology" box) and what a trauma-informed approach looks like. They identify four important assumptions—the 4 R's:

1 Realization: That all involved in the organisation wanting to be trauma-informed understand the factors that can cause trauma and coping mechanisms that are employed at an individual level to manage the effect trauma has had on them.
2 Recognize: How trauma looks, including the signs and that those not directly involved in the event(s) may be impacted as well. Additionally, it is not something that happens to others; people working in the organisation may have experienced abuse and adversity, which have led to trauma. (See the section on self-care).
3 Resist re-traumatisation: Here the focus is on the organisation understanding that their actions can unintentionally re-traumatise. This is an important point for educational settings as the behaviour policy may result in disciplinary actions that reinforce the effects of the trauma a child or young person has experienced.

Consequently, a trauma-informed approach is complex and multilayered and will look different in different organisations. However, as SAMHSA (2014) suggests, this can be addressed by a set of principles that are universal regardless of the setting. They identify six principles, though the terminology used and how they are applied will be 'setting- or sector specific' (SAMHSA, 2014, p. 10). An example of what they mean can be found in Case Studies 1 and 2, where Scotland and Wales have both drawn on the SAMHSA guidance but have framed the levels of knowledge required differently.

The six underpinning trauma-informed principles are as follows:

1 Safety: Staff and those using the organisation feel physically and psychologically safe.
2 Trustworthiness and transparency: Those that work and use the organisation know how decisions are made to support trust building.
3 Peer support: SAMHSA (2014, p. 11) describes 'peers' as 'those with lived experience of trauma … or those who have experienced traumatic events and are key caregivers in their recovery.'
4 Collaboration and mutuality: A trauma-informed approach involves all.
5 Empowerment, voice and choice: There is a strengths approach aimed at empowering, listening to and acting on the voice of those who are employed by or use the organisation.
6 Cultural, historical and gender issues: Works on inclusivity through addressing historical and contemporary issues of, for example, racism and gender inequality.

While the literature review by Maynard *et al.* (2020) indicates the challenges in evidencing that trauma-informed approaches in education settings make a difference, undertaking research in this area and deciding on impact measures is complex. However, smaller research projects have indicated that trauma-informed approaches can make a difference in educational settings. For example, the case study of a school in Australia presented by Stokes (2022) considered how learning and wellbeing could be improved through addressing the training needs of teachers and school leadership. Her work highlighted that change takes time, the importance of leadership, staff training to change mindset and support with 'the creation of classroom environments to enable students to be ready to learn' (Stokes, 2022, p. 11).

The importance of training to support understanding of the effect of trauma on the individual, their engagement with learning and how to create appropriate environments has been highlighted in research conducted by Oxford University. They were commissioned to evaluate the impact of the Alex Timpson Attachment and Trauma Awareness in Schools Programme (2017–2022) (Harrison, 2022). The research was impacted by Covid-19; however, one of the research strands sought the views of headteachers on the impact of the programme. Of the 112 headteachers who returned questionnaires, nearly all believed the programme had had a positive impact on staff confidence, and there had been some 'improvements in the engagement, attendance, learning and attainment of vulnerable children' (Harrison, 2022, p. 1). In fact, one in eight of the headteachers indicated the impact had been 'transformational'.

The vital role of leadership in driving change has also been discussed by Riley (2022). She argues compassionate leadership ensures that 'values shape action, and leadership actions shape belonging' (Riley, 2022, p. 115). Without this strong leadership approach, success of a trauma-informed approach is unlikely (Rees Centre, 2024), especially as a philosophical shift from policies based on managing behaviour to understanding the causes needs a whole school commitment that is led from the top (Berger and Martin, 2020).

Regardless of the limitations in research specifically on the impact of trauma-informed practices in education, the evidence that trauma caused by adverse experiences and abuse has effects on health, wellbeing and outcomes has led to a more proactive approach from different countries. Scotland is an example of a nation with a vision to be:

> A trauma informed and responsive nation and workforce, that is capable of recognising where people are affected by trauma and adversity, that is able to respond in ways that prevent further harm and support recovery and can address inequalities and improve life chances.
> (National Trauma Training Programme, 2023, lines 3–5)

As part of this drive, there has been recognition of the role schools have empowering children and young people through creating nurturing and trauma-informed environments (see Case Study 1). Wales also is proactively focusing on a whole country trauma-informed approach (see Case Study 2)

Case Study 1 Scotland, 'A Whole System Approach'

Part of the Getting it Right for Every Child (GITFEC) (Scottish Government, 2022) legislative and policy direction provides the framework for a whole system approach to create a nation where all children, young people and families can flourish. As part of this, there has been an ongoing focus on understanding the impact of events that lead to trauma or complex trauma and developing systems to promote early intervention. The developments and learning have led to the National Trauma Training Framework (NTTF) initiative. Underpinning the framework is the importance of fostering collaboration, standardising training and promoting trauma-informed practices that respond sensitively and effectively to trauma survivors' needs.

Four levels of incremental training have been identified:

1 Trauma Informed Practice Level: The basic level of knowledge for all of those in the workforce.
2 Trauma Skilled Practice Level: This is for all who have substantial contact with children and young people.
3 Trauma Enhanced Practice Level: This level of training must be undertaken by all who work closely with those who have experienced trauma.
4 Trauma Enhanced Specialist Level: As the name suggests, this level of training is for all those with specialist level involvement in interventions or service development with children and young people who have experienced trauma.

In education, the focus is on translating the policy framework into a whole school nurturing and trauma approach that provides children and young people with learning environments that focus on health, wellbeing and relationships (Education Scotland, 2021, 2023). Schools are supported to deliver these elements of the curriculum through reflecting on their practice (see Activity 8.2) and by supporting staff to develop their confidence and knowledge through professional learning activities that focus on both the cause and impact of traumatic and adverse experiences (Education Scotland, 2023).

Case Study 2 Wales, 'A Trauma-Informed Approach'

Wales, like Scotland, has a societal approach to addressing and preventing trauma and the framework that has been introduced aims 'to support a coherent, consistent approach to developing and implementing trauma-informed practice across Wales, providing the best possible support to those who need it most' (Ace Hub Wales, 2022, p. 8). There is a four-stage approach:

1. Trauma Aware: Aims to ensure all those living in Wales have an awareness of ACEs.
2. Trauma Skilled: For all those working with people who have faced trauma experiences or may have.
3. Trauma Enhanced: For frontline workers.
4. Specialist Interventions: For those providing intense support.

In education, working with families and communities is an essential part of the Welsh approach. The process is ongoing, with a focus on aligning training for staff with the Curriculum for Wales, especially health and wellbeing (Welsh Government, 2020).

Activity

Practice Audit

In *The Compassionate and Connected Classroom: A Health and Wellbeing Curricular Resource for Upper Primary* (Education Scotland, 2021, lines 18–26), four questions are posed to support a whole school approach:

1. To what extent do we have a positive culture and ethos in our school that embraces the principles of nurture, recognises the importance of the United Nations Convention on the Rights of the Child (UNCRC) and supports positive relationships?
2. How aware are staff of safeguarding processes, and do they have the skills to support children who might disclose as part of the discussions within this resource?
3. Has there been sufficient professional learning to support staff's own understanding of adversity and trauma?
4. Are we able to support all staff to have an awareness of the resource so that they will be in a position to support the children through it?

> Consider the first three of these questions in relation to:
>
> - The educational setting in which you work or, if a student, have been/are on placement.
> - Your own learning and development needs.
> - What actions do you think your setting could undertake to develop practice?
> - What actions can you take to enhance your knowledge and understanding?

In summary, a trauma-informed approach in education requires a whole school approach that is proactively led by the compassionate leadership team. All staff in training enables a psychologically and physically safe environment to develop for staff, pupils and their families. It requires a shift from policies that address the consequences of behaviour to ones that reflect behavioural understanding, recognising that some children and young people can be re-traumatised by disciplinary measures.

Staff Wellbeing

Working in a school or other type of education setting is hard for all staff. Traditionally, little training has been afforded on the adverse and abusive situations some children and young people experience. There is also a lack of a formalised supervision structure to allow staff the opportunity to process the day-to-day impact of their work. While this is changing, there is still more to be done to enable all staff to have the knowledge, skills and support structures to address the health and wellbeing of the children and young people who are part of their community. If a school is to have a compassionate and trauma-informed approach, then staff wellbeing needs to be a primary focus.

The Anna Freud Centre (2023) has developed a five-step framework for education settings to promote staff wellbeing, which includes:

1 Leading Change: Includes four area of focus:
   a Preparing for change
   b Health and wellbeing policy
   c Commitment to the development and improvement plan
   d Signpost information

2 Working together: With a focus on improving collaboration with mental health organisations, children and young people and their families and including them in decision-making.

3 Understanding need: Knowing who may be at risk, measuring wellbeing and developing intervention measures.
4 Promoting wellbeing: This includes integrating health and wellbeing in the curriculum, peer support and developing safe environments.
5 Supporting staff: Includes a focus on a confidential support service, training and the promotion of staff wellbeing.

Conclusion

Research evidence reinforces that increasing numbers of children and young people are experiencing challenges with their mental health and wellbeing. Education settings have an important role to play, especially in developing compassionate trauma-informed communities where staff, pupils and their families feel they belong and that relationships matter.

This cannot happen without compassionate leadership that recognises that staff, children and young people may have had experiences that have caused trauma. For those settings wanting to move further than compassionate and nurturing approaches and embrace a trauma-informed approach, they need to appreciate that it is more than words on paper. It is a whole setting approach that benefits from adopting the framework and principles outlined by SAHMSA (2014). These have been the foundation for developments globally, including the whole nation approaches of Scotland and Wales. Central to this is the four R's of *realise, recognise, respond* and *resist re-traumatisation*. If we do not understand what the issues are, know how to recognise their impact, provide the appropriate interventions and know the importance of having structures that do not re-traumatise, then how can we collectively support children and young people improve their life chances?

References

ACE Hub Wales. (2022), Trauma-informed Wales: A societal approach to understanding, preventing and supporting the impacts of trauma and adversity. Available at https://traumaframeworkcymru.com/wp-content/uploads/2022/07/Trauma-Informed-Wales-Framework.pdf (Accessed January 18, 2024).

Action for Children. (2023), Cost of children in crisis: The heightened impact of the cost of living crisis on families with children. Available at https://media.actionforchildren.org.uk/documents/Cost_of_children_crisis_briefing_-_Oct_2023_k4BFayp.pdf (Accessed February 19, 2024).

Al-Ghabban, A. (2018), A compassion framework: The role of compassion in schools in promoting well-being and supporting the social and emotional development of children and young people. *Pastoral Care in Education*, 36(3), pp. 76–188. Available at https://www.tandfonline.com/doi/full/10.1080/02643944.2018.1479221 (Accessed February 19, 2024).

Anna Freud Centre. (2023), 5 steps to mental health and wellbeing: A framework for schools and colleges. Available at https://www.annafreud.org/resources/schools-and-colleges/5-steps/ (Accessed February 19, 2024).

Avery, J.C., Morris, H., Gavin, E., Misso, M., Savaglio, M. and Skoutersis, H. (2021), Systematic review of school-wide trauma-informed approaches. *Journal of Child Adolescent Trauma*, *14*, pp. 381–397. Available at https://www.ncbi.nlm.nih.gov/pmc/articles/PMC8357891/ (Accessed February 19, 2024).

Azevedo, J., Akmal, M., Cloutier, M., Rogers, H. and Wong, Y. (2022), Learning losses during COVID-19: Global estimates of an invisible and unequal crisis. *Policy Research Working Papers*. World Bank. Available at https://elibrary.worldbank.org/doi/abs/10.1596/1813-9450-10.18 (Accessed February 19, 2024).

Berger, E. and Martin, K. (2020), Embedding trauma-informed practice within the education sector. *Journal of Community and Applied Social Psychology*, *31*, pp. 223–227. Available at https://doi.org/10.1002/casp.2494 (Accessed February 19, 2024).

Bellis, A.M., Lowey, H., Leckenby, N., Hughes, K. and Harrison, D. (2014), Adverse childhood experiences: Retrospective study to determine their impact on adult health behaviours and health outcomes in a UK population. *Journal of Public Health (Oxf)*, *36*(1), pp. 81–91. Available at https://www.researchgate.net/publication/236184211_Adverse_childhood_experiences_Retrospective_study_to_determine_their_impact_on_adult_health_behaviours_and_health_outcomes_in_a_UK_population (Accessed February 19, 2024).

Bellis, A.M., Ashton, K., Hughes, K., Ford, K., Bishop, J. and Paranjothy, S. (2016), Adverse childhood experiences and their impact on health harming activities in the Welsh adult population. Available at https://researchonline.ljmu.ac.uk/id/eprint/2648/ (Accessed February 19, 2024).

Children's Commissioner. (2023), Children's mental health services 2021–22. Available at https://assets.childrenscommissioner.gov.uk/wpuploads/2023/03/Childrens-Mental-Health-Services-2021-2022-2.pdf (Accessed November 20, 2023).

Center on the Developing Child. (2016), *From Best Practices to Breakthrough Impacts: A Science-based Approach to Building a more Promising Future for Young Children and Families*. Cambridge: Centre on the Developing Child. Available at https://46y5eh11fhgw3ve3ytpwxt9r-wpengine.netdna-ssl.com/wp-content/uploads/2016/05/From_Best_Practices_to_Breakthrough_Impacts-4.pdf (Accessed February 17, 2024).

Center on the Developing Child. (2017), *8 Things to Remember about Child Development*. Cambridge: Centre on the Developing Child.

Cherry, L. (2021), *Conversations that Make a Difference for Children and Young People: Relationship-Focused Practice from the Frontline*. Abingdon: Routledge.

de Araújo, L.A., Veloso, C.F., Souza, M. de C., de Azevedo, J.M.C. and Tarro, G. (2020), The potential impact of the Covid-19 pandemic on child growth and development: A systematic review. *Jornal de Pediatria*, *97*(4), pp. 369–377. Available at https://pubmed.ncbi.nlm.nih.gov/32980318/ (Accessed December 13, 2023).

Department of Education (DFE). (2023), *Keeping Children Safe in Education 2023: Statutory Guidance for Schools and Colleges*. Available at https://assets.publishing.service.gov.uk/media/66d7301b9084b18b95709f75/Keeping_children_safe_in_education_2024.pdf (Accessed November 11, 2023).

Education Scotland. (2021), Nurture and trauma-informed approaches: A summary of supports and resources. Available at https://education.gov.scot/resources/nurture-and-trauma-informed-approaches-a-summary-of-supports-and-resources/ (Accessed January 31, 2024).

Education Scotland. (2023), The compassionate and connected classroom: A health and wellbeing curricular resource for upper primary. Available at https://education.gov.scot/resources/compassionate-and-connected-classroom/ (Accessed January 31, 2024).

Felitti, V.J., Anda, R. F., Nordenberg, D., Williamson, D.F., Spitz, A.M., Edwards, V., Koss, P. and Marks, J. (1998), Relationship of childhood abuse and household dysfunction to many of the leading causes of death in adults: The adverse childhood experiences (ACE) study. *American Journal of Preventive Medicine*, *14*(4), pp. 245–258.

Gilbert, P. (2013), *Mindful Compassion: Using the Power of Mindfulness and Compassion to Transform our Lives*. London: Robinson.

Gill, T. and Munro, R.M. (2020), *Play during Lockdown*. International Play Association.

Harrison, N. (2022), Attachment and trauma awareness training: Headteachers' perspectives on the impact on vulnerable children, staff and the school. Available at https://www.education.ox.ac.uk/wp-content/uploads/2019/05/Timpson-working-paper-5.pdf (Accessed January 31, 2024).

Lumsden, E. (2018), *Child Protection in the Early Years: A Practical Guide*. London: Jessica Kingsley Publications.

Maynard, B.R., Farina, A., Dell, N.A. and Kelly, M.S., (2020), Effects of trauma-informed approaches in schools: A systematic review. *Campbell Systematic Reviews*, *15*(e1018), pp. 1–18. Available at https://www.ncbi.nlm.nih.gov/pmc/articles/PMC8356508/ (Accessed February 18, 2024).

Murray, J. (2021), Informal early childhood education: The influences of parents and home on young children's learning. *International Journal of Early Years Education*, *29*(2), pp. 117–123.

National Trauma Transformation Programme. (2023), *National Trauma Transformation Programme*. Available at https://www.traumatransformation.scot/ (Accessed February 19, 2014).

Newlove-Delgado, T., Marcheselli, F., Williams, T., Mandalia, D., Davis, J., McManus, S., Savic, M., Treloar, W. and Ford, T. (2022), *Mental Health of Children and Young People in England, 2022*. Leeds: NHS Digital. Available at https://digital.nhs.uk/data-and-information/publications/statistical/mental-health-of-children-and-young-people-in-england/2022-follow-up-to-the-2017-survey (Accessed February 19, 2014).

NSPCC. (2022), The impact of coronavirus (Covid-19): Statistics briefing. Available at https://learning.nspcc.org.uk/research-resources/statistics-briefings/covid/ (Accessed February 19, 2014).

OECD. (2017), *PISA 2015 Results, Volume 3, Students' Well-Being*. Paris: OECD. Available at https://www.oecd.org/education/pisa-2015-results-volume-iii-9789264273856-en (Accessed February 18, 2024); https://dx.doi.org/10.1787/9789264273856-en (Accessed October 25, 2021).

OECD. (2019), *Sense of Belonging at School: PISA 2018 Results, Volume 3, Chapter 9*. Paris: OECD. Available at https://www.oecd.org/publications/pisa-2018-results-volume-iii-acd78851-en.htm (Accessed February 18, 2024).

Office of National Statistics (ONS). (2020), Online bullying in England and Wales statistical bulletins. Available at https://www.ons.gov.uk/peoplepopulationandcommunity/crimeandjustice/bulletins/onlinebullyinginenglandandwales/previousReleases (Accessed February 19, 2024).

Potvin, A.S., Penuel, W.R., Dimidjian, S. & Jinpa, T. (2022). Cultivating skilful means of care in schools through compassion practice and individual and joint inquiry. *Mindfulness*, *14*, pp. 2499–2515. Available at https://link.springer.com/content/pdf/10.1007/s12671-022-01867-x.pdf (Accessed February 18, 2024).

Rees Centre. (2024), School factsheet 2: Successful implementation of attachment and trauma awareness. Available at https://www.education.ox.ac.uk/wp-content/uploads/2019/06/factsheet2_Implementation-guidance.pdf (Accessed January 31, 2024).

Reimers, F. (2022), *Primary and Secondary Education During COVID-19*. Cambridge, MA: Springer. Available at https://library.oapen.org/bitstream/handle/20.500.12657/50965/978-3-030-81500-4.pdf (Accessed January 31, 2024).

Riley, K. (2022), *Compassionate Leadership for School Belonging*. London: UCL Press. Available at https://discovery.ucl.ac.uk/id/eprint/10146072/1/Compassionate-Leadership-for-School-Belonging.pdf (Accessed January 25, 2024).

Robidoux, H., Ellington, E. and Laurerer, J. (2019), Screen time: The impact of digital technology on children and strategies in care. *Journal of Psychosocial Nursing and Mental Health Services*, 57(11), pp. 15–20. Available at https://pubmed.ncbi.nlm.nih.gov/31670830/ (Accessed February 18, 2024).

Royal College of Psychiatrists. (2023), College report CR238–Infant and early childhood mental health: The case for action. Available at https://www.rcpsych.ac.uk/docs/default-source/improving-care/better-mh-policy/college-reports/college-report-cr238---infant-and-early-childhood-mental-health.pdf?sfvrsn=1d8d5efd_12 (Accessed February 19, 2024).

Royal Foundation Centre for Early Childhood. (2020), State of the nation: Understanding public attitudes to the early years. Available at https://royalfoundation.com/wp-content/uploads/2020/11/IpsosMORI-SON_report_FINAL_V2.4.pdf (Accessed February 19, 2024).

Scottish Government. (2019), *Scottish Health Survey 2019 - Volume 1: Main Report*. Available at https://www.gov.scot/publications/scottish-health-survey-2019-volume-1-main-report/pages/11/ (Accessed February 2, 2024).

Scottish Government. (2022), Getting it right for every child. Available at https://www.gov.scot/policies/girfec/. (Accessed January 31, 2024).

Siegel, D. and Payne Bryson, T. (2011), *The Whole-Brainchild: 12 Revolutionary Strategies to Nurture Your Child's Developing Mind*. Bantam Books.

Sinek, S. (2019), *The Infinite Game: How Great Businesses Achieve Long-Lasting Success*. London: Penguin Books.

Shonkoff, J. and Garner A. (2012), The lifelong effects of early childhood adversity and toxic stress. *American Academy of Paediatrics*, 129, pp. 232–246. Available at http://pediatrics.aappublications.org/content/pediatrics/129/1/e232.full.pdf. (Accessed February 16, 2024).

Spratt, J., Shucksmith, J., Philip, K. and Watson, C. (2006), 'Part of who we are as a school should include responsibility for well-being': Links between the school environment, mental health and behaviour. *Pastoral Care in Education*, 24(3), pp. 14–21. Available at https://onlinelibrary.wiley.com/doi/epdf/10.1111/j.1468-0122.2006.00374.x (Accessed February 18, 2024).

Stokes, H. (2022), Leading trauma-informed education practice as an instructional model for teaching and learning. *Education Psychology*, 9(11), pp. 1–14. Available at https://www.frontiersin.org/articles/10.3389/feduc.2022.911328/full (Accessed February 15, 2024).

Substance Abuse and Mental Health Services Administration (SAMHSA). (2014), SAMHSA's concept of trauma and guidance for a trauma-informed approach. Available at https://store.samhsa.gov/sites/default/files/sma14-4884.pdf (Accessed February 18, 2024).

The Children's Society. (2023), The good childhood report. Available at https://www.childrenssociety.org.uk/sites/default/files/2023-09/The%20Good%20Childhood%20Report%202023.pdf (Accessed October 10, 2023).

UNICEF. (2021), Mental health. Available at https://data.unicef.org/topic/child-health/mental-health/#resources (Accessed February 19, 2024).

UNICEF. (2023), Adolescent health dashboards. Available at https://data.unicef.org/resources/adolescent-health-dashboards-country-profiles/ (Accessed February 19, 2024).

Vogels, E. (2022), *Teens and Cyberbullying 2022*. Washington: The PAWS Center. Available at https://www.pewresearch.org/internet/2022/12/15/teens-and-cyberbullying-2022/ (Accessed February 19, 2024).

Ventouris, A., Panourgia, C. and Hodge, S. (2021), Teachers' perceptions of the impact of technology on children and young people's emotions and behaviours. *International Journal of Educational Research Open*, 2, Article 100081.

Welsh Government. 2020, Introduction to the curriculum for Wales. Available at https://hwb.gov.wales/curriculum-for-wales/introduction-to-curriculum-for-wales-guidance/ (Accessed February 17, 2024).

8 The Modern Iliad

Asylum Seeker and Refugee Children's Search for Belonging

Estelle Tarry

Introduction

This chapter's main aim is to support and develop teachers' knowledge and understanding of the trauma asylum seeker and refugee children have experienced, how it has impacted their social and emotional learning including their sense of belonging and the consequence on their mental health and wellbeing. This chapter will also give practical suggestions to help develop teacher trauma-informed practice and discuss how to support children's inclusion and integration into schools and community, so that these children can ultimately flourish and thrive.

Push and pull of migration

For various reasons throughout history, people have always migrated, impacting and changing demographics, culture, religion and language. Recently, there has been a continuing global trend of the displacement of individuals and families through war; political, social or religious persecution; torture; abuse; trafficking; child labour; economics and health risks, including famine, nutrition, water, pandemics, healthcare and vaccinations. Notably, by the end of 2022, 108.4 million people were forcibly displaced worldwide due to 'persecution, conflict, violence, human rights violations or events seriously disturbing public order' (UNHCRa, 2023, p.2). Additionally, climate change—flash floods, drought and wildfires, which in some circumstances have led to conflict—has also exacerbated forced displacement to include 43.1 million children internally displaced due to these 'weather-related disasters' over a six-year period, 2016 to 2021 (UNICEF, 2023, p. 12). As the United Nations High Commissioner for Refugees' Refugee Agency (UNHCRa, 2023, p. 30) highlights, '2.9 million individual asylum applications were registered in 162 countries by States or UNHCR worldwide', 'the highest number of individual asylum applications ever recorded'.

The definition of a migrant is complex. UNHCR 1951 Article 1 (p. 3) defines a refugee as 'someone who is unable or unwilling to return to their country of origin owing to a well-founded fear of being persecuted for reasons of race, religion, nationality, membership of a particular social group, or political opinion'. Arguably, the distinction between asylum seeker and refugee is that an asylum seeker is waiting for their 'refugee status' to be granted by the country they have applied to for protection, whereas a refugee has been formally recognised by that country and has been granted 'refugee status'. The United Kingdom defines an asylum seeker as 'a person who is seeking international protection and has applied for refugee status under this convention, but whose claim has not yet been determined' (United Kingdom, 2022a). In contrast, UNHCR 1951 does not make this distinction and considers an asylum seeker to have already met the criteria of being a refugee.

Asylum seekers and refugees are travelling greater distances in order to seek sanctuary in perceived safe countries. Increasing global migration means that people are travelling through neighbouring safe countries, taking desperate and often life-threatening routes, travelling across mountainous and uninhabitable environments, and crossing dangerous seas, using overcrowded small boats and dinghies, putting themselves at risk to people traffickers and modern slave traders. For those seeking sanctuary, it can be complex; not only are there the push factors, but there are also the host country pull factors: the language, family members, health resources, economics and overall better perceived life chances.

> **What teachers need to know about where asylum seekers and refugees go:**
>
> - Most people who are forced to flee remain displaced in their home country.
> - Neighbouring countries host most refugees and asylum seekers, in the hope they can return to their home country.
> - Most refugees seek sanctuary in low- and middle-income countries.
> - Asylum seekers and refugees are travelling to increasingly farther destinations, including OECD countries.
> - Europe including Turkey hosted 36% of all refugees, with Germany recording the highest number of 2.1 million (6%).
> - Half of asylum seekers and refugees in the UK originate from the Syrian Arab Republic, Ukraine and Afghanistan.
>
> (UNHCRa, 2023)

With the continued influx of asylum seeker and refugee children across Europe and uncontrolled borders, host countries are facing increasing pressures on resources: health, housing and education along with international and national political policies, in what could be described as a humanitarian burden. UNHCR (UNHCRa, 2023) suggests that 'children account for 30 per cent of the world's population, but 40 per cent of all forcibly displaced people' (p. 3).

According to the UNHCR 1951 (p. 3), refugees have minimum basic rights including access to primary education; despite this, the UNHCR (UNHCRa, 2023) suggests that 'at the end of 2022, an estimated 4.4 million people worldwide were either stateless or of undetermined nationality, 90,800 (+2 per cent) more than at the end of 2021' (p. 43) and as they were 'stateless or of undetermined nationality' they were often unable to access essential services, including education. The number of young children has not been identified in these statistics.

British statistics

With the increasing number of schools changing to academies within the UK coupled with the decline of local authority schools, difficulties in accessing school places have increased, and as the Education Policy Institute (EPI, 2023) suggests, this situation has been exacerbated with the complex online application/enrolment systems and language issues (EPI, 2023). Additionally, United Kingdom (2023) statistics have highlighted that the number of all schools has also decreased by 12 to 24,442 schools, and yet recent numbers of school placements for children from outside the UK (UK, 2022b) are now as follows: Ukraine 20,500, Afghanistan 7,900 and Hong Kong 13,100. As the EPI (2023, p. 1) states, 'refugee and asylum seeker children are some of the most vulnerable in the educations system'. However, this chapter does not consider the rights or wrongs of the situation but intends to focus on supporting asylum seeker and refugee children and the society at large.

Trauma-informed practice: Mental health and wellbeing

There is a plethora of research, definitions, and terms for what is meant by trauma:

> Trauma results from an event, series of events, or set of circumstances that is experienced by an individual as physically or emotionally harmful or life threatening and that has lasting adverse effects on the individual's functioning and mental, physical, social, emotional, or spiritual well-being.
> (SAMHSA, 2014, p. 7)

Children during their childhood may have had adverse childhood experiences (ACEs) such as physical, emotional and sexual abuse; neglect; bereavement; domestic violence; broken relationships and separation. Asylum seeker and refugee children will have additional and multiple ACEs during their forced migration (violence, death, loss of home, lack of necessities, etc.), migration journey (traffickers, violence, detention centres etc.) and post-migration (integration into schools and society, care/legal systems etc.).

The impact of ACEs, such as the traumatic events and hardships of being an asylum seeker and refugee child, interrupts child development and has been associated with poor mental health and wellbeing. Young children, due to their cognitive development, are more 'sensitive' to traumatic events triggering fear, stress and anxiety, resulting in maladaptive behaviours (Sims *et al.*, 2000, p. 1). Trauma response behaviour can be short term, long term and complex. Trauma response behaviour can include cognitive (lack of concentration, memory and confusion), emotional (sadness, grief and guilt), interpersonal (withdrawal, avoidance and disconnection) and psychological (fatigue, headaches and appetite change). Heerde *et al.* (2023, p. 9) found in their research that, later in life, young adults who have had ACEs were found to suffer from poor health including 'lower perceived health status, risk for chronic illness, depression and anxiety symptoms, and diagnosed mental health/substance use disorders'. Heerde *et al.* (2023) continue to emphasise how important it is to have strategies and interventions to prevent and reduce ACEs. The cause of the asylum seeker and refugee children ACEs is almost always out of the hands of schools and teachers. However, schools and teachers should develop therapeutic and social interventions strategies to support the children post migration.

Schools and teachers are key players in fostering children's mental health and wellbeing but are not always trained or equipped with the skills along with the knowledge and understanding to support asylum seeker and refugee children's psychological needs. They may be left overwhelmed, daunted and apprehensive.

According to Maslow's hierarchy of needs (Gray and MacBlain, 2015), after the basic physiological needs of nutrition, shelter and the basic need of security/safety are the psychological needs of belonging and relationships, self-esteem and finally self-actualisation. Along with Maslow's hierarchy, social and emotional learning (SEL) is also vital in the children's ability to overcome the ACEs. It is part of the role of schools, teachers and communities to support children in developing the child's five SEL competencies—self-awareness, self-management, social awareness, relationship skills and responsive decision-making skills—to support their emotional regulation. These five social and emotional competencies permeate through the six principles of trauma informed practice.

The term 'trauma-informed' was coined by Fallot and Harris (Harris and Fallot, 2001; Fallot and Harris, 2011), who through their research evolved six principles to trauma-informed practice: safety, collaboration, choice, cultural consideration, trustworthiness and transparency and empowerment. This has led to a plethora of empirical research and literature by academic, government, health and welfare organisations. These six principles are all interconnected, improving school attendance, academic achievement, behaviour, mental health and staff wellbeing (Avery *et al.*, 2023). These principles can be adapted and implemented specifically for asylum seeker and refugee children and for the benefit of all stakeholders, school, teachers, children, parents/carers and community.

- Welcoming environment for children: safe and inclusive (Safety)
- Social integration and cohesion in the classroom (Collaboration)
- Voice and choice; children's communication skills (Choice)
- Culturally responsive learning and teaching (Cultural considerations)
- Parents/carers, family and community support (Trustworthiness and transparency)
- A sustainable future (Empowerment)

Welcoming environment for children; safe and inclusive (Safety)

Before any child can learn, they need to feel safe, in a supportive, nurturing, inclusive and responsive environment. UNESCO (2020, p. 156) highlights 'safe and accessible schools are crucial for inclusion' where 'inclusion in education is about ensuring that every learner feels valued and respected and can enjoy a clear sense of belonging' (UNESCO, 2020, p.v). At this point it is important to highlight the differing language of inclusion (Touray, AlZaabi and Johnson, 2023) and the focus that different countries adopt; for example, inclusion in India addresses the 'caste system', the Caribbean 'colourism' (Rahman, 2020), South Africa 'transformation' (Maguvhe, 2015), Europe 'equity', Japan 'age' (Paschaline, 2023), Nigeria 'inter-ethnic' (Ota and Ecoma, 2021) and the United Arab Emirates 'tolerance' and 'co-existence' (UAE, 2016) . However, regardless of the term and focus, a whole school approach requires strong visionary leadership along with the support of teachers and school staff. The schools' vision and mission statements should reflect the diversity of the whole school (Tarry, 2022), thereby eliciting an atmosphere of shared values, beliefs and common understanding, underpinning the school ethos, which as Cline (2023) highlights supports the children's sense of belonging, crucially for mental health and wellbeing. By developing and maintaining a welcoming, safe and inclusive learning environment, asylum seeker and refugee children will be able to establish and rebuild close and trusting friendships. Many asylum and refugee children will not necessarily have a stable home environment; therefore, a whole school approach should ensure the school, classroom and community include these marginalized and vulnerable children.

> **Activity**
>
> **Suggested strategies to create a welcoming environment**
>
> - Have videos, photographs and maps of the school, and maybe a school app.
> - Ensure that signage and displays are multilingual with pictures.
> - Have clear whole school and class routines/structure.
> - Create a safe and comfortable space for discussion and self-expression.
> - Incorporate nonverbal activities: storyboards, sports, dance, visual art and music.
> - Teachers must act as role models.
> - On induction, develop a buddy system: the asylum seeker/refugee child is supported by a host child, modelling behaviour and building a friendship. However, do not thrust this role on the supporting child. They need to be prepared for the responsibility.
> - After school activities: These will provide a safe environment to further develop the children's interests and supplementary study.
> - Where necessary, have targeted nurture groups.

Integration and social cohesion in the classroom (Collaboration)

The integration of refugee families and their children is the process that helps build cohesive societies (OECD, 2023, p. 17). The OECD (2023) acknowledges that host countries have prioritised the integration of refugees into government agenda. But what is meant by integration? And how can teachers encourage asylum seeker and refugee children's social cohesion in the class?

Integration can be defined as:

> The process through which tensions deriving from inter-group relations come to be managed so as to effect mutual adjustments of these groups to one another, in as much as these adjustments contribute to the effective functioning of society as a whole.
>
> (Isajiw, 1969, p. 511)

According to Manca (2014), there are two dimensions to social cohesion, sense of belonging and relationships. UNICEF Jordan (2019) suggests that social cohesion should not just be considered on the macro-political level but on the micro level of child-led social cohesion. Veerman and Denessen (2021, p. 1) suggest 'social cohesion in schools refers to positive interpersonal relations between students, a sense of belonging of all students and group solidarity'. Therefore, schools and teachers have a major part to play and are a key factor in the integration and social cohesion of asylum seeker and refugee children within the school community and the class.

Arigatou International Geneva (2021, p. 9) points out that many refugee children are victims of 'discrimination and diverse forms of bullying'. Asylum seeker and refugee children are more likely to experience or have experienced, any of the following, rejection, prejudice, harassment, teasing and bullying. Radicalisation Awareness Network (RAN, 2019, p. 2) highlights that these children suffer, 'on a different level' to other children, racism, challenges in building friendships and barriers to their learning. In Italian schools in 2016 (Caravita, 2016), 17.9% of migrant and refugee children experience bullying compared to 11.4% of the other classmates.

Activity

Group asylum seeker and refugee children with other children, ensuring all the children know each other's names and that all the staff in the school can pronounce and spell the children's names correctly. Allow the children to choose activities that they feel comfortable with. Prioritise activities that:

- Are creative and developmentally scaffolded.
- Give the children the opportunity to identify their feelings and express themselves.
- Promote friendships and empathy.
- Are interactive and collaborative.
- Involve cooperation, negotiation and dispute management.
- Involve problem solving, critical thinking and responsive decision making.
- Promote persistence, flexibility and productivity.
- Promote acceptance and appreciation.
- Promote kindness and helpfulness.
- Promote trust and tolerance.

Specifically supporting asylum seeker and refugee children, Reynolds and Bacon (2018, p. 754) advocate that 'broadly programmes and interventions should be sequenced, active, focussed and explicit'. They also recommend asylum seeker and refugee children should have opportunities to explore their premigration, migration and resettlement experiences through art-based creative activities. However, it is suggested that there is caution that the children should do this in their own time and when they are prepared to do so. It is vital for schools and teachers to promote children's self-awareness, social awareness and self-management skills to create a positive classroom community.

Voice and choice; children's communication skills (Choice)

Children need to be confident and proficient in the language of the host country. In England, as Conti (2022) suggests, the impact of language differences is minimal, as in many countries English is a shared language; however, arguably this may not be the case, especially with the high percentage of refugees and asylum seeker children arriving from the Syrian Arab Republic, Ukraine and Afghanistan. According to the United Kingdom Government (2023) statistics for the years 2021/2022 to 2022/2023, the number of children whose first language is 'known or believed to be other than English' attending state-funded nursery has increased from 11,071 to 11,411 (29.1% to 30.4% of the total number of children) while children attending state-funded primary schools has increased from 987,252 to 1,022969 (21.2% to 22% of the total number of children). These numbers do not distinguish between asylum seeker/refugee children and non-asylum seeker/non-refugee children.

Speaking and listening are the prerequisite of literacy, making them vital for not only the child's academic progress but also for the children to be able to express themselves, socially and emotionally. Teachers must nurture opportunities for children to develop their oracy skills.

Gozcu and Caganaga (2016) emphasize that games are an effective and vital pedagogical approach to learning a language. Stress and trauma affect children's ability to learn. Games-based learning, which are games for education and learning purposes, are a motivating and an experienced-as-fun way of learning a language, whether English as an additional language (EAL), host country first language or developing the first language of the asylum seeker refugee child, which is part of the child's identity. Children learn through game-based play, informally and formally, whether in the playground or in the class. Game-based learning initially does not always require language skills, for example matching games or games using photographs, pictures and emoji, but can be used as vehicles for speaking, reading and writing and building vocabulary and grammar.

Board games give children the opportunity to learn and use the eight parts of speech, nouns, verbs, adjective, adverb, pronoun, conjunctions, prepositions, and interjections. Children can talk about the board game pictures, where their pieces are on the board 'I am near …', 'I have got to get past …', anticipatory language 'I hope I get red', 'I hope I land on a space' and the expression of emotion 'Oh wow'. Board games can be designed with specific language aims and objectives, whether for speaking, reading or writing. They are flexible, adaptable and can be differentiated to the cognitive, language and physical ability levels and the emotional and social needs and interests of all children.

Asylum seeker and refugee children need to be able to make choices; they need a voice; they need to be heard. This is supported by one of the key findings of UNICEF Jordan (2019) for asylum seeker and refugee children: For a child to feel the sense of belonging, they need to be heard.

Picture books are a powerful tool to start conversations and discussion not only to support the young children's speaking and listening skills but also to give young children social and emotional support and a voice. By sharing a picture book, young children can express their ideas, thoughts, feelings and emotions, and of course be creative and imaginative. There are picture books specifically for young children, focussing on asylum seeker and refugee children's experiences. Not only will these books support refugee and asylum seeker children, but they will enable children without a refugee background to engage and empathize. By sharing picture books, relationships and trust can be built. This links very closely to the following section on culturally responsive pedagogical practices.

Activity

Sharing picture books

Try *Sunny and the Birds* (Meddour, 2023), *A Counting Book of Kindness* (Kurman, 2020) and *A Suitcase* (Naylor-Ballesteros, 2019). These picture books are about asylum seekers and refugees, and they foster understanding, kindness and empathy. Share the book and allow the children to start the conversation and discussion. Ask the children open questions about the picture book that will elicit their thoughts and feelings. Be respectful and sensitive.

- What is going to happen next? Why do you think that?
- Have you seen something like this before?
- How does it make you feel?
- What would you do if you were in that situation?
- What have you discovered?

Culturally responsive learning and teaching (Cultural considerations)

When asylum seeker and refugee children arrive in the host country, they will have had varying and different cultural, social and educational backgrounds. They may:

- Have limited knowledge of the host country and culture.
- Have limited language abilities of the host country and their mother tongue.
- Have limited or disrupted schooling.
- Be familiar with more conservative social norms, where liberal openness between children and teachers, such as group work and open discussion, is not present or encouraged.
- Be familiar with pedagogy that is more teacher-centred and less child-centred, for example, critical thinking and problem solving.

Teachers may have low expectations of immigrant children (Saeed, 2022, p. 203). To overcome this, teachers must be culturally responsive in their practice, be open to diversity and recognise the experiences and abilities of these children. Cultural responsiveness is when the teacher knows, understands, respects and accepts the cultural diversity of the children, integrating this into education policies, planning, curriculum, assessment and pedagogy (Gay, 2021). For teachers to be culturally responsive, they need to be aware of their own cultural lens, that is, the social and cultural norms that affect the way they feel, think and act, and examine their own prejudices and biases. Once teachers know and understand themselves, they can develop their own intercultural competencies and embrace their own curiosity for 'personal cultural trajectories' (Conti, 2022).

Teachers must be facilitators in intercultural dialogue, enabling children to construct their identity by sharing their culture, related experiences, curiosity, opinions and feelings. Active participation in intercultural dialogue, collaboration and peer-to-peer learning will foster self-awareness, inclusion and sense of belonging. Teachers must encourage children's intercultural engagement; therefore, teachers must be sensitive, build partnerships and trust and know when to give children the opportunity and choice to express themselves, thus enabling children to feel respected and appreciated. Teachers must master active listening and open questioning, and be able to reflect back on the children's feelings while being unjudgmental—and as Conti (2022) advocates, teachers need to know and be able to withdraw from the exchange.

Through fun and engaging child-centred activities, play and recreation, children can develop their communication, social and emotional skills and are more motivated to learn. Learning resources such as educational toys, puppets, materials and books should be culturally appropriate to reflect the class and the world diversity. Opportunities to explore cultural fairy tales, traditional stories, playground games, languages, singing and dancing, to name but a few, should be embedded into the curriculum. For example, include Arabic books so that children can know and appreciate the fact that Arabic is written from right to left and Middle Eastern books open in reverse to Western books. Teachers and children can use puppets to explore relationships, emotions, empathy and social and emotional language, which underpin emotional regulation. This has been developed further by The Sesame Workshop and International Rescue Committee (IRC), who co-created the mass media intervention *Ahlan Simsim* TV Program in Pre-Primary Classrooms. This intervention targeted children affected by the Syrian conflict and refugee crisis in countries in the Middle East and North Africa. The Global TIES for Children at New York University (2023), through their evaluation of this mass media intervention incorporating the use of puppets, had a positive impact on the children's ability to identify emotions and apply simple emotional regulation and coping strategies.

Good quality, culturally responsive assessment is vital and should not exclude any learners. A formative approach, such as projects or portfolios, should encourage and motivate learners, with constant feedback both orally through questions and written comments or marking. Extra time should be given for tests but also for oral assessment, giving the children time to comprehend (UNESCO, 2020, p. 112).

UNESCO (2020, p. 156) states that 'assistive technology can make a difference between participation and marginalisation'. Pynnönen *et al.* (2022) found that digital learning games (DLG) were a positive way of supporting refugee children's progress in literacy for Bangladeshi and Pakistani five- to eight-year-olds in refugee camps and urban slums (Dhaka and Karachi). Tahir and Wang (2022) emphasised how beneficial Arabic focussed DLG are in non-traditional contexts for motivation, engagement, curiosity, critical thinking, acquisition of digital experience skills and enjoyment. However, that is not to say that these opportunities should not be given to asylum seeker and refugee children in host country schools.

Parents/carers, family and community support (Trustworthiness and transparency)

Parents are major stakeholders in their child's academic attainment, mental health and wellbeing. Parents influence children's academic performance. The OECD (2023, p. 24) found that immigrant children's academic performance was lower in schools where the schools had 'high proportions of children with a low educated mother'; arguably this could be considered an issue for host country mothers. It is vital that there are strong home–school links to support these families, building partnerships with good quality two-way communication. This should be a priority for all parents and especially parents of asylum seeker and refugee children who face additional barriers. Unfortunately, there may be barriers as to why parents of asylum seeker and refugee children are not willing or able to be involved in their child's education and wellbeing, in schools. These possibly include:

- The parents' limited spoken and written communication skills of the host country.
- The parents' limited knowledge of the curriculum, teaching and learning strategies and education system.
- The schools' use of school education jargon.
- The parent's hierarchical notion that teachers are the experts, and it is the role of the school and teacher to educate their children.
- The parents' lack of academic qualifications and educational experience.
- The parents' concern that 'too deep involvement in a mainstream secular society could have the corrupting effect on lowering one's moral standards' (Saeed, 2022, p. 169).
- The parents, perhaps due to their previous experiences, being suspicious and mistrusting of government services and schools.

It must be noted that many asylum seekers and refugees do hope to return to their home country. For example, the UNHCR (UNHCRb, 2023) reported that 62% of Ukrainian refugees had the long-term hope of returning home. Schools and teachers must have empathy, knowledge and understanding (comprehending) to embrace, involve and empower the asylum seeker and refugee children's parents and the community. They need to support and guide asylum seeker and refugee parents in the host country while, as UNHCR (UNHCRb, 2023) acknowledges, their lives are on hold.

Activity

Suggested strategies to create parents/carers, family and community support

- Gather a learner profile, where possible: Include the child's family background and experiences, language proficiency in first language/host country language and education experience. Avoid having parents and children as interpreters for sensitive and personal meetings or details. Access professional interpreters; funding needs to be assessed. Have a designated welcoming and calming area for private conversations and discussion.
- Give a tour of the school: Give the family a tour of the school, highlighting expectations for example attendance, transport, uniform, meals and homework. Provide a simple map.
- Explain the school system: Discuss the structure and expectations of the school system. Include information of where to get uniform and equipment and resources the children will require. Write in different languages.
- Explain the school routines: Discuss the daily structure, times for start/end of the school day, lessons, official play, lunch and after-school activities.
- Have flexible joining dates: Agree, verbally and written, on a start date, as children will be arriving at different points during the academic year.
- Identify staff roles and responsibilities: Identify appropriate staff with relevant expertise. Consider academic and wellbeing support.
- Emphasise the importance of parental communication and engagement: Provide parent/carer workshops on the curriculum, assessment, language support, behaviour, special educational needs and disability (SEND), care/social/wellbeing support and governance. Highlight the importance of the parents' involvement and commitment in their child's learning journey.
- Provide school newsletters in various languages: Give school and curriculum information and details of festivals and events to build a strong school community.
- Highlight support services: Provide information and contact details of organisations, charities and community support who can provide language and asylum/refugee advice and other services.
- Connect community and religious leaders: Develop positive relationships early on with community and religious leaders to bridge the gap between school and parents. Identify and address potential barriers to parents' engagement.

A sustainable future (Empowerment)

For a sustainable future, schools must develop a whole-school framework to encompass inclusion, diversity, equity and access to build a sense of belonging. As the influx of asylum seekers and refugees is expected to increase, interconnection is going to be paramount. Schools, as part of the social sustainability framework, must recognise and identify misalignments and consequential tensions, and take action to address the issues.

Teachers need to empower the next generation; empower teachers, empower children. Teachers require training and professional development to improve their expertise in knowledge, skills and understanding, to remove barriers such as bias and prejudice and to unlearn assumptions. They need to be able to listen and truly understand the children's experiences, feelings and emotions, adopting a sustainable, culturally responsive and inclusive pedagogy and providing a flexible, accessible and differentiated curriculum with appropriate and motivating assessment.

In a rapidly changing world, teachers need to be lifelong continuous learners and researchers reflecting on own practice, embracing peer-to peer-learning and participating in mentor programmes and teacher-led workshops. Teachers need to be prepared to teach children with diverse backgrounds and abilities. UNESCO (2020, p. 136) identified that, '25% of teachers in middle- and high-income countries reported a high need for professional development on teaching students with special needs', and the need for mainstream and specialised teachers to train together to ensure positive perceptions of inclusion are maximised. This is supported by Barrett and Berger (2021), who through their research found that teachers had had little or no training on supporting refugee children and that they would benefit from specific targeted training.

Surprisingly, only a 'few countries' provide training for pre-service teachers 'from a broad perspective' (UNESCO, 2020, p. 140). The European Commission Review of Initial Teacher Education (Caena, 2014, p. 12) identifies four key areas of concern: teaching literacy and numeracy, information computer technology (ICT), assessment and diversity and the role of research. In summary, the European Commission Review of Initial Teacher Education recommended, as also mentioned earlier in the chapter, the need to embed technology into teaching practice, the use of assessment for learning by adopting portfolios as a means of assessing student teachers—an approach they could themselves use in assessing children, and student teachers' need to research and reflect on their own practice to identify areas of improvement. Finally, the teaching profession workforce lacks diversity and does not always mirror the diversity of the children (UNESCO, 2020). Therefore, schools must take opportunities to encourage all to consider teaching as a meaningful, rewarding and valued career.

Conclusion

This chapter has shown that children and their families, whether asylum seekers or refugees, require a whole school framework, encompassing the revised trauma-informed principles, enabling seamless inclusion into the education system and integration into their host country.

Schools and teachers need to build strong, trusting relationships with children, parents and community/religious leaders, which will support the development of a cohesive school community. However, asylum seeker and refugee parents must also take responsibility and positive action in engaging with the school and their child's learning journey. They need to become familiar with the school curriculum and pedagogy.

Teachers and student teachers require training and continued support, so that they can adopt new ways of teaching and adapt to the changing circumstances of this marginalized and vulnerable group. What is imperative is that teachers must learn and embrace teaching strategies and interventions that will empower children to enter the education system, enabling them to overcome language and cultural differences and develop a sense of belonging.

As a closing remark: No matter what the reasons are for the arrival of asylum seeker and refugee families, these families require safety, security and support. Asylum seeker and refugee children have experienced trauma through forced migration and during their migration journey and should, can and need to be supported post-migration, through providing a welcoming environment, which fosters inclusion, social integration and social cohesion, so that these children can flourish and thrive.

References

Arigatou International Geneva. (2021), *Inclusive Education for Migrants and Refugees*. 47th session of the Human Rights Council. June 24, 2021.

Avery, J.C., Galvin, E., Deppeler, J., Skouteris, H., Roberts, J. and Morris, H. (2023), Raising voice at school: Preliminary effectiveness and community experience of culture and practice at an Australian trauma-responsive specialist school. *Trauma Care*, *3*, pp. 331–351. Available at https://doi.org/10.3390/traumacare3040028 (Accessed January 17, 2024).

Barrett N. and Berger, N. (2021), Teachers' experiences and recommendations to support refugee students exposed to trauma. In *Social Psychology of Education*, *24*, pp. 1259–1280. Available at https://doi.org/10.1007/s11218-021-09657-4 (Accessed January 16, 2024).

Caena, F. (2014), *Initial Teacher Education in Europe: An Overview of Policy Issues*. European Commission Directorate-General for Education and Culture School policy/Erasmus+ ET2020 Working Group on Schools Policy. Brussels: European Commission Publications.

Caravita, S. (2016), Migrant and refugee children face higher rates of bullying. UNICEF Office for Research. Available at https://www.unicef-irc.org/evidence-for-action/migrant-children-face-higher-rates-of-bullying/ (Accessed January 12, 2024).

Cline, T. (2023), School ethos and student identity: When is wearing a uniform as badge of honour? In T. Cline, A. Gulliford and S. Birch (eds.), *Education Psychology: Topics in Applied Psychology* (pp. 306–324). New York: Routledge.

Conti, L. (2022), Dealing with intercultural issues. In C. Balraldi, E. Joslyn and F. Farini (eds.), *Promoting Children's Rights in European Schools; Intercultural Dialogue and Facilitative Pedagogy*. London: Bloomsbury Academic, Bloomsbury.

Education Policy Institute. (2023), What impact will the nationality and borders act have on the educational outcomes of refugee and migrant pupils? EPI and Paul Hamlyn Foundation's Event Series, Spring 2023. Accessed at https://epi.org.uk/wp-content/uploads/2023/05/EPI_PHF_Impact-of-the-NABA_summarypaper_Apr23_-1.pdf (Accessed September 23, 2023).

Fallot, F. and Harris, M. (2011, November), Creating cultures of trauma-informed care (CCTIC): A self-assessment and planning protocol. *Community Connections* Version 2.3/11-11. https://doi.org/10.13140/2.1.4843.6002

Gay, G. (2021), Culturally responsive teaching. In H.R. Milner and K. Lomotey (eds.), *Handbook of Urban Education*. London: Routledge. Available at https://www.routledgehandbooks.com/doi/10.4324/9780429331435-16 (Accessed October 22, 2023).

Global TIES. (2023), Lessons and impacts of *Ahlan Simsim* TV program in pre-primary classrooms in Jordan on children's emotional development: A randomized controlled trial Available at https://figshare.com/articles/preprintlessons_lessons_and_impacts_of_em_ahlan_simsim_em_TV_program_in_pre-primary_classrooms_in__on_children's_emotional_development_jordan_a_randomized_controalled_trial/22770929/1 (Accessed December 29, 2023).

Gozcu, E. and Caganaga, C.K. (2016), The importance of using games in EFL classrooms. *Cypriot Journal of Educational Science*, 11(3), pp. 126–135.

Gray, C. and MacBlain, S. (2015), *Learning Theories in Childhood* (2nd Ed). London: Sage Publications.

Harris, M. and Fallot, R. (eds.) (2001), Using trauma theory to design service systems. *New Directions for Mental Health Services*. San Francisco: Jossey-Bass.

Heerde, J.A., Merrin, G.J., Le, V.T., Toumbourou, J.W. and Bailey, J.A. (2023), Health of young people experiencing social marginalization and vulnerability: A cross-national longitudinal study. *International Journal of Environmental Research and Public Health*, 2023(20), p. 1711. https://doi.org/10.3390/ijerph20031711.

Isajiw, W.W. (1969), The process of social integration: The Canadian example. In *dalrev* (Dalhousie University), 48(4), pp. 510–520. Available at https://dalspace.library.dal.ca/handle/10222/59265 (Accessed November 1, 2023).

Kurman, H. (2020), *A Counting Book of Kindness*. Hereford: Otter-Barry Books.

Maguvhe, M. (2015), Inclusive education: A transformation and human rights agenda under spotlight in South Africa. *African Journal of Disability*, 4(1), pp. 183. https://doi.org/10.4102/ajod.v4i1.183. PMID: 28730034; PMCID: PMC5433483 (Accessed November 15, 2023).

Manca, A.R. (2014), Social cohesion. In A.C. Michalos (eds.), *Encyclopedia of Quality of Life and Well-Being Research*. Dordrecht: Springer. Available at https://doi.org/10.1007/978-94-007-0753-5_2739 (Accessed January 16, 2024).

Meddour, W. (2023), *Sunny and the Birds*. Oxford: Oxford University Press.

Naylor-Ballesteros, C. (2019), *A Suitcase*. London: Nosy Crow.

Organisation for Economic Co-operation and Development (OECD). (2023), *Indicators of Immigrant Integration 2023: Settling In*. Paris: OECD Publishing. https://doi.org/10.1787/1d5020a6-en

Ota, E.N. and Ecoma, C. (2021), The presentness of the past: Pre-colonial inter-ethnic relations and the challenges of national integration in contemporary Nigeria. *Saudi Journal of Humanities and Social Sciences*, pp. 227–284. https://doi.org/10.36348/sjhss.2021.v06i08.004

Paschaline, F.F., Prastita, R.A. and Mega, E. (2023), Japan's aging society: A challenge to Japan's diversity & social inclusion. In *Jurnal Transformasi Global*, 10(3), pp. 20–34.

Pynnönen, L., Hietajärvi, L., Kumpulainene, K. and Lipponen, L. (2022), Overcoming illiteracy through game-based learning in refugee camps and urban slums. *Computers and Education Open*, 3, 10113.

Radicalisation Awareness Network. (2019), Safeguarding troubled refugee children in the classroom. *Ex Post Paper; RAN EDU and H&SC joint meeting, October 3–4, 2019, Zagreb, Croatia.*

Rahman, M. (2020), The causes, contributors, and consequences of colorism among various culture. Honors College Theses. 71. Available at https://digitalcommons.wayne.edu/honorstheses/71 (Accessed November 15, 2023).

Reynolds, A.D. and Bacon, R. (2018), Interventions supporting the social integration of refugee children and youth in communities. *Advances in Social Work*, 18(3), pp. 745–766.

Saeed, A. (2022), *Education, Aspiration and Upward Social Mobility: Working Class British Women*. Cham, Switzerland: Palgrave MacMillan.

Sims, M., Hayden, J., Palmer, G. and Hutchins, T. (2000), Working in early childhood settings with children who have experienced refugee or war-related trauma. *Australasian Journal of Early Childhood*, 25(4), pp. 41–46. https://doi.org/10.1177/183693910002500408

Substance Abuse and Mental Health Services Administration (SAMHSA). (2014), SAMHSA's *Concept of Trauma and Guidance for a Trauma-Informed Approach*. HHS Publication No. (SMA) 14-4884. Rockville, MD: Substance Abuse and Mental Health Services Administration.

Tahir, R. and Wang, A.I. (2022), Evaluating the effectiveness of game-based learning for teaching refugee children Arabic using the integrated LEAGUÊ-GQM approach. *Behaviour & Information Technology*. https://doi.org/10.1080/0144929X.2022.2156386 (Accessed November 22, 2023).

Tarry, E. (2022), More than just dressing up in a sari: International schools in a multicultural world. In E. Tarry (ed.), *Challenges in Early Years and Primary Education: Employing Critical Thinking Skills During Turbulent Times*. London: Routledge.

Touray, F., AlZaabi, S. and Johnson, H. (2023), Sustainable practices in building inclusive academic communities: Insights from NYU Abu Dhabi's 'Journey to Belonging'. *The 10th Biannual GCES Symposium*, November 2023, United Arab Emirates.

United Arab Emirates. (2016), *National Program for Tolerance and Co-existence and Peace*. Ministry of Tolerance and Co-existence.

United Kingdom Government. (2022a), Refugees and asylum-seekers: UK policy. United Kingdom House of Lords policy. United Kingdom Government. Available at https://lordslibrary.parliament.uk/refugees-and-asylum-seekers-uk-policy/#heading-1 (Accessed September 8, 2023).

United Kingdom Government. (2022b), School placements for children from outside the UK. Accessed athttps://explore-education-statistics.service.gov.uk/find-statistics.school-placements-for-children-from-outside-of-the-uk (Accessed November 27, 2023).

United Kingdom Government. (2023), Academic year 2022-2023: Schools, pupils and their characteristics. Available at https://explore-education-statistics.service.gov.uk/find-statistics/school-pupils-and-their-characteristics/2022-23 (Accessed November 27, 2023).

United Nations High Commissioner for Refugees (UNHCR). (1951), *UN Convention and Protocol Relating to the Status of Refugees*. UNHCR Communications and Public Information Service P.O. Box 2500 1211 Geneva 2 (Text of the 1951 Convention Relating to the Status of Refugees).

United Nations High Commissioner for Refugees: The Refugee Agency (UNHCRa). (2023), *Global Trends: Forced Displacement in 2022*. United Nations High Commissioner for Refugees (Statistics and Demographics Section). Copenhagen: Denmark.

United Nations High Commissioner for Refugees: The Refugee Agency (UNHCRb). (2023), Lives on hold: Intentions and perspectives of refugees and IDPs from Ukraine. *Regional Report #4 June 2023.* UNHCR Regional Bureau for Europe/ UNHCR Ukraine and IPSOS.

United National Educational, Scientific and Cultural Organisation (UNESCO). (2020), *Global Education Monitoring Rreport: Inclusion and Education; All Means All.* Paris: UNESCO.

United Nations Childrens Fund Jordan (UNICEF). (2019), *Towards a Child-Led Definition of Social Cohesion.* Amman, Jordan: UNESCO.

United Nations Children's Fund (UNICEF). (2023), *Children Displayed in a Changing Climate, Preparing for a Future Already Underway.* New York: United Nations.

Veerman, G-J. and Denessen, E. (2021), Social cohesion in schools: A non-systematic review of its conceptualization and instruments. *Cogent Education, 8*(1), 1940633. https://doi.org/10.1080/2331186X.2021.1940633

9 Ecology and Embodiment
Engaging Children and Young People with Nature

Marie Hale

Introduction

Situated at the very heart of Schumacher College's mission to engage students in embodied and experience-led practice at the intersection of arts, ecology, and environmental justice. The Masters in Arts Degree (MA) in movement, mind and ecology (MME) represents a radical deterritorialization of both pedagogies and more-than-human entanglements in an emergent interspecies interactions embedded within a diversity of movement-led enquiries.

By empowering postgraduate students to actively engage with, interrogate and facilitate community action that can change children's, young people's and communities' relationships with the natural world, this programme reaches across international, ethnic, gender, socioeconomic and ecological boundaries (Nicol and Higgins, 2021).

The broad spectrum of more-than-human forms of existence, and their interconnections with and within human embodiments, have drawn attention from across a range of disciplines and practices. Attentiveness, openness, curiosity and response-ability (Haraway, 2012) are core values at the heart of MME students' learning experiences.

The aims explored within this MA are to interrogate, explore and redevelop ways to connect with socioecological systems and understand how they can positively impact humans' and nonhumans' wellbeing. By triangulating theory (involving seminars related to indigenous knowledge, complexity, interspecies collaborations and more), field research, practice-led learning and group discussion, students are reimagining networks from the liveliness around us, across species and beings, engaging in deep-field interrogations of human centrality.

Drawing from students' experiences of the learning content of the MA in MME, this chapter seeks to unveil how they have transposed their learning experiences within their own professional settings and work with children and young people. This chapter aims to understand how children and young people engage with nature and how the framework developed within the scope of the MME subject can reconfigure children's entanglements with place, nonhumans, and more-than-humans (Abrams, 1996).

Drawing from course materials and embodied practices, this chapter will investigate different intervention strategies that have been explored with MME students to reconnect children and young people with more-than-human worlds. It will draw on examples and case studies developed during the MA to demonstrate how nurturing these connections can have positive impacts on children's wellbeing (Capaldi *et al.*, 2015; Martin *et al.*, 2020). These activities and approaches can be applied and transferred to children and young people who are known to be spending less time outdoors due to increasing urbanisation processes (Louv, 2008). However, the opportunity for children and young people to connect with nature has been proven to be crucial for their personal development, and also for their wellbeing and general health condition (Louv, 2008).

From a methodological perspective, this chapter is based on students' experiences and designed activities for their first module, as well as a series of semi-structured interviews with alumni students to explore if and how they have transposed with children and young people they are working with, as well as what they have learnt on the course within their own professional settings.

This chapter will focus on means and ways to empower practitioners who are working with children to actively engage with, interrogate, and facilitate community action that can change children's and young people's relationships with the natural world.

Ecology and embodiment: place-responsive pedagogy

Students are required to frame conceptual debates with a particular emphasis on agency, the role of embodiment, movement ecology and more-than-human geographies in the context of addressing issues related to global environmental crises. Human engagement with the more-than-human world in the context of socioecological systems is at the heart of the teaching content.

Learning content is centred around the ways in which movement practices entangle humans with the more-than-human world, and the exploration of the relationship between ecology, movement and place is central to students' learning experiences.

At the heart of their learning experience are the principles of Schumacher College's ways of teaching: 'There is a double learning process at issue here: cultural and educational systems need to engage in deep change in order to facilitate deep change, that is, they need to transform in order to be transformative' (Sterling, 2004, p. 9). Students are encouraged to engage with learning content that is conceived as being 'transformative' and not 'transmissive' for them to develop their individual potential, as well as their socioecological wellbeing. The idea of interdependency is central to the teaching practice of the Schumacher College (Sterling, 2004). These principles of transformative education, which encourage a holistic, emotional, reflexive and experiential approach to learning, as well as place-based learning, can be applied and beneficial for all learners, regardless of their age.

Movement, mind and ecology students come from very different backgrounds, which is why ecology and embodiment are conceived to develop an ecology of practice, where students can interact with parts of their environment that are the most important to them, so they can embed them within their own creative practice (Jackson and Barnett, 2019).

The transformative learning philosophy and methodology of Schumacher College is based on the triangulation of 'Head, Heart, and Hands' as a systemic approach to learning and impulse for socioecological changes (Islam et al., 2022).

Movement, mind and ecology students are encouraged as much as possible to engage with the outdoors and nature during all the workshops. After all, as stated by Gunter Pauli, 'How can you learn from Nature and not be inside Nature?' (Pauli, 2021, p. 90).

Sterling suggests that education is key to progress towards a sustainable, regenerative, transformative and ecological paradigm to empower each person to become a learning leader at different scales, from one's family to the wider community (Sterling, 2004).

In designing ecology and embodiment, a wide range of sources and concepts are explored (Figure 9.1). Students are encouraged to explore concepts of deep mapping and slow residencies (Modeen and Biggs, 2021). Positioned between the natural and the social sciences, ecology and embodiment is using a lens of human geography to understand and deconstruct the relationship between nature, space and society (Castree and MacMillan, 2001).

Figure 9.1 Ecology and embodiment field trip to Dartmoor National Park, a contested landscape

> **Activity**
>
> **Practice for children and young people: Your breathing landscape**
>
> Everybody sits in a comfortable position. Become aware of the air around your nostrils.
>
> As you take a breath in, interlock your fingers and turn your palms outwards so they're facing away from you. As you breathe out, push your hands forwards, straighten your arms and pull your spine backwards so your upper back curves. Then drop your chin, relax your neck and keep your hands pushing forwards.
>
> What is the quality of that air? Is it warm? Is it cold? Is it dense or is it light? Does it have a scent?
>
> Place your awareness on the aroma of the air on every inhale. Become aware of the smell that is close to your nose.
>
> Bring the aromas into your body. Now try to tune in a different aroma, perhaps something further away. On the inhale bring these new aromas into your body. You can now open your eyes.

Attention in nature: Raising children's and young people's awareness to the natural world

One of the key aspects explored with MME students is the importance of paying attention in nature. From the beginning, students are encouraged to follow Ingold's phenomenological approach of sensing and attuning to the world through their whole body, experiencing it from an embodied perspective, not just as a cognitive process (Ingold, 2004). Kimmerer (2013) refers to the act of listening to engage in a system of lateral relations as an invitation to listen to what 'speaks to us'. As Rubin highlights (2023), 'when noticing the wisdom in nature, it awakens possibility in us. Nature also transcends our tendencies to label, classify, to reduce and limit'. When asked for feedback about one of the striking elements that MME brought to alumni MA students, sense of attentiveness in nature resonated all the interviews.

As one student stated,

> Being in nature, near the river or in the red woods allowed me to go back to my inner childhood and to just be curious and more opened to what is out there. It is this sense of curiosity and openness that I try to share with the young people I work with. Being in nature helps them to let go.
>
> (Interview 3, 2023)

Lewis (2009) highlights this attention that children have when they are in nature, being attentive and curious of what the world has to offer. Feedback from the students also highlighted that letting children play spontaneously within nature allowed them to develop a more embodied experience compared to when they followed a planned schedule of activities (Skar et al., 2016).

Robin Wall Kimmerer (2013) is one of the key voices that supports the learning experience on the MA in movement, mind and ecology. By fostering 'reciprocal restoration', students are encouraged to develop mutually beneficial partnership with nature, whether it be the river, the forest, the hedgerows or the gardens.

These partnerships with nature and this attentiveness also help children and young people to be more open to challenging existing labels or reductionist approaches that they may have.

> I noticed when I took the kids out in nature that it allows them to think outside of the box, they can just let go of who is in charge or not and reflect on their own feelings. That sense of going back to nature is really helpful for young people to escape the pressure of society and just relax.
> (Interview 4, 2023)

Rubin (2023) reflects that nature has this ability to help humans to 'transcend their tendencies to label, classify, to reduce and limit'.

Activity

Practice in a box: Starter activity; noticing nature

'I am noticing': Ask children to pick or choose something they are noticing while they are outside.

It can be as simple as 'a flower' or 'the wind'. Ask them why they have noticed this element.

Ask children to close their eyes and focus on the nearest sound they can hear.

Ask children to close their eyes and focus on the furthest sound they can hear.

Ask children to opening their eyes, then to explore around them and come back with a small object that draws their attention. In pairs, ask them to explain why they were drawn to this object. Is it because of its texture, colour or smell?

This sense of awareness (Petitmengin, 2021) can be a very powerful tool for children and young people to enhance their quality of life and to improve their creative skills. Triangulating learning between indoor exploration of theories, outdoor practice-as-research, and peer discussion reinforces the learning experience of MA students. The process of learning becomes intuitive, emotional, cognitive and embodied.

> **Activity**
>
> **Practice for children and young people: Intention in nature**
>
> Taking the children or young people outside, ask them to form a pair and set up an intention for the day with your partner. At the end of the day, bring the children or young people back together so they can reflect on their intention.

Place-based nature connectedness for children

Nature connectedness refers to when a person identifies themselves as being a part of nature, also defined as a 'sense of oneness with the natural world' (Mayer and Frantz, 2004, p. 504). These connections are fundamental to preserving ecosystems and connecting spaces within cities and beyond to foster resilient linkages between urban, rural and natural areas. The benefits of nature contact for children have been outlined within research that demonstrated that green and other natural areas are 'essential elements of healthy communities for children' (Chawla, 2015, p. 433).

> Something else I learnt on MME is the fact that we need connections with nature to be able to understand the world we live in. Taking children out of cities is so important for them to understand where their food is coming from, where their water is coming from. Understanding how everything is connected is key for children.
> (Interview 2, 2023)

Connectivity and accessibility to these natural spaces in cities are therefore central to fostering children's nature connections with the environment. A study of preschool children in an urban setting found that nature connectedness was positively associated with enhanced psychological functioning (Sobko et al., 2018). Rautio and Jokinen (2016), conducted some interesting work in Finland with children to understand their connections with nature within their urban lives. They found that children's nature connections are very much place-based in their approach, and these connections emerge depending on the context of where they live.

> **Activity**
>
> **Task for children and young people: Sensorial experience**
>
> Close your eyes, place your hand on your tummy, focus on your breathing and feel the weight of your skull, the movement inside of your body and the weight on your knees. Join your hands together and rub them against each other to create warmth. Finishing the experience, place your hands on your eyes; when you open your eyes, focus on this shadow and how the light is trying to move through your hands.
>
> Looking around you, create a 360-degree circle and verbally name what is around you, not focusing on the names, more looking at the texture and the colours.

Engaging with water: A sensorial experience for children and young people

Movement, mind and ecology students are encouraged to develop their practice around water. Having the river Dart on site is a key element to explore, at various scales, how humans interact with water. Engaging in activities like swimming, surfing and simply being near water, among other water-based interactions, has been central in the learning experience of MME students. Place-based learning is pivotal in the delivery of the MA; therefore students are taken to both Dartmoor National Park, the source of the river Dart, and to the coast to explore concepts such as intertidal zones like beaches, key sociocultural spaces, and hybrid 'borderland' (Preston-Whyte, 2004, p. 348).

Figure 9.2 Water bodies in Plymouth

Indeed, an entity like the river Dart helps students to understand the relationships between ecological, political, cultural, ethnic, gender, urban/rural and other boundaries, binaries and borders in the context of embodiment and ecological systems (Figure 9.2). Students also engage with water through different medium such as poems, literature and art, all proven to be beneficial for humans' health (Buxton *et al.*, 2021).

By exploring Nature's rights and especially legal personhood given to rivers (Magallanes, 2015), students are encouraged to interrogate their understanding of boundaries and the ways in which movement can play an essential role in deconstructing limits, both socially constructed and bioregionally limned. Exploring how indigenous communities engage with nature is central to the learning content of this MA, and challenging anthropocentric views of nature is central (Jeong et al., 2018). Understanding their balanced and harmonious relationships with natural component such as rivers is key to deconstruct western approaches that value nature as a resource (Mehltretter *et al.*, 2023).

Activity

Practice in a box: Body of water and water bodies

Place your hands in the water—it can be a lake, a river or a puddle—and play with the water.

- What do you notice? How does it feel to sense the water on your hands?
- Do you have a personal memory connected to a body of water?
- Do you know a myth or a story attached to this body of water?

Please choose two sounds relating to your experience of the water that for you reflect or rhythmically illustrate your interactions with water. You can write these sounds in words or draw what they represent.

It is also important to mention here that 'When we rely on going outside to teach and tell environmental stories we are missing the point. We forget how mysterious everything that surrounds us is; the mundane is alien and special and strange and wonderful' (Scott, 2021, p. 46). McCormick has shown how accessing green space, especially water and mountain landscape, can have restorative benefits for children's and young people's mental wellbeing (McCormick, 2017). This chapter argues that engaging children, young people and adults with nature can be facilitated in all environments, urban, rural and natural, although recognising the creativity challenges that can arise in the most urban and nature-deprived areas. As Kimmerer (2013) maintains, 'The exchange of recognition, gratitude and reciprocity for these gifts is just as important in a Brooklyn flat as under a birch bark roof' (Kimmerer, 2013, p. 240).

148 *Principles and Practice to Help Young Children Belong*

Learning about and with nonhumans: Encountering others

The idea of kinship and symbiosis is a key aspect to the notion of becoming together rather than becoming in isolation, meaning we look out for the survival of all beings, not just our own (Kimmerer 2013).

Students in ecology and embodiment are asked to conduct a formative assignment on an encounter with another species. Students were encouraged to engage with species present on site (Figure 9.3). This includes rich encounters with grey squirrels, swallows, pine trees, red woods, pigeons, and many others.

Figure 9.3 A formative assignment on human/nonhuman interactions

Several steps need to be followed to be able to engage in the encounter with a nonhuman, as related in the practice box.

Activity for young people

Practice in a box: Encountering others

Calm your mind and focus on your breathing.
  Reflect on the form of being of the other species you are encountering.
  Ask permission to engage with it in a respectful manner.
  Observe in compassion.
  Explore if and how you can enter in a dialogue.
  Observe their environment and draw a map of their movement and interactions with other species while you observe them.
  Come back in the classroom and do some research on the species you have encountered.
  Is there anything you noticed that is similar or may not be in the articles you are reading?

These multispecies encounters are based on the idea that participatory research with nonhumans and more-than-humans should be conducted according to ethical principles that can be explained for children and young people. As Bastian highlights, the main qualities of this participatory research method need to be 'attentive, open, invitational, redistributive, informed, responsive, respectful, curious and humble' (Bastian, 2017, p. 194).

> Embodying nature and having the time and space to understand plants and animals has completely transformed my perspective on relating to other species and how important it is for humans to not think themselves at the top of the pyramid but as part of a whole.
> (Interview 3, 2023)

More-than-human practices were recognised in Eben Kirksey's *The Multispecies Salon* (2014), which is widely regarded as a landmark work in this subject. The book explores the relationships between humans and various nonhuman species and highlights the importance of recognizing and respecting these interdependent connections. Bergold and Thomas (2012) summarised the purpose of more-than-human participatory research processes by explaining that this form of research allows co-production of knowledge where humans are encouraged to step away from their routines to allow new forms of interaction to take shape and critically engage with power relationships.

> Ecology and embodiment has allowed me to actively consider other worlds and how other beings interact differently with their environments. I was curious to see how I could do this with the children I work with at school, and I find that sometimes the simplest approaches are the easiest. We did it with insects by just lying on the ground and stepping into the insect's world. It allows children to change their perspective and develop empathy.
>
> (Interview 4, 2023)

As noted by Harvey *et al.* (2020), observing animals within their natural environment is one of the most attractive and popular interactions in nature for children and young people to develop their ability to connect with nature.

This approach to nonhumans is based on several theories, including that of Bennett (2010), who put forward a theory of 'agency of assemblages' to explore the vital materiality intrinsic to human and more-than-human agents. The idea is that assemblages are living, moving, evolving confederations, but each actor has individual agency.

Students, while being invited to research and engage with other species, are being taught the principles and challenges of anthropomorphism (Noorani and Brigstocke, 2018) when it comes to listening to the voices of nonhumans while doing participatory research (Kirksey, 2014). Students are encouraged to approach this experience with mindfulness and respect to explore how different species interact and co-create in varied ways through collaboration and reciprocal care. This is an opportunity to challenge traditional anthropocentric perspectives, which place humans as separate from and superior to the nature world.

Being based at Schumacher College, students can engage through their formative assignment with very different species, which allows students to shift their values towards an ecological balance, build dynamic relationships and reflect on their perspectives of the nonhuman and more-than-human world while challenging instrumentalist and exploitative approaches to nature (Villanueva, 2021).

It is frequent that students who are encouraged to observe, research and present their assignment on another species choose to do it with plants or trees. This aspect, of researching with rather than on, is a key step to recognising that knowledge is co-produced (Noorani and Brigstocke, 2018). This formative assignment follows what Pitt (2017, p. 93) describes as 'research as apprenticeship' where humility is a key value (Taylor, 2011). That is the reason why this assignment is called 'nonhuman teachers'; it is an opportunity for students to become apprentices and learn from a teacher who knows about themselves and the world around them.

> **Activity**
>
> **Practice for children and young people: The limits of the tree**
>
> Ask children or young people to find the furthest point of the tree, the end of a branch or a root. and walk towards it.
>   Once they have reached the furthest point, look back and see where their classmates are.
>   Reflect on the width of the tree.
>   At the beginning of the week, ask children or young people to draw or write their wish for the week on a piece of paper and hang it on a branch or on a tree.

Teaching about the importance of trees to children is widely recognised within research (Hadzigeorgiou *et al.*, 2011), especially regarding the benefit for their health (Lovasi *et al.*, 2008). Children's relationships with trees help them to reinforce their place-making (Cele, 2019), especially in urban environments where play is more and more defined.

> I work with young people and the assignment we did with you in Ecology and Embodiment gave me the idea of exploring the concept of invasive animals and plants. I thought it was such a great way to explore movement but also explore the stories humans create around animals. It allows me to explore concepts of resilience, transformation, and adaptation with young people. We also deconstruct labels and prejudice, this leads to useful channelled discussion.
> (Interview 5, 2023)

As highlighted in this interview, engaging children in nature with these values should help to make them realise that the environment around them is not just a backdrop (Lyons, 2020). Being in nature is also a relevant opportunity for practitioners to engage children with ethical and gender debates, challenging preconceptions around female and male roles and expected behaviours in the outdoor (Cosgriff *et al.*, 2009).

> I enjoyed exploring and decolonising names in MME activities, we did a lot of work on how to call something and I found that, in the end, understanding naming can be a powerful tool to teach children how to connect with nature.
> (Interview 7, 2023)

Challenging students to learn from other epistemologies can be useful when working with children and developing new pedagogies on interconnectedness between different human cultures and the more-than-human world (Ritchie, 2012). An example of how some students have transposed this into their own practice is the initiative of a 'plant bingo' with children:

> I hosted a game of 'Plant Bingo' in a park near our school as a fun educational tool that encourages children to explore the world of local plants in an urban environment. By turning plant identification into a game of recognition, I hope to engage children with a sense of connection that might inspire responsibility. Through the act of searching for and identifying different plants, children are encouraged to develop their observational skills and develop their knowledge of ecology, their sense of community and belonging.
>
> (Interview 7, 2023)

Stemming from children's geographies is the practice of sustaining focus also on how things matter rather than only on what they mean (Horton 2010). Hillevi Lenz Taguchi (2010), has argued for a reconceptualization of early childhood pedagogy as an intra-active material/discursive practice, in which agency, meaning and thus potential transformation are produced in the intra-actions between children and the material 'things' with which they are engaged.

Conclusion: Embodied ecologies for children and young people

This chapter has demonstrated how practitioners who followed the module on ecology and embodiment are incorporating the agencies of nonhumans and more-than-human into their teaching practice and learning experiences (Lynch and Mannion, 2021). By promoting new notions of interconnectedness and attentiveness in nature, this chapter has shown how to equip practitioners who are working with children and young people with learning experience of contemporary theories across environmental humanities, place-based practices and peer learning to develop their socioenvironmental synthesis approaches. This ability to frame conceptual debates, with particular emphasis on agency, embodiment and empathy, can help to shape positive and creative relationships while working with children and young people from diverse backgrounds.

This relational view of learning, and the importance of attuning with the more-than-human, within children's and young people curriculums is considered more necessary than ever across research (Lynch and Mannion, 2021).

Following on from Smith *et al.*'s conclusions (2022), the activities and subject areas explored during the MA in movement, mind and ecology offer professionals who are working with children and young people the tools to notice and connect with nature and to mediate socioecological boundaries. By engaging with concepts such as class, race and gender (Smith, Pitt and Dunkley, 2022), alumni students are equipped to navigate arising debates with children and young people to understand how nature, and societies, are sociospatially produced and constructed.

References

Abram, D. (ed.). (1996), *The Spell of the Sensuous: Perception and Language in a More-than-Human World*. Pantheon.

Bastian, M. (2017), Towards a more-than-human participatory research. In M. Bastian, O. Jones, N. Moore and E. Roe (Eds.), *Participatory Research in More-than-Human Worlds* (pp. 19–37). London: Routledge.

Bennett, J. (2010), *Vibrant matter: A political ecology of things*. Durham: Duke University Press.

Bergold, J. and Thomas, S. (2012), Participatory research methods: A methodological approach in motion. *Historical Social Research/Historische Sozialforschung*, pp. 191–222.

Buxton, R.T., Pearson, A.L., Allou, C., Fristrup, K. and Wittemyer, G., (2021), A synthesis of health benefits of natural sounds and their distribution in national parks. *Proceedings of the National Academy of Sciences*, 118(14), p. e2013097118.

Capaldi, C.A., Passmore, H.A., Nisbet, E.K., Zelenski, J.M. and Dopko, R.L. (2015), Flourishing in nature: A review of the benefits of connecting with nature and its application as a wellbeing intervention. *International Journal of Wellbeing*, 5(4).

Castree, N. and Macmillan, T. (2001), Dissolving dualisms: Actor-networks and the reimagination of nature. In N. Castree & B. Braun (Eds.), *Social Nature: Theory, Practice, and Politics* (pp. 208–224). Malden, MA: Blackwell Publishers.

Cele, S. (2019), Trees: A tale of two trees: How children make space in the city. In P. Rautio and E. Stenvall (eds.), *Social, Material and Political Constructs of Arctic Childhoods: An Everyday Life Perspective* (pp. 1–15). Singapore: Springer.

Chawla, L. (2015), Benefits of nature contact for children. *Journal of Planning Literature*, 30(4), pp. 433–452.

Cosgriff, M., Little, D.E. and Wilson, E. (2009), The nature of nature: How New Zealand women in middle to later life experience nature-based leisure. *Leisure Sciences*, 32(1), pp. 15–32.

Hadzigeorgiou, Y., Prevezanou, B., Kabouropoulou, M. and Konsolas, M. (2011), Teaching about the importance of trees: A study with young children. *Environmental Education Research*, 17(4), pp. 519–536.

Haraway, D. (2012), Awash in urine: DES and Premarin® in multispecies response-ability. *Women's Studies Quarterly*, 40(1/2), pp. 301–316.

Harvey, C., Hallam, J., Richardson, M. and Wells, R. (2020), The good things children notice in nature: An extended framework for reconnecting children with nature. *Urban Forestry & Urban Greening*, 49, 126573.

Horton, J. (2010), 'The best thing ever': How children's popular culture matters. *Social & Cultural Geography*, 11(4), 377–398.

Ingold, T., (2004), Culture on the ground: The world perceived through the feet. *Journal of Material Culture*, 9(3), pp. 315–340.

Islam, M.A., Haji Mat Said, S.B., Umarlebbe, J.H., Sobhani, F.A. and Afrin, S. (2022), Conceptualization of head-heart-hands model for developing an effective 21st century teacher. *Frontiers in Psychology*, 13, 968723.

Jackson, N. and Barnett, R., (2019), Introduction: Steps to ecologies for learning and practice. In R. Barnett and N. Jackson (eds.), *Ecologies for Learning and Practice* (pp. 1–16). London: Routledge.

Jeong, S., Britton, S., Haverkos, K., Kutner, M., Shume, T. and Tippins, D. (2018), Composing new understandings of sustainability in the Anthropocene. *Cultural Studies of Science Education*, 13, pp. 299–315.

Kimmerer, R. (2013), *Braiding sweetgrass: Indigenous wisdom, scientific knowledge and the teachings of plants*. Minneapolis: Milkweed Editions.

Kirksey, E. ed. (2014), *The multispecies salon*. Durham: Duke University Press.

Lewis Jr, T.G. (2009), *Youth and nature: Assessing the impact of an integrated wellness curriculum on nature based play and nature appreciation for youth in out-of-school time recreation programming*. University of Minnesota.

Louv, R. (2008), *Last Child in the Woods: Saving Our Children from Nature-Deficit Disorder*. Algonquin Books.

Lovasi, G.S., Quinn, J.W., Neckerman, K.M., Perzanowski, M.S. and Rundle, A. (2008), Children living in areas with more street trees have lower prevalence of asthma. *Journal of Epidemiology & Community Health* 62(7), pp. 647–649, PMID: 18450765, https://doi.org/10.1136/jech.2007.071894

Lynch, J. and Mannion, G. (2021), Place-responsive pedagogies in the Anthropocene: Attuning with the more-than-human. *Environmental Education Research*, 27(6), pp. 864–878.

Lyons, K. (2020). Nature, sensory integration, and pediatric occupational therapy. In K. Lyons (ed.), *Outdoor Therapies* (pp. 134–145). London: Routledge.

Magallanes, C.J.I. (2015), Nature as an ancestor: two examples of legal personality for nature in New Zealand. In *VertigO-la revue électronique en sciences de l'environnement* (Hors-série 22). Available at https://papers.ssrn.com/sol3/papers.cfm?abstract_id=3532319 (Accessed March 12, 2024)

Martin, L., White, M.P., Hunt, A., Richardson, M., Pahl, S. and Burt, J. (2020), Nature contact, nature connectedness and associations with health, wellbeing and pro-environmental behaviours. *Journal of Environmental Psychology*, 68, p. 101389.

Mayer, F.S. and Frantz, C.M. (2004), The connectedness to nature scale: A measure of individuals' feeling in community with nature. *Journal of Environmental Psychology*, 24(4), pp. 503–515.

McCormick, R. (2017), Does access to green space impact the mental well-being of children: A systematic review. *Journal of Pediatric Nursing*, 37, pp. 3–7.

Mehltretter, S., Longboat, S., Luby, B. and Bradford, A. (2023), Indigenous and Western knowledge: Bringing diverse understandings of water together in practice. *Global Commission on the Economics of Water*. Available at https://watercommission.org/publication/indigenous-and-western-knowledge-bringing-diverse-understandings-of-water-together-in-practice/ (Accessed February 12, 2024).

Modeen, M. and Biggs, I., (2021), *Creative engagements with ecologies of place: Geopoetics, deep mapping and slow residences*. London: Routledge.

Nicol, R., & Higgins, P. (2021). Transformative learning. Reflections on 30 years of head, heart and hands at Schumacher College: By Satish Kumar and Pavel Cenkl (eds.), New Society Publishers, 2021, 9781771423410. *Environmental Education Research*, 28(1), pp. 160–167. https://doi.org/10.1080/13504622.2021.1991280

Noorani, T. and Brigstocke, J. (2018), More-than human participatory research. Available at https://orca.cardiff.ac.uk/id/eprint/119017/1/J%20Brigstocke%202018%20more%20than%20human%20report.pdf (Accessed February 25, 2024).

Pauli, G. (2021), Nature has no waste. In Kumar, S. and Cenkl, P. (eds.), *Transformative Learning: Reflections on 30 Years of Head, Heart and Hands at Schumacher College* (pp. 89–93). Canada: New Society Publishers.

Petitmengin, C. (2021), On the veiling and unveiling of experience: A comparison between the micro-phenomenological method and the practice of meditation. *Journal of Phenomenological Psychology*, 52(1), pp. 36–77.

Pitt, A. (2017), *The experienced worker, the student, and the information gap: What are the information needs of vocational trades students while on work experience?* Victoria University of Wellington. Available at https://ir.wgtn.ac.nz/handle/123456789/20157 (Accessed February 15, 2024).

Preston-Whyte, R. (2004), The beach as a liminal space: In A. Lew, M. Hall, and A. Williams (Eds.), *A companion to tourism* (pp. 349–359). Oxford: Blackwell.

Rautio, P. and Jokinen, P. (2016), Children's relations to the more-than-human world beyond developmental views. *Play and Recreation, Health and Wellbeing*, 9, pp. 35–49.

Ritchie, J. (2012), Early childhood education as a site of ecocentric counter-colonial endeavour in Aotearoa New Zealand. *Contemporary Issues in Early Childhood*, *13*(2), pp. 86–98.

Rubin, R. (2023), Nature as teacher. In *The Creative Act: A Way of Being, Nature as Teacher* (p. 432). Penguin US.

Scott, J.W. (2021), Cognitive geographies of bordering: The case of urban neighbourhoods in transition. *Theory & Psychology*, *31*(5), pp. 797–814.

Skar, M., Gundersen, V. and O'Brien, L. (2016), How to engage children with nature: Why not just let them play? *Children's Geographies*, *14*(5), pp. 527–540.

Smith, T. A., H. Pitt, and R. A. Dunkley, eds. (2022), *Unfamiliar Landscapes: Young People and Diverse Outdoor Experiences*. London: Palgrave Macmillan Cham.

Sobko, T., Jia, Z. and Brown, G. (2018), Measuring connectedness to nature in preschool children in an urban setting and its relation to psychological functioning. *PloS One*, *13*(11), p. e0207057.

Sterling, S. (2004), Sustainable education: Revisioning learning and change. Schumacher Briefings (pp. 96).

Taguchi, H.L. (2010), Rethinking pedagogical practices in early childhood education: A multidimensional approach to learning and inclusion. In N. Yelland (ed.), *Contemporary perspectives on early childhood education*. Maidenhead: Open University Press, pp. 187–206.

Taylor, A. (2011), Reconceptualizing the 'nature' of childhood. *Childhood*, *18*(4), pp. 420–433.

Villanueva, E. (2021), *Decolonizing wealth: Indigenous wisdom to heal divides and restore balance*. Oakland: Berrett-Koehler Publishers.

Part III
All schools and all practitioners

10 Towards a Needs-Led Approach to Inclusion

Questions and Challenges for the Ideology of Inclusive Practice

Cathie Burgess

What is inclusion?

'Inclusion' and 'inclusive practice' have become buzzwords in the field of education both within the UK and globally over the past 30 years, but what these mean and whether a truly inclusive classroom can be achieved remain, for the most part, undefined and unchallenged. This is largely because 'inclusion' is one of the most elusive concepts in education. Coached in an idealism that is rarely reflected in everyday practice, its implementation has become embroiled with other issues such as participation, integration and anti-discrimination, with the outcome that inclusion often means very different things to different people (Ainscow, 2020). Soan (2021) addresses this, pointing out that, even without diagnosis of a specific need, there will always be times when children do not learn as quickly or as easily as their peers or, conversely, may not be stretched and challenged when they find something easy and quick to grasp. So, in examining inclusion, one must consider the differing perspectives of what this means for different children and young people and, in turn, how to improve pedagogy based on this.

It is probably no surprise to educational practitioners that a reflective approach is necessary to consider how practice can be made more inclusive, acknowledging the positionality not only of the teacher but also of the educational sector and communities of practice within it. Brookfield (2017), however, warns against an approach that observes only the teacher's own reflections as this is likely to skew the perspective, particularly in considering a concept as broad and dynamic as inclusion. Instead, the use of 'critical lenses' through which one can examine how diverse perspectives may converge and their meaning for praxis allows for this personal experience to be compared and contrasted with students' experiences, colleague's perceptions and theoretical or academic literature that provides context within both a national and global arena. Indeed, it is important to consider the latter as this very often has a direct impact on educational policy, focus of regulation and government agenda.

Inclusion as a global citizen

In 1989, the United Nations Convention on the Rights of the Child (UNCRC) stipulated that children under the age of 18 have a right both to an education and for that education to nurture:

- The development of the child's personality, talents and mental and physical abilities to their fullest potential.
- The development of respect for human rights and fundamental freedoms and the principles enshrined in the Charter of the United Nations.
- The development of respect for the child's parents, his or her own cultural identity, language and values, the national values of the country in which the child is living, the country from which he or she may originate and civilisations different from his or her own.
- The preparation of the child for responsible life in a free society in the spirit of understanding, peace, tolerance, equality of sexes and friendship among all peoples, ethnic, national and religious groups and persons of indigenous origin.
- The development of respect for the natural environment.

(UNICEF, 2023)

Enshrined within this article is an appreciation of the diversity of children from different countries, social and economic backgrounds, religions, cultures and abilities. Ratified in every country in the world, barring the United States of America due to legal complexities, this right is supported through law wherever children and their families dwell; however, to implement such an approach requires structural and economic support in the political arena. At a global level, the requirement for educators to rise to this challenge is also evident in the manifesto of the Global Education Council, who also acknowledge the need for partnership working between governments, the state, nongovernmental organisations and the private sector to achieve a 'high quality education for all'. Perhaps most telling, though, is their first assertation that 'global radical transformation in education is possible and starts with the belief that everyone has the potential to learn' (Global Education Council, 2021). This suggests that the education system, internationally, is not yet at a point where the rest of their aims are being met, necessitating transformational change. McGuckin and Síoráin (2021) also recognise this within their work, suggesting that

> In this era of international accountability and change, we belong to a collective voice for education to be transformative in actions and outcomes and to rectify previous inequalities.
>
> (p. 15)

They draw their reader's attention to the Sustainable Development Goals, specifically SDG4 (quality education) and SDG10 (reduced inequalities), part of an agenda of 17 goals designed to improve health and education, reduce poverty and inequality and tackle global issues of deforestation and climate change that threaten the wellbeing of the planet. Indeed, this global interconnectedness is reflected at every level of Bronfenbrenner's ecological systems theory, which can be used to contextualise practice and understanding of a practitioner's (and indeed children's) place within the wider world and within the rapidly changing climate of education (Aubrey and Riley, 2023).

Type in the terms 'global' and 'inclusion' or 'inclusion on a global scale' in any internet search engine and the majority of results will pertain to the economy, organisational practices and cultural differences. The Organisation for Economic Co-operation and Development (OECD, 2018) notes that to promote this excellence in practice at an organisational level, education must do its part in teaching children from an early age about their interconnectedness in the world. This is more than just a lesson in citizenship. The OECD (2018) suggest that the knowledge, skills, attributes and values for global competence need to be embedded throughout the curriculum, the culture of the setting and how practitioners encourage students to participate as meaningful changemakers to tackle global economic and environmental challenges. This means equipping children with an understanding of their place and benefits of being part of the global community while also giving them the tools to access it, to change it and to claim it as their own—in short, to be included within it.

Reflection

- How do you embed global citizenship within your current curriculum?
- How do you and your setting extend activities offered to encourage children to look outside of their immediate community to others?

Example: A lesson that looks at Henry VIII or Queen Victoria could also be extended to look at how their interconnectedness with the wider world influenced our own British culture and how their influence in turn affected other countries around the world, both in a positive and a negative way.

Examining your schemes of learning can help to identify where opportunities to include the global perspective may help to embed the idea of individuals of change-makers within the wider world.

Educators and policy makers face several challenges in promoting inclusion within the global community, not least the sheer scope of information available. There is an inherent bias in selecting what should be included within the curriculum and how to address this, just as there is a cultural bias in access to the means to engage with education as a whole (Moore, 2012). As Ferguson and Brett (2023) posit, the concept of global citizenship is just as multifaceted as that of inclusion, with different interpretations, theoretical frameworks and political agendas. The untangling of this knotty discourse cannot simply rely on teachers to integrate a global view into each aspect of their scheme of learning; it requires the tools, time and curricular support to do so. As a starting point, it is helpful to recognise that there is already a growing range of resources in place to help children to engage with others on a worldwide scale.

Johnson and West (2018) cite regional case studies from across the world where children have conducted their own research and interventions to tackle change. Their work demonstrates a commitment from adults to be accountable to children, not to just give them voice but to adequately hear and act on the views and opinions expressed by children and young people. However, it is also noted that such studies could also ignore the power relationships exercised in a world where children and young people are given opportunities to participate based on the will of adults rather than as equal agents of change (Johnson and West, 2018). This is a key message in Friere's (1970) work where he cautions against tokenistic approaches that work 'for' certain groups in favour of pedagogical approaches developed 'with' these groups. Hart (2008) notes that often adults have created opportunities or programmes with the outcome of children's voice but need to go further in recognising children's natural curiosity and abilities to construct and influence their own worlds. He notes that 'children also build competencies from their participation in play or work with one another, often without adults' (Hart, 2008, p. 20). Whilst participation itself must not become entangled with the concept of inclusion, there is no denying it is part of it, as children's voices are not only recognised but given agency within a world where they are included. Hart (2008) suggests that this is more evident within informal education than within the classroom, and therefore it can be useful to acknowledge where children are already exercising this wider participation.

One of the most far-reaching developments of the past 30 years in education has been the increased access to online resources. While this poses significant and unique challenges for those introducing children and young people to the world of technology and the internet (Burgess, 2022), it also furnishes learners with greater control over what and how they learn (OECD, 2018). The Global Digital Citizenship Foundation (2015) suggest that children and young people's engagement as global digital citizens relies on five tenets, those of personal responsibility, global citizenship, digital citizenship, altruistic service and environmental stewardship. Furthermore, Kidron and Ruskin (2017) suggest that a lack of access to the digital world disadvantages children, not only on a global scale, but also in their own personal development, and children are ill equipped to attain the level of digital literacy that is required to navigate the online world as a global citizen. Livingstone *et al.* (2019) conducted a study into what children do online and activities that may indicate that they are interacting as global citizens. For instance, they suggest that certain activities such as becoming involved in a campaign or protest, discussing politics, searching for resources about their neighbourhood, talking to people who are different and looking at news and work or study opportunities offer a higher level of digital citizenship integration than posting photos or comments online, playing games or using social networking sites. Researching with children across three different countries from the ages 9 to 17, their findings suggest that,

> While most children in the three countries are already enjoying some of the opportunities of internet access in sizeable proportions, most children do not reach the point where they commonly undertake many of the civic, informational and creative activities online that are heralded as the opportunities of the digital age.
> (Livingstone *et al.*, 2019, p. 7)

The implications of this research suggest that, within the curriculum, opportunities could be sought to encourage children to make better use of the potential offered through online spaces. As Kidron and Ruskin (2017) note and as the foregoing study confirms, digital literacy often increases in line with other areas of development and age. In acknowledging this, educational policy makers are in a unique position not only to construct a curriculum that introduces children to the possibilities that global online participation offers but also to stretch and challenge all children to participate online in a meaningful way.

Perhaps one of the most useful tools at children and young people's disposal is defined by Packham (2008) as 'social capital'. This is the notion of creating a network of people with different interests, expertise and knowledge that can be called upon. This, Packham (2008) suggests, is strongly linked with active citizenship as individuals can play a part not only in gaining support but in providing support to one another. Online, this can take the shape of looking up instructions, learning about something that interests you or participating in discussions. Communities of practice spring up around different hobbies and interests, different views and common goals—for instance, when one shares how to approach a certain challenge within an online game. Evans-Greenwood, O'Leary and Williams (2015) suggest that this approach marks the disruption of traditional pedagogy and that the practitioner's role in helping children to navigate this environment is to optimise their skills in utilising these digital and cyber-connective resources. Indeed, the UK Council for Internet Safety (2020) recognises this and suggests that the curriculum should be adapted in support of children's online use, helping them to make sense of their connectivity through frameworks designed specifically for them.

Of course, the potential benefits of digital connectivity are themselves subject to the same inequalities that plague education. Gottschalk and Weise (2023) for instance note disparity in access, infrastructure and support for children who may have come from low-income backgrounds or experience special educational needs. Thus, the notion of inclusion needs to be underpinned by the practicalities of equity. To examine this, one must inspect the policies and legislation in place to support and remove barriers both to learning and to wider citizenship. While underpinned by both the Human Rights Act (1998) and the United Nations Convention on the Rights of the Child (1989), to examine legislation, it is necessary to narrow the focus to a national scale.

The link between inclusion and equity

Within the UK, Ofsted (2023) approaches inclusion as an aspect of equality, diversity and inclusion, recognising the links between these concepts and with a focus on how those with protected characteristics under the Equality Act (2010) may be disadvantaged. They highlight an inequality of opportunity 'between boys and girls, Gypsy, Roma and Traveller pupils, Black Caribbean pupils, Mixed white and Black Caribbean pupils and pupils from other ethnic groups' and between 'pupils who have a disability and those who do not' (Ofsted, 2023). The currency of this article suggests that, despite over 13 years where equality has been the goal, supported through legislation and school inclusion policies, UK schools are struggling to adequately meet the needs of all pupils and to equalise opportunity in a meaningful way that addresses future inequalities. It is argued, however, by Imerai (2022) that the inequalities described are symptomatic of a wider disparity across society as a whole between those with different financial means, geographic variations and gender inequality. This is supported by Lynch (2018), who suggests that equality of opportunity is frequently intertwined with the ideology of meritocracy, but that this is highly misleading where the 'opportunities to be meritorious are based on non-meritocratic factors (including inheritance and the circumstances of birth)' (Lynch, 2018, p. 7). Imerai (2022) agrees, pointing to 'the unequal distribution of academic resources, including but not limited to school funding, qualified and experienced teachers, books, and technologies to socially excluded communities' (Imerai, 2022). Sherrington (2015) agrees, pragmatically pointing out that while a child having their needs met is entitlement, not privilege, there is often a blurring of the lines when one considers such aspects of school life as educational trips. Where there is financial disadvantage, children may also be excluded from opportunity simply because there is a cost involved in taking part. As Lynch (2018) suggests, schools can enhance life chances and capabilities, but this will not address the wider social structures that heavily influence children and young people's academic and educational experiences.

To do so requires systemic change. This is recognised in the HM Government's (2022) 'Levelling up' white paper, which recognises the need for financial investment in both digital connectivity and education. However, there is little recognition of the interactivity between the two or the recognition that connection requires often very expensive devices, furnished with subscription-based software platforms including anti-virus software. The financial investment in such devices again differentiates those with financial means from those without. Furthermore, the Children's Code (Information Commissioner's Office, 2020) also examines providers' responsibilities around keeping children safe online and acknowledges the risks associated with some online communities, technology companies preying on children's buying power and exposure to inappropriate content and activities. Neither is the online environment a substitute for education delivered through school, but as Gottschalk and Weise (2023) note, it can go some way to creating opportunities for children and young people to operate some autonomy within their educational experience.

The National Curriculum of England

In England specifically, the National Curriculum is the four-stage curriculum offered on a statutory basis through maintained schools with academies and free schools free to choose, although many opt for this as they still must deliver a 'broad and balanced' curriculum including core subjects of English, maths, sciences and religious studies. They must also, regardless of the curriculum offered, participate in the national Standard Assessment Tests (Roberts, 2022). The debates and contentions around standardised testing are incredibly complex, but Gray (2015) points to the potential for exclusion, shame and emotional turmoil exacted upon children by such tests. From a psychological viewpoint, he suggests that the competitive nature of tests can lead to those who do well to feel excessive pride from shallow accomplishments and those who do not do well to disengage. This is, seemingly, the antithesis to growth mindset, and yet the reliance on this as a measure of children's and schools' performance still stands. This approach clearly disadvantages a number of children, specifically those with special educational needs and disabilities (SEND) and children who may have come into the UK from other countries where they may not have studied the same curriculum or even have the same language. Furthermore, as Radford *et al.* (2014) assert, since the National Workload Agreement of 2003, the UK has seen an unprecedented increase in teaching assistants, making up around a quarter of the education workforce, and Blatchford (2012) claims that many of these will become the primary educators of the lowest attaining pupils in order that the teacher can give overall support to the majority of the class. This serves to further segregate those with SEN or who face other exclusionary factors such as poverty from their peer group. After the suspension of UK Standard Assessment Tests through the Covid pandemic, the subsequent consultation with the National Association of Head Teachers suggested that,

> Teachers don't need SATs results to tell them about a pupil's progress. They are already constantly assessing that and are more aware than ever of what each child needs to help them recover any lost learning from the pandemic. SATs are not something teachers find valuable for assessment and are simply a distraction during a time when there is still significant disruption in schools.
> (National Association of Head Teachers, 2022)

This does appear to be mirrored in a more international perspective in the OECD's vision for education in the approach to 2030 as they propose that,

> Curriculum design and learning progression is shifting from a 'static, linear learning-progression model' to a 'non-linear, dynamic model', which recognises that each student has his/her own learning path and is equipped with different prior knowledge, skills and attitudes when he/she starts school. And, student assessment has thus also shifted from standardised testing only to different types of assessments for different purposes.
> (OECD, 2019, p. 11)

The academic expectations of the National Curriculum were first set out in Callaghan's 1976 speech where the goals of education were claimed to be,

> To equip children to the best of their ability for a lively, constructive, place in society, and also to fit them to do a job of work. Not one or the other but both. For many years the accent was simply on fitting a so-called inferior group of children with just enough learning to earn their living in the factory. Labour has attacked that attitude consistently, during 60 or 70 years and throughout my childhood. There is now widespread recognition of the need to cater for a child's personality to let it flower in its fullest possible way.
> (Callaghan, 1976, cited in Gillard, 2010).

In 1976, this was heralded as a radical concept; however, looking back on this, the rhetoric is not significantly different from what today's educational practitioners are aiming for. The complication arises from the assumption that education means learning solely academic skills and behaviours, an idea that appears contested by UNICEF (2017), which defines inclusive education as 'an education system that includes all students, and welcome and supports them to learn, whoever they are and whatever their abilities and requirements.' Such a definition considers an understanding of children as having multiple intelligences (Gardner, 1999) and a range of talents, interests and values. As the late Ken

Robinson (2010) suggested, it is important that education should not alienate children and young people by ignoring all the things they feel are important about themselves. This is supported Harter (2012), who claimed that self-esteem is shaped not only by scholastic competence but also social acceptance, physical appearance, athletic competence, romantic appeal, close friendships, job competence and behavioural conduct. Moreover, Bialecka-Pikul *et al.* (2019) assert that these domains are dynamic and ever-changing as the child enjoys positive experiences or is affected by negative ones. Many of these domains of self-esteem have the potential to be positively impacted by a school where children feel accepted and valued for their individual differences.

Carnie (2017) suggests that in teaching a subject-by-subject curriculum, schools are ignoring the more integrated and holistic approach of the wider world, both in terms of industry and life skills. In exploring a range of alternatives including well-recognised systems of education such as Steiner and Montessori, Carnie (2017) suggests that a more holistic approach, where problem solving is at the heart of the approach, leads to a deeper level of learning and removes much of the stress associated with the more traditional curriculum. Indeed, examples of how the National Curriculum may not have suited various learners are peppered throughout Knight's (2016) books about Forest School, Mercogliano's (2007) defence of children's rights to be children, as well as through a variety of campaigns around lesbian, gay, bisexual and transgender rights (Bradlow *et al.*, 2017). Perhaps as with any 'one size fits all' approach, a universal curriculum is just not able to be inclusive to everyone.

That said, there are various considerations made through the National Curriculum that at their heart have intentions of inclusion. The process of learning through which information is imparted can be understood to occur in two key ways; the first, biologically primary knowledge relates to those skills that are picked up through cultural and familiar cues. Sweller, Merrienboer and Paas (2019) use the example of learning to listen as biologically innate but differentiate this from secondary or domain-specific skills such as learning to read. These latter skills require conscious cognitive commitment on the part of the child. While some children will develop their skills at home, much of what they learn is through their school and education, and therefore a generic curriculum supports equality of access to such skills. Furthermore, a spiral curriculum such as that proposed by Bruner allows for the development of schemas and scaffolding information, an essential part of breaking down tasks in a way to allow for children to engage with the material so that it does not overwhelm them (Aubrey and Riley, 2023). This acknowledgement of cognitive load theory (Sweller and Levine, 1982) suggests that planning the curriculum requires an understanding of how to best organise information into domain-specific content that can explicitly provide instruction and opportunities for learning both from one's own experiences and from that of others. The curriculum, separated into subjects, equips children with basic tools with which to build schemas, and it evolves each concept to become steadily more complex as the child grows. To fail to provide such as curriculum also poses challenges for inclusivity as some children would surely not have the same opportunities to access the same information as their peers. This is challenged by Gray (2015), who argues that as the school curriculum cannot possibly hope to teach children everything they can know, there is no reason or use for all children to learn exactly the same thing.

Gray's (2015) point emphasizes the need to reassess the National Curriculum in terms of how it prepares all children to be included in later life. Certainly, there are arguments that vital skills are missing from the standard curriculum. Interestingly, a research study was undertaken by the Department for Education between 2018 and 2019, whereby 'Essential Life Skills' were delivered as extracurricular interventions with groups of disadvantaged young people (Cutmore, Llewellyn and Atkinson, 2020). Noted outcomes included improved confidence, greater resilience, emotional intelligence and even benefits for the schools such as better community partnerships. This is something mirrored through Knight's (2016) work around Forest Schools, adding to the argument that the existing standard curriculum is not achieving this without additional intervention despite inclusion of many aspects of these in personal social and health education (PSHE). This was recently debated within the House of Lords where Baroness Garden of Frognal (2023) pointed to the lack of relevance of many of the National Curriculum topics and suggested that life skills were not being taught to the depth required for many children to use these skills into adulthood. The relevance of this to inclusion for children, and indeed adults, is that many children are finding education a lot harder because of an increased cognitive load of skills that are unhelpful for them in later life. The accompanying standardised tests of knowledge, memory and learning do not adequately assess what Bloom's taxonomy describes as 'deeper learning' whereby learners are encouraged to apply such knowledge and fully engage with it in ways that have relevance to their lives (Aubrey and Riley, 2023). This means that rafts of children who have not yet learned how to pass tests may be shown to be at a lower level than peers despite having great practical abilities. This is also evident through the recent introduction of exam-based 'T-levels' within vocational subjects for 16- to 19-year-olds, which can represent societal barriers for some learners (Thorley, 2017).

The tensions around inclusivity within the National Curriculum stand in contrast to the strengths-based approach advocated through the Special Educational Needs and Disabilities Code of Practice (2014), within the Every Child Matters agenda which developed the Children Act (2004) as well as through classic humanistic theories, such as Maslow's hierarchy of needs, which points to the importance of 'belonging, love and acceptance' (Aubrey and Riley, 2023). Clearly there is a legislative and indeed theoretical structure in place to promote inclusive pedagogy but, as has been examined, systemic change may be required if inclusion is not to become confused with integration.

Inclusion versus integration

The 'Excellence for all children: Meeting special educational needs' (DfEE, 1997) green paper created a focus within the UK on including children with special educational needs (SEN) in mainstream provision. This emphasized a needs-led approach and the role of practitioners in ensuring children with SEN can 'join fully with their peers in the curriculum and life of the school' (Department for Education and Employment, 1997, p. 44). Rodriguez and Garro-Gil (2015), however, recognise that there is confusion between the term 'integration', taken to mean incorporating children into the mainstream but with alternations to their learning, and 'inclusion', which sets out to ensure equality of access and provision from the start. This, Warnes, Done and Knowler (2021) argue, is largely due to failures to adequately define fully inclusive education and, more importantly, to provide the structural and political means for this to be achieved. As has been argued previously, if access to the curriculum requires specific adaptations to be made, if it is not flexible and responsive to the needs of learners, then it does not promote or allow for truly inclusive practice (Schuelka, 2018).

UNICEF's (2017) definition is similar to the Department for Education and Employment's (1997) assertion, claiming that 'Inclusive education means all children learn together in the same schools.' However, the majority of these mainstream UK schools are offering, as a bare minimum, the core subjects of the National Curriculum, a broad set of subjects with expectations set across age groups and regular testing to benchmark schools and pupils against national averages. Academic achievement is most often measured in the UK through academic achievements such as league tables, grades, dropout rates and university entrance data. While these measurements pertain to opportunity, they fail to provide an adequate picture of what is happening in the classroom to either perpetuate or to reinforce inequality. Robinson's *Changing Education Paradigms* (2010) argued that inequality is, unfortunately, rooted in the very foundations of the education system with preconceptions of what it means to achieve academic success, expectations of ability based on nothing more than age and a curriculum that poses challenges in preparing children for a rapidly changing, unpredictable economy. This curriculum, he argued, was restrictive in both its content and delivery, and the newest iteration of 2014 has not appeared to overhaul many of the characteristics that Robinson (2010) criticised. While Evans-Greenwood, O'Leary and Williams (2015) concur, they also point out that at a pedagogical level change is happening with practitioners increasingly encouraged to think of children as active agents in their own learning. Their argument is that, from an international perspective, education is moving away from the traditional model of transmission of knowledge from teacher to student into a structure that recognises knowledge as a construct, reframed and reimagined between individuals and where learning should be focused more on problem-solving than finding the answer.

Evans-Greenwood, O'Leary and Williams (2015) propose that, just as industry has changed from the linear institutions of post-war Britain to social-led communities of co-operation and practice, so it is possible to reimagine education in this image. They suggest that this necessitates a paradigm shift in acknowledging the skillset necessary for innovation, creativity, informal and work-integrated learning.

Co-operative learning structures between children and others in the learning environment are also suggested by Emerson (2013) as a more inclusive environment where children have accountability for their own learning and come together with other students to share their knowledge in mixed ability communities of practice. This approach incorporates some of the best known developmental and learning theories around growth mindset (Dweck, 2014) and Vygotsky's idea that learning happens in the presence of a more knowledgeable other. The practicality of this is encouraged within Sherrington and Caviglioli's (2020) teaching walkthrus, which suggest collaborative methods such as 'think, pair, share' and Rosenshine's principles around scaffolding information (Rosenshine, 2012). On the surface, getting children to work collaboratively seems a great strategy; however, in considering how these strategies may aid inclusion, it is also necessary to consider the dichotomy of exclusion and what it is within education that poses the risk of exclusion for children and young people.

In planning a lesson, the teacher may consider which groups will work together, key strategies that may be employed and whether particular resources are employed to support children with specific needs. However, the expectation for these children simply to take part may, itself, fail to meet these needs. Consider the following example.

Activity

Anneka has autism. She is a quiet and studious learner and listens attentively in class, often writing notes of what the teacher has said. The teacher implements the cold calling strategy often in class. While this has been integrated in class from the beginning, and most students accept this as a low-risk strategy, Anneka feels cold and sweaty every time the teacher asks a question because she is scared she will be the next to be asked. She is not worried about getting the answer wrong. Growth mindset is well embedded in the class and the culture of the school, and she appreciates that mistakes are part of learning, but she doesn't want to speak out loud in class. She doesn't like the way her voice sounds. The teacher has understood this fear and Anneka is encouraged instead to share her ideas with another learner, but this too fills Anneka with dread. This is just not how she feels comfortable learning. Eventually she is asked the question. Her mind is so filled with confusing thoughts that she cannot answer. The teacher assumes that she has not learned or understood the material, so she is encouraged to join a group with some others who will help to explain it to her. The other children kindly do explain it to her, but the concept has become diluted in Anneka's mind because they are not explaining it the way she imagines it or has learned it. She becomes overwhelmed and fails to learn anything else that lesson.

- Are the strategies that have been employed here inclusion or integration?
- What could be done differently to make Anneka feel that her needs are also valued and to remove the risk to her self-esteem?
- The teacher has understood Anneka's fears due to her education and health care plan (EHCP) and has put some adaptations in place based on this, but would you, as an educational practitioner, put these changes in place for a learner where no EHCP exists?
- What strategies has the practitioner employed that you think are inclusive and helpful to all children in the class?

It should be noted that many strategies, cold calling included, should be warm invitations to participate (Sherrington, 2021); however, for this to be the case, children and young people need to already feel included in an environment where there is no risk to them from volunteering a response. Regardless of whether the child knows the answer or feels happy that they know what to say, the nature of this practice could still elicit a negative feeling in them. As the OECD (2018, p. 20) claims, 'It is likely that the students will assimilate the culture of the classroom more readily than they will learn the curriculum.' This does mean that, regardless of the curriculum, the inclusive ethos of the school and classroom can still have a positive effect on the child's educational experiences.

Exclusivity in inclusion

Practitioners today face a number of complex challenges not only in planning, delivering and assessing learning but also in understanding and developing a myriad of skills with which to successfully teach. Pedagogical concepts include theory, research, legal perspectives and organisational culture, all of which must be integrated into some form of professional identity before a teacher even walks through the classroom door. Katz and Miller (2016) point out that practitioners need to be conscious of their own culture and the biases that affect their viewpoints, both conscious and unconscious. However, this can be problematic for the practitioner. How does one know what they are not aware of? Reflection, learning from wider research, and use of peer learning can all be useful ways to cast a lens over these assumptions and provide insight into previously unconscious thoughts and feelings.

The simple place to start to look at one's own perspectives on inclusion is the legislative framework of the Equality Act (2010). Developed to take into account nine protected characteristics, it lays out the legal obligations for both organisations and practitioners to ensure that needs are met and rights are protected. Helpfully, within schools, this information is usually enshrined through inclusion or equality and diversity policies which, again, point to the differences that individual children may experience, often accompanied by the importance of celebrating diversity. This is important because, as HM Government (2022) points out, the UK is a rich, multicultural nation where difference is a fundamental part of the collective identity, and respect for these differences is part of the fundamental British values underpinning the education system within the UK. The tension though comes not from the difference itself but from the need to diagnose, label and legitimise this difference, an approach still couched in the medical model of disability (Zaks, 2023). Across this country, and in many others, children and families struggle with systems that require them to receive an assessment of being 'different' to be included.

While it is evident that children in school may have any number of protected characteristics (or none at all but still experience differences from peers), it is helpful to illustrate the problem of inclusion through looking specifically at the experience of high needs learners. Indeed, these children are a specific category for Ofsted's inspection framework (2023), and their diagnosis and provision is often the subject of much data analysis and funding allocation. Often, entitlement to specific support and certainly to adaptations such as exam access arrangements require an assessment of learning need. SEN support can be provided without a diagnosis, but the Children's Commissioner for England notes that current support for SEN is insufficient, claiming that almost 400,000 pupils have an education and health care plan with a further 1,182,384 pupils receiving SEN support without one in place. While the process of applying for an EHCP does not always require a diagnosis from a medical professional, the process of requesting an EHCP is a lengthy process with the deadline of 20 weeks from application for local authorities to issue an EHCP only being met in around 51% of cases (Children's Commissioner, 2023). Calling for a radical overhaul of the SEN system, the Children's Commissioner for England (2023) states:

> In our report last year on Special Educational Needs and/or Disabilities (SEND) we found that children want support to help them do well, but they often experience a system which is more interested in asking 'what is wrong with you?' than 'how can we help?'

This is poignant for the topic of inclusion as these children are faced with a curriculum that they cannot access for a sizeable proportion of the school year. This could mark them as different to peers, affecting not only cognitive development but also social and emotional development. Even with an EHCP and significant SEN support in place, Warnes, Done and Knowler (2021) suggest that methods of integration, where teachers adapt practice to each individual student's needs, is demanding of time and energy and requires significant planning, all of which are firmly within the domain of the teacher without recognising the benefits of providing a more inclusive structure to begin with.

The Children's Commissioner (2022) addresses some of the issues of inclusive practice within SEND in 'Beyond the labels: A SEND system which works for every child, every time', but there is still a division between 'mainstream school' and 'alternative provision'. Not that attending a specialist provision is less inclusive; for many children, this is often a more inclusive environment as learning is personalised to their individual needs, but there are large numbers of children whose barriers to learning are not SEND related. Furthermore, Robinson (2010) notes that some children simply learn in different ways, at different times of the day and with aptitudes for different topics. Within this parameter, it could be argued every child who enters a classroom will experience some kind of learning need, either in the short or long term. If this is accepted, then every child, regardless of protected characteristics, diagnoses or EHCP, could be considered to require some kind of individual learning plan. This would not necessarily be a written document or pen portrait but something that fosters mutual respect, a relationship between practitioners and children and between children themselves, extending to the wider family and community in which the school operates.

Relational and restorative practice and the ethos of inclusion

Hopkins (2018) promotes an inclusive approach through restorative classroom practices. This includes getting to know every child and acknowledging everyone's ideas and contributions. Here the teacher moves away from the authoritarian role and instead makes meaningful and real connections to find out about their interests, their hopes and dreams, their concerns and their personalities. Zaks (2023) also proposes such an approach as avoiding the medical and social models in view of utilising universal design to maximise accessibility for everyone. Schuelka (2018) agrees that there is indeed hope for inclusive practice to be implemented at a pedagogical level if supported by successful implementation strategies employed at every level of the school and within initial teacher training. Pointer, McGoey and Farrar (2020) point out that restorative practices have the ability to redress some of the imbalances in power existing within a social space. This provides children with an all-important sense of belonging, both of their space and their education, encouraging autonomy and agency, which supports their rights under the UNCRC (UNICEF, 2017). With the role of the teacher becoming one of facilitator, individuals are encouraged to share their experiences and learning, showing respect for each individual within the classroom. Hopkins (2018) suggests that inclusion, mutual respect, collaboration, joint problem solving, open communication, accountability and trust are at the heart of the restorative classroom and asserts that there is a link between attainment, social inclusion and mental health and wellbeing of children in school. However, Hopkins (2018) also acknowledges that classrooms exist within the wider culture of the school, something underpinned by the ethos and values of the setting.

Sadler (2022) notes the relationship between a school's ethos and the feelings of citizenship enjoyed by students attending that school. The link between the ethos, leadership of the school and values is also scrutinised. Dimitrellou (2017) suggests that schools with an emphasis on inclusion within their ethos need to also have a strong behavioural strategy to differentiate for those with additional needs but should acknowledge that all students, irrespective of SEN (or other protected characteristics), have the right to be included. This brings back Sherrington's (2021) point about creating a warm and inviting environment when cold-calling students. If students feel included and a sense of belonging, they are much more likely to engage, both with peers and with one another, so the setting itself must also promote a restorative and relational approach to working with children and young people.

At the heart of an inclusive school is the feeling of safety. Recognised within Maslow's hierarchy of need (Aubrey and Riley, 2023) as a prerequisite, psychological models also support the idea that for a child to learn effectively, they cannot be in fight-or-flight mode (Vogel and Schwabe, 2016). They must feel comfortable in their environment. Inclusion, nurtured by a sense of belonging, makes that possible, as does lowering the risk to students from engaging in learning practices. Growth mindset emphasizes the power of 'yet', the supposition being that mistakes are part of learning rather than a catastrophic failure leading to shame (Dweck, 2014). This has widely become adopted into schools where terminology around effort and achievement is changing. Instead of praising the outcome, the focus is on the process of learning, with deeper questions being asked to assess the way that the learner is engaging with the knowledge. Dweck (2015) is quick to point out that praising effort is not the same as praising learning and that, fundamentally, learning needs to be the end goal. This highlights the fact that interactions with all children should not be tokenistic, but instead should recognise where the child is at in their learning and how they should be encouraged to move beyond their zone of actual development into the zone of proximal development where 'yet' can happen. This can be supported through a number of paraprofessionals including teaching assistants, but this should not happen at the expense of time spent with the teacher or others within the classroom as peer learning from mixed ability groups is also incredibly valuable.

Most schools will also play host to a range of children of different ages and stages of development. This presents a unique opportunity for children to be included outside of their immediate class or year group. Robinson (2010) suggests that the structure of the education system is incorrect in grouping children according to age, pointing out that many children will perform consistently above or below their peer group. This is also apparent when comparing.

Inclusion reimagined

This chapter has investigated inclusion and inclusive educational practice through Brookfield's critical lenses, looking at inclusion on an international level, underpinning it with theoretical perspectives, examining the legislative structure of English education and narrowing it down to the ethos and culture of the school and peering through the doors of classrooms. What has become apparent is that there is no one 'catch all' approach. If the OECD's (2019) proposals are to be believed, then transformation is necessary across the micro, meso and macro levels of Bronfenbrenner's systems model (Aubrey and Riley, 2023). As Robinson (2010) argued, the whole idea of education needs to be reimagined to align with the needs of 21st-century industry and a world in which knowledge is not simply passed from teacher to child but flows between individuals in a way that allows for true collaboration and, in turn, inclusion as individuals find their place based on their own strengths, interests and abilities. The National Curriculum itself poses challenges for inclusion. As Gray (2015) suggests, in separating subjects delivered in a linear mode, many children fail to develop the skills needed to be adequately prepared for life, lacking the problem-solving ability or social skills required for inclusion in a variety of adult communities and activities. Furthermore, Mercogliano (2007) points to the medicalisation of behaviour increasingly viewed as noncompliant within mainstream schools. To truly include children, one must dispense with labelling and the need for diagnosis to accompany interventions and adaptations. This, as the Children's Commissioner (2023) has pointed out, would mean overhauling existing processes such as the education and health care plans and exam access arrangements in favour of a tailored system that recognises every child's individual needs and abilities.

Nonetheless, it is not only possible but beneficial for educational practitioners to create an inclusive environment through restorative practice where 'decisions are shared and problems are addressed together' (Hopkins, 2018, p. 7). Looking at the child holistically allows each practitioner to show that they are valued for the skills and attributes that they have. This is closely aligned to the humanistic perspective, and Swan, Chen and Bockmier-Sommers (2020) advocate that Rogers' core conditions of empathy, genuineness and unconditional positive regard effectively underpin person-centred education in a way that allows the classroom to become a community of inquiry where everyone recognises one another as an agent in their learning. As Batsleer (2008) asserts, simply making the human connection and 'being there' for children can have hugely positive impacts on their sense of self-esteem and mental health. The benefits of such an approach in creating a sense of community are clear, but there are further implications for learning such as reducing extraneous cognitive load (Sweller, Merrienboer and Paas, 2019) given over to simply trying to engage with the instructional model. However, Codina and Fordham (2021) do point out that such an approach presents challenges for practitioners, not least their own ability to be resilient within their classroom practice. They point out that teaching operates within an interpretivist paradigm, through which everyone's classroom becomes a construct of their own attitudes, beliefs, assumptions, prejudices and habits (Bolton and Denderfield, 2018; Codina and Fordham, 2021).

As with many aspects of education, changing instructional models from the whole school to the wider community and at a national level requires a significant investment of time and reflexivity. Changing one's approach, on the other hand, can happen swiftly. Restorative practice is something that can be learned and applied with relative ease yet can have far reaching positive consequences for children who struggle to feel included within educational systems for a variety of reasons. A restorative classroom will teach lessons around respect and diversity and provide a sense of belonging that will go on to influence children into adulthood (Hopkins, 2018). From one classroom, you, your colleagues and the children you teach can strive for inclusion within an ever-changing world.

Reflection

- How do you promote shared ownership and sense of belonging within your classroom space?
- How do you promote showing interest in each other's ideas and contributions?
- How can you embed school values into your own classroom culture?
- What do you do to actively look for positive role models which reflect your children's diversity and beyond?
- How do you cultivate a meaningful growth mindset where children are actively encouraged to give and receive constructive feedback?

Looking forward

Consider your class.

- How much do you know about each of them and the people they are?
- If there are some class members you feel you don't know as well, what can you do to redress this balance?
- How will you show that you value everyone within your space, and how will you work with and challenge learners who do not show this respect themselves?

References

Ainscow, M. (2020), Inclusion and equality in education: Making sense of global challenges. *Prospects*, *49*, pp. 123–134.

Aubrey, K. and Riley, A. (2023), *Education Theories for a Changing World*. London: Sage Publications Limited.

Baroness Garden of Frognal. (2023), 'Life skills and citizenship', *Hansard: House of Commons debates*, September 7, 832, c.609. Available at https://hansard.parliament.uk/Lords/2023-09-07/debates/FD43353F-BE41-4A2C-8E01-577DD4AB2995/LifeSkillsAndCitizenship (Accessed February 5, 2024).

Batsleer, J. (2008), *Informal Learning in Youth Work*. London: Sage Publications.

Bialecka-Pikul, M., Stepien-Nycz, M., Sikorska, I, Topolewska-Siedzik, E. and Cieciuch, J. (2019), Change and consistency of self-esteem in early and middle adolescence in the context of school transition. *Journal of Youth and Adolescence*, *48*(8), pp.1605–1618.

Blatchford, P., Russell, A. and Webster, R. (2012), *Reassessing the Impact of Teaching Assistants: How Research Challenges Practice and Policy*. Abingdon: Routledge.

Bolton, G. and Denderfield, R. (2018), *Reflective Practice: Writing and Professional Development*. London: Sage Publications Limited.

Brookfield, S. (2017), *Becoming a Critically Reflective Teacher* (2nd ed.). San Francisco: Jossey-Bass.

Bradlow, J., Bartram, F., Guasp, A. and Jadva, V. (2017), *School Report: The Experiences of Lesbian, Gay, Bi and Trans Young People in Britain's Schools in 2017*. Cambridge: University of Cambridge Centre for Family Research and Stonewall.

Burgess, C. (2022), Walking the online learning tightrope: Education reimagined through pandemic learning. In E. Tarry (ed.), *Challenges in Early Years and Primary Education: Employing Critical Thinking Skills During Turbulent Times* (pp. 67–80). Abingdon: Routledge.

Callaghan, J. (1976). "A rational debate based on the facts." Speech delivered at Ruskin College, Oxford, October 18, 1976.

Carnie, F. (2017), *Alternative Approaches to Education: A Guide for Educators and Parents*. (2nd ed.). Abingdon: Routledge.

Children Act. (2004), UK, Chapter 31. London: The Stationery Office. Available at: https://www.legislation.gov.uk/ukpga/2004/31. (Accessed December 10, 2023).

Children's Commissioner. (2023), New statistics on education, health and care plans (EHCP) for children with special educational needs. Available at https://www.childrenscommissioner.gov.uk/blog/new-statistics-on-education-health-and-care-plans-ehcp-for-children-with-special-educational-needs/ (Accessed February 10, 2024).

Children's Commissioner. (2022), Beyond the labels: A SEND system which works for every child, every time. Available at https://assets.childrenscommissioner.gov.uk/wpuploads/2022/11/cc-beyond-the-labels-a-send-system-which-works-for-every-child-every-time.pdf (Accessed February 15, 2024).

Codina, G. and Fordham, J. (2021), Resilience, reflection and reflexivity. In S. Soan (ed.), *Why Do Teachers Need to Know About Diverse Learning Needs? Strengthening Professional Identity and Well-being* (pp. 119–136). London: Bloomsbury Academic.

Convention on the Rights of the Child. (1989), Treaty no. 27531. *United Nations Treaty Series*, 1577, pp. 3–178. Available at https://treaties.un.org/doc/Treaties/1990/09/19900902%2003-14%20AM/Ch_IV_11p.pdf (Accessed February 3, 2024).

Cutmore, M., Llewellyn, J. and Atkinson, I. (2020), *Process Evaluation of the Essential Life Skills Programme: Final Evaluation Report*. Ecorys UK. Available at https://assets.publishing.service.gov.uk/media/5fd0c218d3bf7fd02b21962/ELS_Process_Evaluation.pdf (Accessed January 12, 2024).

Department for Education and Employment. (1997), *Excellent for All Children: Meeting Special Educational Needs*. Available at https://education-uk.org/documents/pdfs/1997-green-paper.pdf (Accessed February 10, 2024).

Dimitrellou, E. (2017), Does an inclusive ethos enhance the sense of social belonging and encourage the social relations of young adolescents identified as having social, emotional and mental health difficulties (SEMH) and moderate learning difficulties (MLD). Available at https://core.ac.uk/download/pdf/111005426.pdf (Accessed December 10, 2023).

Dweck, C. (2015), Carol Dweck revisits the 'growth mindset'. Available at https://austinlearningsolutions.com/images/stories/growth-mindset/Dweck_Growth_Mindsets.pdf (Accessed January 10, 2024).

Dweck, C. (2014), The power of believing that you can improve. Available at https://www.ted.com/talks/carol_dweck_the_power_of_believing_that_you_can_improve?language=en#t-318964 (Accessed July 25, 2021).

Emerson, L. (2013), Co-operative learning in inclusive classrooms: Students who work together, learn together. Available at https://education.wm.edu/centers/ttac/resources/articles/inclusion/cooperativelearning/ (Accessed January 12, 2024).

Equality Act. (2010), UK, Chapter 15. London: The Stationery Office. Available at https://www.legislation.gov.uk/ukpga/2010/15/contents/enacted (Accessed December 10, 2023).

Evans-Greenwood, P., O'Leary, K. and Williams, P. (2015), *The Paradigm Shift: Redefining Education*. Australia: Deliotte.

Friere, P. (1970), *Pedagogy of the Oppressed*. London: Penguin

Ferguson, C. and Brett, P. (2023), Teacher and student interpretations of global citizenship education in international schools. *Education, Citizenship and Social Justice*. Available at https://journals.sagepub.com/doi/full/10.1177/17461979231211489 (Accessed February 16, 2024).

Gardner, H. (1999), *Intelligence reframed*. New York: Basic Books.

Gillard, D. (2010), A rational debate based on the facts: Speech by James Callaghan at Ruskin College Oxford on 18th October 1976. Available at https://education-uk.org/documents/speeches/1976ruskin.html (Accessed February 15, 2024).

Gottschalk, F. and Weise, C. (2023), Digital equality and inclusion in education: an overview of practice and policy in OECD countries. *OECD Education Working Papers*, 14(299), pp. 2–75.

Global Digital Citizenship Foundation. (2015), The global digital citizen: QuickStart guide. Available at https://www.gcedclearinghouse.org/sites/default/files/resources/180102eng.pdf (Accessed February 2, 2024).

Global Education Council. (2021), The GEC manifesto: The Global Education Council believes. Available at https://www.bettshow.com/global-education-council (Accessed January 17, 2024).

Gray, P. (2015), *Free to Learn*. New York: Basic Books.

Hart, R. (2008), Stepping back from the ladder: Reflections on a model of participatory work with children. In A. Reid, B. B. Jensen, J. Nikel, & V. Simovska, (eds.), *Participation and Learning* (pp.19–31). Dordrecht: Springer.

Harter, S. (2012), *The Construction of the Self: A Developmental Perspective* (2nd ed.). New York: Guildford Press.

HM Government. (2022), *Levelling up the United Kingdom: Executive summary*. Available at https://assets.publishing.service.gov.uk/media/62e7a429d3bf7f75af0923f3/Executive_Summary.pdf (Accessed January 19, 2023).

Hopkins, B. (2018), *The Restorative Classroom: Using Restorative Approaches to Foster Effective Learning*. Abingdon: Routledge.

Human Rights Act. (1998), UK. London: The Stationery Office. Available at https://www.legislation.gov.uk/ukpga/1998/42 (Accessed December 10, 2023).

Imerai, F. (2022), Explaining the attainment gap and education inequality in the UK. Available at https://actiontutoring.org.uk/explaining-the-attainment-gap-and-education-inequality-in-the-uk/ (Accessed January 15, 2024).

Information Commissioner's Office. (2020), About this code. Available at https://ico.org.uk/for-organisations/guide-to-data-protection/key-data-protection-themes/age-appropriate-design-a-code-of-practice-for-online-services/about-this-code/#code2 (Accessed June 25, 2021).

Johnson, V. and West, A. (2018), *Children's Participation in Global Contexts: Going Beyond Voice*. Oxon: Routledge.

Katz, J. and Miller, F. (2016), Defining diversity and adapting inclusion strategies on a global scale. *OD Practitioner*, *48*(3), pp. 42–47.

Kidron, B. and Ruskin, A. (2017), Digital childhood: Addressing childhood development milestones in the digital environment. Available at https://5rightsfoundation.com/uploads/digital-childhood---final-report.pdf (Accessed July 11, 2021).

Knight, S. (2016), *Forest School in Practice*. London: Sage Publications Limited.

Livingstone, S., Kardefelt-Winther, D., Kanchev, P., Cabello, P., Claro, M., Burton, P. and Phyfer, J. (2019), Is there a ladder of children's online participation? Findings from three global kids online countries. Available at https://www.unicef-irc.org/publications/pdf/IRB_2019-02%2013-2-19.pdf (Accessed December 19, 2023).

Lynch, K. (2018), 'Inequality in education: what educators can and cannot change'. In M. Connolly, D. Eddy-Spicer, C. James and S. Kruse (eds.), *The Sage Handbook of School Organization*. London: Sage Publications Limited.

McGuckin, C. and Síoráin, C. (2021), The professional self and diverse learning needs. In S. Soan (ed.), *Why Do Teachers Need to Know about Diverse Learning Needs? Strengthening Professional Identity and Well-being* (pp. 15–32). London: Bloomsbury Academic.

Mercogliano, C. (2007), *In Defense of Childhood: Protecting Kids Inner Wildness*. Boston: Beacon Press.

Moore, A. (2012), *Teaching and Learning: Pedagogy, Curriculum and Culture* (2nd ed.). London: Routledge.

National Association of Head Teachers. (2022), SATs results this year will be 'useless' and tests should be cancelled, say school leaders. Available at https://www.naht.org.uk/News/Latest-comments/Press-room/ArtMID/558/ArticleID/1558/SATs-results-this-year-will-be-'useless'-and-tests-should-be-cancelled-say-school-leaders (Accessed January 16, 2024).

Organisation for Economic Co-operation and Development (OECD). (2018), *Preparing our Youth for an Inclusive and Sustainable World: The OECD PISA Global Competence Framework*. Available at https://www.oecd.org/education/Global-competency-for-an-inclusive-world.pdf (Accessed December 12, 2023).

Organisation for Economic Co-operation and Development (OECD). (2019) *OECD Future of Education and Skills: OECD Learning Compass 2030: A Series of Concept Notes*. Available at https://www.oecd.org/education/2030-project/teaching-and-learning/learning/learning-compass-2030/OECD_Learning_Compass_2030_Concept_Note_Series.pdf (Accessed December 12, 2023).

Ofsted. (2023), Consultation outcome: Equality, diversity and inclusion statement: Ofsted's role as quality assurance body for the Department for Education's online education accreditation scheme. Available at https://www.gov.uk/government/consultations/consultation-on-ofsteds-role-in-the-online-education-accreditation-scheme/equality-diversity-and-inclusion-statement-ofsteds-role-as-quality-assurance-body-for-the-department-for-educations-online-education-accreditation#fn:1 (Accessed November 22, 2023).

Packham, C. (2008), *Active Citizenship and Community Learning*. Exeter: Learning Matters Limited.

Pointer, L., McGoey, K. and Farrar, H. (2020), *The Little Book of Restorative Teaching Tools: Games, Activities, and Simulations for Understanding Restorative Justice Practices (Justice and Peacebuilding)*. New York: Good Books.

Radford, J., Bosanquet, P., Webster, R., Blatchford, P. and Rubie-Davies, C. (2014), Fostering learner independence through heuristic scaffolding: a valuable role for teaching assistants. *International Journal of Educational Research*, *63*, pp. 116–126.

Roberts, N. (2022), *Assessment and Testing in Primary Education (England)*. Available at https://researchbriefings.files.parliament.uk/documents/CBP-7980/CBP-7980.pdf (Accessed December 10, 2023).

Robinson, K. (2010), *Changing Education Paradigms*. Available at https://www.ted.com/talks/sir_ken_robinson_changing_education_paradigms (Accessed January 10, 2024).

Rodriguez, C. and Garro-Gil, N. (2015), Inclusion and integration on special education. *Procedia–Social and Behavioural Sciences*, *191*, pp. 1323–1327.

Rosenshine, B. (2012), Principles of instruction: Research-based strategies that all teachers should know. Available at https://files.eric.ed.gov/fulltext/EJ971753.pdf (Accessed January 10, 2024).

Sadler, A. (2022), *Crossing the Gap: An Examination of School Ethos and its Potential Impact on Citizenship* [Prof Doc Thesis]. Australian Catholic University.

Schuelka, M. (2018), Implementing inclusive education. Available at https://assets.publishing.service.gov.uk/media/5c6eb77340f0b647b214c599/374_Implementing_Inclusive_Education.pdf (Accessed December 12, 2023).

Sherrington, T. (2021), Cold-calling: The #1 strategy for inclusive classrooms—remote and in person. Available at https://teacherhead.com/2021/02/07/cold-calling-the-1-strategy-for-inclusive-classrooms-remote-and-in-person/ (Accessed January 10, 2024).

Sherrington, T. (2015), Inclusion and exclusion in a community school. Available at https://teacherhead.com/2015/01/04/inclusion-and-exclusion-in-a-community-school/ (Accessed January 15, 2024).

Sherrington, T. and Caviglioli, O. (2020), *Teaching Walkthrus: Five Step Guides to Instructional Coaching*. Woodbridge: John Catt Educational Limited.

Soan, S. (2021), Setting the context. In S. Soan (ed.), *Why Do Teachers Need to Know about Diverse Learning Needs? Strengthening Professional Identity and Well-being* (pp. 1–14). London: Bloomsbury Academic.

Swan, K., Chen, C. and Bockmier-Sommers, D. (2020), Relationships between Carl Rogers' person-centered education and the community of inquiry framework: A preliminary exploration. *Online Learning*, *24*(3), pp. 4–18.

Sweller, J., Merrienboer, J. and Paas, F. (2019), Cognitive architecture and instructional design: 20 years later. *Educational Psychology Review*, *31*, pp. 261–292.

Sweller, J. and Levine, M. (1982), Effects of goal specificity on means-ends analysis and learning. *Journal of Experimental Psychology: Learning, Memory and Cognition*, *8*, pp. 463–474.

Thorley, C. (2017), *Final Report: Tech Transitions: UTCs, Studio Schools, and Technical and Vocational Education in England's Schools*. Available at https://www.nuffieldfoundation.org/sites/default/files/files/Tech_transitions_May17.pdf (Accessed February 12, 2024).

UK Council for Internet Safety. (2020), *Education for a Connected World – 2020 edition*. Available at https://assets.publishing.service.gov.uk/government/uploads/system/uploads/attachment_data/file/896323/UKCIS_Education_for_a_Connected_World_.pdf (Accessed July 24, 2021).

UNICEF. (2023), The right to education: Introducing Articles 28 and 29. Available at https://www.unicef.org.uk/rights-respecting-schools/the-rrsa/the-right-to-education/ (Accessed December 29, 2023).

UNICEF. (2017), Inclusive education. Including children with disabilities in quality learning: What needs to be done? Available at https://www.unicef.org/eca/sites/unicef.org.eca/files/IE_summary_accessible_220917_brief.pdf (Accessed January 2, 2023).

Vogel, S. and Schwabe, L. (2016), Learning and memory under stress: Implications for the classroom. *NPJ Science of Learning*, *1*, pp. 16011. Available at https://doi.org/10.1038/npjscilearn.2016.11 (Accessed February 11, 2024).

Warnes, E., Done, E. and Knowler, H. (2021), Mainstream teachers' concerns about inclusive education for children with special educational needs and disability in England under pre-pandemic conditions. *Journal of Research for Special Educational Needs*, 22(1), pp. 31–43.

Zaks, Z. (2023) Changing the medical model of disability to the normalisation model of disability: Clarifying the past to create a new future direction. *Disability and Society*. Available at https://www.tandfonline.com/doi/pdf/10.1080/09687599.2023.2255926 (Accessed February 10, 2024).

11 Developing a Mentally Healthy Culture for All in Schools

Issues and Possible Solutions

Andy Smith

The underpinning context: Warnings and stress!

First warning: This is a particularly Anglo-centric chapter that may not appeal to an international audience; however, child mental health and wellbeing isn't limited by geographical boundaries, and so I hope that all readers will find some of this chapter useful as transferrable information, if only for comparative reasons. Second warning: This chapter isn't written as a carefully balanced and unbiased academic paper as it is opinionated and written in the 'first person' as I am talking directly to 'you', aiming to provoke and challenge you; at first, I'm going to paint something of a rather negative picture in the hope that you can take issue with it in order to formulate your own counter-argument supporting a brighter context or at least generating a 'silver lining' around the dark clouds that are presented here.

This is a stressful world for children and young people as, daily, they experience news and events that impact on their mental health. There is global terrorism, war in the Middle East and Ukraine, whole populations uprooted, global warming with its associated climatic results and growing economic poverty at home. The crises keep on coming: cost of living, affordable housing, refugees, food, the NHS and fuel; there is dysfunctional government, protest marches in the streets, the lingering threat of Coronavirus and the fall-out from months of shut-down still to be resolved. These are only a few of the stressors which fill our TV/laptop and smartphone screens, newspapers, podcasts and 24-hour revolving news programmes. This mixture has added complications generated by another list: invidious social media, the spread of dangerous or spurious conspiracy theories, too powerful social media influencers and reality TV shows allied with constant heavy-duty marketing playing on perceptions of 'ideal self'. We have crumbling school buildings and the always present pressures associated with just being a young person trying to make sense of an increasingly confusing world—what a toxic climate! No wonder that the Children's Commissioner reported one in five children being unhappy with their mental health (Children's Commissioner, 2023). This dire picture is also recognised by the National Health Service, whose 2022 data recorded that 18% of children aged 7 to 16 had mental health issues; their data for

DOI: 10.4324/9781032716190-15

young people aged 17 to 19 were even more alarming in that this percentage increased to 26% (NHS, 2022). This situation doesn't show any improvement as their 2023 data reports that more than 10% of 17- to 19-year-olds in England (who took their survey) had an eating disorder, overall data indicating that 20% of 8- to 16-year-olds had probable mental health needs, rising to almost 25% among 17- to 19-year-olds (NHS England, 2023).

Schools are places where issues can emerge; unfortunately, we have an education system which exists within a high-stakes assessment and overly inspected regime where schools sit firmly in a quasi-marketplace. In short, it's not easy for pupils today as they become increasingly anxious in response to these (and other) situations. Schools should, of course, be places where pupils' mental health and wellbeing flourish; school should provide a sense of purpose, enabling them to develop their knowledge, understanding, expertise and skills for independence. This positive combination of skills, empathy, and understanding is being then employed to enable pupils to make their own informed decisions and to make many inter-actions and friendships with others. School should be a safe place where pupils can be protected from harm, and then taught and guided to manage their progress by supporting the development of resilience but, unfortunately, school isn't a pleasant experience for some pupils as school-induced anxiety has been reported as a problem. However, there has been some very well-intentioned national, regional and local policy and action to address these identified issues over the past few years that has had a positive effect on pupil mental health and overall wellbeing. One of the most recent interventions being the deployment of education mental health practitioners (EMHPs) in schools—but I'm 'jumping the gun' here as, before we explore the EMHP role in more detail, it might be useful to present a brief picture of some of the factors that influence a school's policy, provision and practice.

The 'psychological contract', OFSTED, the limited curriculum and teacher burnout

Műller and Goldenberg (2020) stated that teachers, although not trained as mental healthcare professionals, play a vital role in the identification and support of children with mental health needs. Due to this key, untrained role, it makes sense that if teachers have concerns about their pupils' mental health both parents and mental health professionals should be involved. It is encouraging to see that mental health and wellbeing is a significant factor in all schools' policies and practices; one of the main external influences for this development is the Office for Standards in Education, Children's Services and Skills (OFSTED) because, in their school inspection regime, they have a focus on how well learners are supported, protected and kept safe (OFSTED, 2023a). Although this key aspect isn't separately graded, inspectors do make a judgment that appears in their written commentary on school leadership and management. According to the OFSTED (2019) Education Inspection Framework, in order for schools to gain 'good' status, children must enjoy learning about how to stay healthy and about emotional and mental health, including understanding about safe and positive relationships. To be 'outstanding', schools must enable students to be able to make their own informed choices about healthy eating, fitness and their emotional and mental wellbeing.

OFSTED's focus, at heart, is a sound one as they state that in creating an emotional wellbeing-friendly and resilient culture, schools should raise awareness and provide support to foster emotional wellbeing and then sustain this culture through a range of practices, strategies and close partnerships within the school and with external organisations such as the Child and Adolescent Mental Health Service (CAMHS) and general practitioners. An additional factor to this positive mix is that emotional wellbeing should be embedded within school policies and in teaching across the curriculum. OFSTED call this a whole school approach to mental health with the objective of improving achievement by creating a positive, nurturing and supportive school environment, which reduces barriers to learning, risk factors and poor mental health. This is linked to enhancing the way the curriculum is delivered with increasing parental engagement in their children's learning at school and home. This focus on positive mental health through universal approaches combined with targeted individual/bespoke and therapeutic interventions is designed to enable schools to develop a 'mentally healthy culture' for pupils and staff.

All good so far—but unfortunately, the process of the OFSTED inspection itself has been identified as a serious concern in terms of its detrimental impact on the mental health and wellbeing of headteachers and their staff; the tragic suicide of headteacher Ruth Perry (Court and Tribunals Judiciary, 2023; OFSTED, 2023b) who saw her school downgraded by OFSTED inspectors to 'inadequate' due to some quickly and easily rectifiable issues in around pupil wellbeing (followed by the deluge of righteous anger at OFSTED malpractice) became the catalyst for change in their inspection regime, the main one being the need for improved inspector training (although there remains some intransigence in terms of changing the damning 'one-word' summary judgment of a whole school, which was a significant contributory factor). Thankfully, the January OFSTED (2024) school inspection handbook makes a clear statement about the conduct of their inspections, and so, from now on,

> Inspectors will uphold the highest professional standards in their work. They will treat everyone they meet during inspections fairly and with the respect and sensitivity they deserve. Inspectors will work constructively with leaders and staff, demonstrating professionalism, courtesy, empathy and respect at all times.
>
> (para. 9)

It will be interesting to see if this will be sustained over the next few years, but let's take this concept of the school environment as a 'mentally healthy culture' and consider the factors at play, both positive and negative.

Perhaps the most positive factor is the school staff itself. Generally the contribution that teachers and teaching assistants (TAs) make goes far beyond what is expected of them in their formal job descriptions and duties as laid out in legislation, I call this their 'legal contract', but the focus here is the significant amount of additional time, effort, care and thought that any teacher/TA gives to their pupils, particularly to the most vulnerable: kindness, attention, proper listening, empathy, interest, support—in short, their blood, sweat and tears (literally in many cases, because if you're a teacher or TA you know this to be true). I call this their 'psychological contract'—the essential 'stuff' that doesn't appear in any formal contract of employment. This helps form the bedrock of any 'mentally healthy school' as it is based on caring and doing what's right and best for pupils. This involves a full commitment that, in the vast majority of cases, is freely given by teachers/TAs. This psychological contract is a positive force—unfortunately, it's also a two-edged sword, as the amount of time and energy given by a teacher/TA that is beyond their legal contract, although providing a source of professional and personal pride, can also be the very source of teachers'/TAs' stress, particularly in relation to lack of time, excessive workload, a lack of resources and a performativity-ridden school system that conforms to a high-stakes inspection and assessment-driven culture—with poor pay! This commitment and its effect upon work–life balance isn't new as it's been recognised for years; 20 years ago, Wedell (2004), when writing about special educational needs coordinators (SENCos), stated that they had a 'tremendous commitment to their work and that, in some instances, this led them to accept very unreasonable workloads' (p. 105). Although this commentary is about SENCos, it applies to teachers/TAs in general as many school staffrooms across the country are filled with exhausted and stressed staff. A study by MacBride (1983) explored the misconceptions of job burnout, a term describing a condition in which a person changes in their work situation from a state of high motivation and efficiency to apathy and inefficiency and may even demonstrate mild or severe psychological disturbance; these misconceptions include the belief that it is a sudden and dramatic happening that is inevitable in certain high-pressured professions (e.g., teaching). More gradual burnout was thought to be indicated by certain signals such as loss of job satisfaction, frequent sickness and minor medical ailments, loss of morale, gradual loss of confidence and deteriorating productivity accompanied by depression. Brill (1984) suggested that stress could lead to burnout but not all who are stressed became a 'victim'—a victim being someone who had functioned adequately for a time in their job but who would not recover to previous levels of high performance without external help or environmental rearrangement. MacBride's list of burnout symptoms was supported by Lowenstein (1991), who identified, among some teachers, symptoms including physical, emotional and attitudinal exhaustion leading to irritability and that,

> Others include feelings of helplessness, hopelessness, disenfranchisement as well as somatic states of physical exhaustion including proneness to accidents and increased susceptibility to illness. To these may be added a sense of guilt, depression, a feeling of disorganisation, shock, volatile emotion and loneliness.
>
> (p. 12–13)

These references are old, but I challenge anyone working in a school today to deny the continuing issues relating to teacher/TA stress and burnout; perhaps there is a strong argument to make that it's actually worse now, particularly as OFSTED inspection is another two-edged sword. It has already been stated that the focus on pupil wellbeing is to be welcomed as it provides some pertinent factors for a school to use in underpinning and strengthening its inclusive policies, practices and culture; these include supporting the development of an effective school plan, which will be particularly important when reviewing, auditing and interrogating how a school engages with its wider school community when establishing priorities, setting goals for improvement, implementing strategies and evaluating progress. But—it's OFSTED, isn't it! This means that the positive focus on wellbeing comes with the 'gut-churning' reality of high stakes scrutiny as an inspection team descends and passes judgment based on a snapshot view of school life. This isn't a deep critique of this somewhat performativity-driven process where schools feel forced into second guessing what the team might choose to place their 'lens' on according to the whims of its individual members, but how many school leaders and their staff actually welcome this imposed regime in its current evolution? Such a stressful experience has a significant impact on a school, no matter if judged outstanding or requires improvement, it leaves school leaders, teachers and pupils stressed and exhausted. In short, I believe OFSTED generates an undercurrent of fear in schools felt by all school staff; this influences the overall climate in the school which, in turn, affects the pupils.

There is plenty of anecdotal evidence from schools that supports this idea of fear at the heart of our education system fuelling anxiety for staff and pupils. Alongside critiques and research by other educationalists, the journalist and political commentator Polly Toynbee writing for the *Guardian* (2024). states that children became unhappier in this past decade, quoting data from the Childrens Society's (2023) Good Childhood Report Summary, which identified that the number of 8- to 16-year-olds with mental health issues has risen significantly. The summary report points out that this unhappiness and distress is due, in the main, to their life at their schools. Toynbee focuses on the unrelenting concentration on exams at the expense of subjects such as art, drama, music, sport and design/technology with the English baccalaureate, forcing secondary schools to follow its subject-limited content due to a lack of funding for anything else, plus the hard fact that a school's standing in the league tables is judged on the results. Toynbee writes that this is driving the 'fun' out of teaching and learning, thus affecting absence levels, which, like anxiety levels, also significantly rose.

I've mentioned 'anxiety' and 'fear' several times, perhaps this is a good time to provide a definition: Müller (2023) argues that being anxious isn't at all the same as being diagnosed with an anxiety disorder, and the American Psychological Association (n.d.) presents the view that anxiety is a normal part of responding to the stresses of everyday life, and when the stress or event passes, so does the anxiety, usually. However, there is plenty of real-life evidence to show that, for some children, anxiety persists. This can become excessive, even debilitating, leading to both clearly seen and sometimes difficult to recognise internalised panic attacks, physical symptoms, obsessions, dissolving self-concept, withdrawal and a whole range of other behaviours (NHS, 2023).

So, what can we do to help, support, advise and guide our vulnerable pupils in our schools? There has been a clarion call for this for years as, in 2014, the Department for Education (DfE, 2014) recognised that in order to help their children succeed, schools have a role to play in supporting them to be resilient and mentally healthy, while OFSTED (2013) has highlighted that children and young people themselves say that they want to learn more about how to keep themselves emotionally healthy. The report of the Department of Health (2015) identified a national commitment to 'encouraging schools to continue to develop whole school approaches to promoting mental health/wellbeing' (p. 19). So—since 2015, how well are we doing in rising to the challenge?

Eight key principles and the importance of a whole school approach

This isn't a comprehensive investigation into all of the strategies and provisions available to support positive pupil and staff mental health and wellbeing, but it does touch on three important facets: The first has already been presented, teachers/TAs' knowledge of what is best for their pupils (their psychological contract). I keep emphasising this, and so my advice to any teacher and/or TA who doesn't have any empathy with, or interest in, the positive mental health and emotional wellbeing of their pupils is to leave the profession—now—for self-preservation or before you cause a negative effect on the learning experience of your pupils!

The second facet is to use what is already available. Over the past few years, pupil mental health and wellbeing has had a significant lens focused upon it. There is plenty of advice and guidance for schools that has been published; examples include the Department of Health and NHS England's (2015) report entitled 'Future in Mind'. This detailed publication engaged with the national situation, policy and work-force development in regard to promoting, protecting and improving outcomes for children and young people's mental health and wellbeing. Although now historical, it does provide some useful background context for any current strategies and approaches, particularly if appraising how effective we've been so far in addressing the recommendations given in this report. Other useful publications include the Children Society's (2023) Good Childhood Report, which draws on children and young people's own views and subjective narratives in order to generate an informative summary with attached recommendations, the DfE's (2018) departmental advice on mental health and behaviour in schools (including information on the school's responsibilities and setting up a whole school culture), the DfE (2023) statutory guidance on keeping children safe (relating to safeguarding) while the DfE and Brown's (2018) research-based report, which had mental health and wellbeing policy and provision in mainstream and special schools as its subject, critically interrogated areas such as whole school values and aims, how the school promotes equality, diversity and tolerance and behaviour, anti-bullying and establishing a respectful school community. A useful publication by Public Health England (2016) is their paper on the mental health of children and young people in England; this included accessible data and information that provides a suitable resource for teacher/TA professional development.

The foregoing list is only a small selection; however, there is one publication that does provide a very workable model for a school needing to set up (or strengthen or audit) its whole school approach. Surprisingly, it isn't from the DfE or OFSTED; it is Public Health England's (2015) 'Promoting children and young people's emotional health/wellbeing'; this has since been updated by the Young People's Mental Health Coalition (2021). At the heart of this publication is a clear model presenting eight key principles for establishing a whole school approach to promoting mental health and wellbeing. These principles aren't in a hierarchy as they inter-relate with, and complement, each other; however, school leadership does take a central role.

School leadership

These eight principles start with the school's senior leadership. School leaders or senior leadership teams (SLT) are recognised as having an executive role in advocating for the needs of children within the context of wider strategic planning. This includes the need to have a school governor with an understanding of mental health and wellbeing issues in order to champion organisation-wide practices. Having a commitment to addressing and referencing social and emotional wellbeing in improvement plans across a range of school policies is identified as a key function of school leaders. A recommendation is that a lead on mental health is assigned, being responsible for linking school policy and practice with external expertise, identifying issues and making referrals. Schools engaging with this principle will find that they address these questions, which OFSTED might pose.

Developing a Mentally Healthy Culture for All in Schools 189

> *Questions OFSTED might pose*
> - What is the school's vision for mental health and wellbeing?
> - How effective is it?
> - How is the school providing visible senior leadership for emotional health and wellbeing?
> - How well is mental health and wellbeing referenced and integrated within the school's strategic priorities, goals, aims, policies and practice?

School environment and ethos

The importance of the school environment and ethos or culture has been noted and commented upon for many years; Jamal (2013) stated that the physical, social and emotional environment has been shown to affect the physical, emotional and mental health and wellbeing and attainment of both pupils and staff. Relationships between staff and pupils, and between pupils, are identified as being critical in promoting wellbeing and in helping to engender a sense of belonging to, and liking, school. So, it's obvious that a toxic school environment underpinned by fear, where bullying goes unchallenged, with limited opportunities for pupils and with crumbling buildings strays far from the ideal. Returning to OFSTED, the inspection team will look for evidence of a positive ethos that fosters improvements in the school as well as the promotion of safe practices and a culture of safety. To assess this, inspectors may interrogate the school's records and analysis of bullying (including racist, disablist and homophobic/sexist) and will probably ask the children about their experiences of learning and behaviour as the school will be judged on the effectiveness of its actions to prevent and tackle all forms of bullying and harassment. The questions that an inspection team might pose could be as discussed in the following box.

> *Questions OFSTED might pose*
> - How does the school's culture promote respect and value diversity?
> - How are staff already supporting the pupils' mental health through day-to-day contact and through building a sense of belonging?

Curriculum, teaching and learning

This principle focuses on the curriculum, teaching and learning and how programmes of social and emotional learning have the potential to help pupils acquire the skills to make good academic progress as well as benefiting their mental health and wellbeing. The importance of lessons that are of practical application with a high degree of relevance to the pupils (e.g., managing feelings, actions and relationships, and using problem-solving and group working) are noted for improved pupil engagement, particularly as there may be opportunities over the school year for a specific focus (e.g., learning skills for coping with transitions, managing examination pressures or a focus on pertinent local issues/events). Of course, OFSTED will look for learning and teaching that promote both learning and spiritual, moral, social and cultural development, so the questions they might ask could be as follows.

> *Questions OFSTED might pose*
> - What focus is given across the curriculum to social and emotional learning and promoting resilience?
> - Is it sufficiently intensive and ongoing with learning goals and themes being reinforced and threaded throughout the curriculum?

The Pupil voice

This principle presents the view that schools should have a firm commitment to the 'pupil voice'. This involves pupils being able to engage in decisions that impact them with a particular emphasis on helping them to feel part of the school. A school might very well have formal processes for this (e.g., councils, class representatives), but how often do teachers/TAs actually spend quality time really listening with interest to what pupils actually say, particularly as time to do this during the school day is at a premium? A pupil who really feels that their ideas, views and worries have been listened to with understanding and empathy by their teacher or TA who has spent the time to do so feels that they count. The same feelings apply to teachers/TAs too, in their interactions with senior leadership and their colleagues! For our most vulnerable pupils, their voice sits at the heart of the DfE/Department for Education and Health (2015) Code of Practice for Special Educational Needs: 0 to 25. OFSTED inspectors will have regard to the views of pupils and will probably ask these sorts of questions:

> *Questions OFSTED might pose*
> - How are pupils involved and listened to?
> - What does the school do to encourage children to talk about how they feel?
> - What is the school doing to give children the skills to know how, and when, to ask for help?

Staff development, health/wellbeing

This is a welcome focus on the staff and their mental health/wellbeing needs with an emphasis on schools providing and supporting effective staff development and training (both in-house and externally) with the particular need to increase teacher/TA knowledge of pupils' development and emotional wellbeing and to equip them to identify mental health difficulties. This should enable teachers/TAs to refer vulnerable pupils to relevant support either within the school or from external services. Promoting staff health and wellbeing is also a key element of a whole school approach with commitment being shown by appraising the needs of staff, taking positive and long-term action to enhance staff wellbeing and promoting a positive work–life balance. An excellent intention! However, in our current climate where overworked, underpaid and poorly recognised teachers with a disrupted work–life balance try to function, perhaps this is something that the whole education profession should make a priority as this is a national issue! OFSTED probably won't ask directly about staff wellbeing, but they will investigate the extent to which all staff benefit from professional development and that professional performance review and development is based on the needs of staff, with particular notice paid to the induction of staff new to the school. The questions they might ask include the following:

Questions OFSTED might pose

- What is the staff confidence in identifying children's needs early and mobilising protective support for children at risk of poor mental health?
- How much does professional and personal development focus on mental health and wellbeing?

Identifying needs and monitoring impact

This principle engages with the essential area of identifying needs and monitoring the impact of strategies and provisions put in place. Defining a pupil's needs can help to inform decisions at school level, across school clusters or at a local authority level, and then, after suitable provision has been implemented, the process of recording or monitoring and review is undertaken to make sure that the impact of any intervention is making a positive difference. This is particularly important in the case of provision, which is assessed as not working as well as it should, so that suitable amendments can be made. It is also essential that teachers/TAs recognise that what works well for one pupil may not prove successful for another and so together, and in partnership with external agencies, bespoke programmes of support for each pupil can be devised and implemented.

There are a number of validated tools and audits available that are designed to measure mental wellbeing, but perhaps the most effective process will always be careful observation by teachers and TAs, knowing the pupils and then being alert by noticing any changes in their normal routines and behaviours. In terms of OFSTED the questions they might pose are as follows:

> **Questions OFSTED might pose**
> - How is the school assessing the needs of all pupils: the progress of those who need support, and the difference made by programmes or interventions being used to improve mental health and wellbeing?
> - Is the school building on data collected as part of the school health profile, analysing needs of children and families?

Working with parents and carers

This principle recognises that the family plays the major role in influencing children and young people's mental and emotional health and wellbeing with a strong evidence base indicating that well-implemented interventions supporting parenting and family life, offering a combination of emotional, parenting and practical life circumstances, have the potential to yield social as well as economic benefits. Through the DfES (2005a), there used to be the Extended Schools initiative, which was promulgated alongside other initiatives such as Sure Start (DfES 2004) and Excellence in Cities (DfEE, 1999), all designed to address social factors impacting negatively on vulnerable children and their families; the coordination of professional and voluntary services (DfES, 2005b) was a key part of this process. This was allied with the core principles of Every Child Matters (DfES, 2003) and the drive for multi-agency teams, which, as Rose and Smith (2009) stated, were 'responsive to community needs and are seen as both accessible and welcoming to families who have previously felt distanced from the services offered' (p. 57). The Extended School programme, with school-based case workers attached to vulnerable families, operated until the raft of changes introduced by the Coalition Government in 2010 removed them almost immediately upon taking office; as this valuable intervention is now gone, it is vital that each school should now maintain a high degree of effective parent partnership not only in meeting the mental health needs of individual children but also involving parents/carers in policy review and development so that they remain live documents that are responsive to the evolving needs of the school community.

OFSTED expects schools to engage parents in supporting pupils' achievements, behaviour and safety as well as their spiritual, moral, social and cultural development. Inspectors have a duty to have regard for the views of parents, so an inspection team will need to know the answer to this question:

> **Question OFSTED might pose**
> - How does the school engage and work with parents and carers to reduce risks and de-escalate needs?

Targeted support

The final principle focuses on how some pupils are at greater risk of experiencing poorer mental health than others. Some examples are those who are in care, young carers, those who have had previous access to CAMHS, those living with parents/carers who have a mental illness and those living in a household with domestic violence. Delays in identifying and meeting any emotional mental health and wellbeing needs evolving from these (and other) factors can have far-reaching effects, as a result this principle sets out that schools need to have timely and effective processes that identify pupils who would benefit from specifically targeted support (with referral to the appropriate support services when required) as well as the wide range of 'universal' support and provision and interventions offered by the school. OFSTED will be interested in how this is done, particularly how interventions are secured so that the pupils receive the support they need (including those provided through effective partnerships with external agencies) and how staff identify, support and refer pupils who may need extra help at an early stage.

So—these are the eight key principles that provide, I believe, a sound framework to adopt and adapt if a school needs to remodel their own response to meeting the mental health and wellbeing needs of their whole school community. Across these principles there are several references to 'expertise' and 'external services', so it will be useful to conclude with a brief description of a fairly new intervention that is starting to show a great deal of positive potential in helping to support pupils who are feeling excessive levels of anxiety; this is the work of the education mental health practitioner.

The education mental health practitioner (EMHP): The school and the expert working in partnership

Education mental health practitioners (EMHPs) work across education and healthcare to provide mental health support for pupils and students in schools and colleges. EMHPs are trained, both academically and on work-practice, at an institute of higher education or university, on a 12-month long specialist course at first degree or master's degree level (if they already have a first degree or equivalent). The core purpose of this professional training is to prepare an EMHP to help children and young people to manage common mental health problems, particularly mild to moderate symptoms of anxiety and depression, plus some focus on behaviour. Many EMHPs come from a school-based professional background (but certainly not all), so it wasn't surprising that, in my professional conversations with EMHPs in training, the main reason most gave for changing their career pathway was to make a real difference for vulnerable pupils—it was clear that the psychological contract 'force', to quote a well-known cinema film, 'was strong with them'!

EMHPs are not employed directly by a school but through a healthcare organisation to work in schools, colleges, special schools and pupil referral units as part of a mental health support team (MHST) designed to help meet the mental health needs of those from 5 to 18 years old. These teams usually consist of around four EMHPs with therapists, a team manager and administrative support. When an EMHP is assigned to a school (or family of schools), pupils will be referred to them for a set (limited) number of sessions only, and so this focus on 'mild to moderate' is an important distinction as the work of an EMHP is an early intervention, or at least the next step after a school has already started their own interventions. This early support for vulnerable pupils usually takes the form of low-intensity approaches such as cognitive therapy–based interventions in order to address emerging mental health needs (e.g., working with pupils to help them manage their stress, anxiety, or depression, advising on panic attacks and problem-solving). As a result of this, the potential for using the specialist skills and knowledge held by an EMHP is huge, particularly as their work impacts on the future progress of their case study pupils and with the development and enhancement of the whole school's approach to mental health and wellbeing.

What do EMHPs say about their role?

In a series of professional conversations with EMHPs, during their work-based training and with those already in practice, I discovered that there was a high level of agreement that they found their training to be relevant and engaging in terms of preparing them for the rigours of working within a school setting. However there were concerns, expressed by those already working in schools, around heavy work/case-loads comprising of a lot of limited time allocated individual pupil cases. Many stated that this approach was proving difficult to manage as the set number of sessions per pupil, many of whom had a comorbidity of need, were felt to be too few as the EMHPs wanted to do more, particularly with pupils identified as being in most need. In short, despite feeling pressurised by their heavy caseloads, the EMHPs would have preferred fewer cases but with more time allocated to each one. Some EMHPs did, initially, have difficulties around being able to manage their own feelings and emotions when listening to some of the disturbing narratives presented by their pupils, even though they knew that this was to be an underpinning part of their role; however, over time, their increasing experience in role helped to address this—in short, it's their psychological contract coming into play again, but this time carefully managed according to the protocols and remit of the role. Early intervention by schools in effectively identifying then referring pupils was recognised as being essential particularly when inter-related with the second aspect of the EMHP role, which involved them advising class and subject teachers and SENCos on further provision for the pupils.

Not all EMHPs had an equitable experience in their schools, but they expected this difference as 'not all schools are the same'. This was evidenced in terms of the availability of resources for supporting mental health and wellbeing needs, with some schools identified as being well-resourced while in others resources were few or out-of-date. Schools procuring and designing suitable resources for mental health and wellbeing (assessments, texts, physical resources, ICT, etc.) was a key area several EMHPs recommended for development. Issues also arose, in some schools, about not having a suitable space to hold confidential sessions with pupils, particularly spaces free of disturbance; this was a difficulty particularly as safety and comfort were felt to be key elements in helping to gain trust. Those EMHPs who reported that they were provided with a dedicated safe and confidential space rather than having to keep 'moving their base' felt that it had a significantly positive impact on their interactions with the pupils and on their own wellbeing. However, those EMHPs who didn't have this security of space stated that their schools did try and provide as best as they could, particularly in smaller schools where space was at a premium. Interesting commentary arose related to the EMHP's 'place' in their schools; those who had previously been teachers or TAs managed to understand and engage with general school culture as they were well-versed in the whole process of policy, administration and processes and knew the many procedures, practices and sometimes seemingly esoteric unwritten behaviours which underpin school life. Those EMHPs who didn't have this background did take a longer period of time to feel at home in such an environment. There was a degree of contextual variety in terms of the status of the EMHP in the school as some felt that they were fully embedded within the whole school culture, working in close partnership with the SENCo, the school mental health lead, the SLT and other staff by having their role very well defined and explained, while other EMHPs felt that they were accepted and treated well, but more as a form of 'bolt-on' external service. In the most positive cases, the EMHPs' role (and wellbeing) was best supported by the school when they had the opportunity to regularly meet and collaborate with professional colleagues, external services and parents/carers in order to freely discuss (formally and informally) pupil progress, to review interventions and to undertake staff development. The importance of being able to brief or advise their colleagues and take part in wider school events and activities, particularly investigating how their case study pupils engaged in the classroom and in supporting the identification of potential pupils for referral (contributing their expertise to the whole referral process), was highlighted. A few EMHPs had the opportunity to work with teachers/TAs in classrooms and found this experience rewarding and very useful.

A vital point that emerged from these discussions with EMHPs was that they all felt that this career choice was a good choice to have made; in short, in spite of the emotional and work-load stress, they all thoroughly enjoyed their role and gained a great deal of job satisfaction from it!

Overall, these discussions with this small group of EMHPs presented a positive picture of how they are used as key staff in a whole school approach, but points for improvement in how they are managed did emerge. It will be interesting to see how the EMHP role develops nationally with, hopefully, future political change not sweeping it away like the previous Extended Schools agenda.

I've just realised—I think I may have created my own 'silver lining' after all!

Finally, if you are a teacher, TA or parent/carer, here are some questions to ask about your own school or setting:

- How is the setting providing visible senior leadership for emotional health and wellbeing?
- How does the setting's inclusive culture promote respect and value diversity, and how is this celebrated?
- What focus is given within the curriculum to social and emotional learning and promoting personal resilience?
- How is this recognised and assessed?
- How does the school ensure all pupils have the opportunity to express their views and influence decisions?
- How is the staff supported in relation to their own health and wellbeing?
- How does the setting assess the needs of pupils and the impact of interventions to improve wellbeing?
- How does the setting work in partnership with parents/carers to promote emotional health?
- How does the setting ensure the timely and effective identification of pupils who would benefit from targeted support (with appropriate referral to support services)?
- If the setting works in partnership with an EMHP, how does the school inter-relate their skills or expertise and remit within its culture, policies and practices?

References

American Psychological Association. (n.d.) Anxiety. Available at https://www.apa.org/topics/anxiety/ (Accessed November 10, 2023).

Brill, P.L. (1984), The need for an operational definition of burnout. *Family and Community Health*, 6(4), pp. 12–24.

Children's Commissioner. (2023), *Children's Mental Health Services 2021–22*. Available at https://www.childrenscommissioner.gov.uk/resource/29751/ (Accessed November 10, 2023).

Children's Society. (2023), *Good Childhood Report*. Available at https://www.childrenssociety-.org.uk/information/profesionals/resources/good-childhood-report-2023 (Accessed November 10, 2023].

Court and Tribunals Judiciary. (2023), *Ruth Perry: Prevention of Future Deaths Report*. Available at https://www.judiciary.uk/prevention-of-future-death-reports/ruth-perry-prevention-of-future-deaths-report/ (Accessed February 5, 2024).

Department for Education and Employment. (1999), *Excellence in Cities*. London: HMSO.

Department for Education and Skills. (2003), *Every Child Matters*. Nottingham: DfES Publications.

Department for Education and Skills. (2004), *Working Together: A Sure Start Guide to the Curriculum and Early Education Field*. Nottingham: DfES Publications.

Department for Education and Skills. (2005a), *Extended Schools: Access to Opportunities and Services for All*. Nottingham: DfES Publications.

Department for Education and Skills. (2005b), *Extended Schools Remodelling Programme*. Nottingham: DfES Publications.

Department for Education. (2014), *Mental Health and Behaviour in Schools: Departmental Advice for School Staff*. London: DfE.

Department for Education and Department for Health. (2015), *The Special Educational Needs and Disability Code of Practice: 0 to 25 years*. Ref: DfE-00205-2014. Available at https://assets.publishing.service.gov.uk/government/uploads/system/uploads/attachment_data/file/398815/SEND_Code_of_Practice_January_2015.pdf (Accessed March 10, 2023).

Department of Health. (2015), Future in mind: Promoting, protecting and improving our children and young people's mental health/wellbeing. Available at https://assets.publishing.service.gov.uk/media/5a80b26bed915d74e33fbe3c/Childrens_Mental_Health.pdf (Accessed November 10, 2023).

Department for Education. (2018), Mental health and behaviour in schools. Available at https://assets.publishing.service.gov.uk/government/uploads/system/uploads/attachment_data/file/1069687/Mental_health_and_behaviour_in_schools.pdf (Accessed November 10, 2023).

Department for Education and Brown, R. (2018), *Mental Health and Wellbeing Provision in Schools Review of Published Policies and Information Research Report*. Available at https://assets.publishing.service.gov.uk/government/uploads/system/uploads/attachment_data/file/747709/Mental_health_and_wellbeing_provision_in_schools.pdf (Accessed November 10, 2023).

Department for Education. (2023), *Keeping Children Safe in Education: Statutory Guidance for Schools and Colleges*. Available at https://assets.publishing.service.gov.uk/media/66d7301b9084b18b95709f75/Keeping_children_safe_in_education_2024.pdf (Accessed November 10, 2023).

Jamal, F., Fletcher, A. and Wells, H. (2013), The school environment and student health' *BMC Public Health*, *13*(798), pp. 1–11.

Lowenstein, L. (1991), Teacher stress leading to burnout: It's prevention and cure. *Education Today*, *41*(2), pp. 12–13.

MacBride, A. (1983), Burnout: Possible? Problematic? Preventable? *Canada's Mental Health*, *3*(1), pp. 2–3, 8.

Műller, L.M. (2023), Supporting pupil mental health and wellbeing: Understanding the complexity. *Impact*, *19*(Autumn), pp. 70–72.

Műller, L.M. and Goldenberg, G. (2020), *Education in Times of Crisis: The Potential Implications of School Closures for Teachers and Students*. Chartered College of Teaching. Available at https://my.chartered.college/wp-content/uploads/2020/05/CCTReport070520_FINAL.pdf (accessed November 10, 2023).

National Health Service (NHS). (2022), *Mental Health of Children and Young People in England 2022—Wave 3 Follow-Up to the 2017 Survey.* Available at https://digital.nhs.uk/data-and-information/publications/statistical/mental-health-of-children-and-young-people-in-england/2022-follow-up-to-the-2017-survey (Accessed November 10, 2023).

National Health Service. (2022), *The NHS website: NHS.* Available at https://www.nhs.uk/Tools/Documents/Wellbeing%20self-assessment.htm (Accessed November 10, 2024).

National Health Service (NHS). (2023), *Anxiety in Children.* Available at www.nhs.uk/mental-health/children-and-young-adults/advice-for-parents/anxiety-in-children (Accessed November 10, 2023).

Office for Standards in Education. (2013), *Not Yet Good Enough: Personal, Social, Health and Economic Education in Schools.* Available at www.ofsted.gov.uk/resources/130065. (Accessed November 10, 2023).

Office for Standards in Education (OFSTED). (2019), Education inspection framework. London: Office for Standards in Education, Children's Services and Skills. Available at https://www.gov.uk/government/publications/education-inspection-framework (Accessed March 10, 2024).

Office for Standards in Education. (2023a), *Framework for Inspection.* Available at https://www.gov.uk/government/publications/education-inspection-framework/education-inspection-framework-for-september-2023 (Accessed February 5, 2024).

Office for Standards in Education. (2023b), *A Statement from Ofsted's Chief Inspector, Amanda Spielman.* Available at https://www.gov.uk/government/news/statement-from-his-majestys-chief-inspector (Accessed February 5, 2024).

Office for Standards in Education. (2024), *School Inspections Handbook.* Available at https://www.gov.uk/government/publications/school-inspection-handbook-eif (Accessed February 5, 2024).

Public Health England. (2015). *Promoting children and young people's emotional health/wellbeing.* Available at https://www.gov.uk/government/publications/promoting-children-and-young-peoples-emotional-health-and-wellbeing (Accessed March 10, 2024).

Public Health England. (2016), *The Mental Health of Children and Young People in England.* Available at https://assets.publishing.service.gov.uk/media/5a80c3e240f0b62305b8d06c/Mental_health_of_children_in_England.pdf (Accessed March 12, 2023).

Rose, R., Smith, A. and Feng, Y. (2009), Supporting pupils and families: A case study of two English extended secondary schools. *Management in Education,* 23(2) pp. 57–62.

Toynbee, P. (2024), The Tories have sucked the joy from the education system. Available at https://www.theguardian.com/commentisfree/2024/feb/29/ (Accessed February 29, 2024).

The Childrens Society. (2023), *Good Childhood Report Summary.* Available at https://www.childrenssociety.org.uk/Good-childhood-report-summary-2023_0.pdf (childrenssociety.org.uk) (Accessed February 29, 2024).

Wedell, K. (2004), Life as a SENCo. *British Journal of Special Education,* 3(12), p. 105.

Young People's Mental Health Coalition. (2021), *Promoting Children and Young People's Emotional Health and Wellbeing.* Available at https://assets.publishing.service.gov.uk/government/uploads/system/uploads/attachment_data/file/1020249/Promoting_children_and_young_people_s_mental_health_and_wellbeing.pdf (Accessed March 12, 2023).

12 Wellbeing in the Modern World

Jodie Rossiter

Introduction

For the best part of the 20th century, the field of psychology was dominated by efforts to understand what is 'wrong' with human beings and how they could be 'fixed'. If the problem was unconscious, psychoanalysts could help to make it conscious. If the problem was learned, behaviourists could offer positive modelling and reconditioning experiences. Physiological imbalances could be addressed with medication, and in the extreme, electroconvulsive therapy or a good old-fashioned lobotomy. Unhelpful thinking strategies could be challenged and repressed with cognitive behavioural theory (CBT), while relational issues could be examined through the lens of attachment theory and alleviated through social intervention.

The contributions of psychology, as a science of mind and behaviour, have been exponential and have unquestionably influenced attitudes, societal norms, legislation, health care, education and social discourse for over a century. The field is vast, multidisciplinary, and seemingly infinite in capacity to develop new ways of understanding and addressing individual and social issues. Psychology has both informed and been informed by what it is to be human, throughout the most rapid period of social evolution in the history of the species. However, until the turn of the 21st century, psychology was permeated by narratives about what is wrong with people.

This chapter picks up the mantle of 'positive psychology', which emerged in the 1990s, asking a new set of questions that can be broadly summarised as 'what is right with people'? As a lecturer, with over two decades of experience teaching key approaches in psychology, this positive shift in direction has illuminated a new path in my life and work. Being well versed in the contributions of psychodynamic, cognitive, behaviourist, biological and social psychology had provided me with a wealth of knowledge about human distress and deficit, yet this had generated a sense of disenchantment and disempowerment about what it is to be human. All that was about to change!

Underpinned by humanist values, this chapter will explore ways in which practitioners, parents and children can set forth on a journey of self-discovery, healing, empowerment and connection. Incorporating the person-centred beliefs that human beings know themselves best and have the capacity to flourish under the right conditions, readers can engage in activities designed to draw out their true nature and to identify what really matters to them. The chapter is also informed by ancient practices, which demonstrate the natural wisdom that human beings possess and the cross-cultural lessons that have been passed down through generations. Furthermore, contributions from third-wave CBT are included, as they offer tools for self-acceptance and self-regulation that do not require external intervention.

As an integrated counsellor and trauma informed psychologist and psychotherapist in training, I have cultivated intentions to move towards a way of seeing and being in the world that is motivated by identifying strengths, skills, positive qualities and innate knowledge of self and other. This is a journey, with no clear beginning or end, which can be undertaken by any human being at any age and stage in life. The invitations in this chapter can be accepted or declined as the reader sees fit. Practitioners can apply what they learn to inform their own development, and they can also adapt the activities for the classroom. The invitations are offered without expectation and with a belief that they are applicable to anyone who wishes to explore them. Barriers of culture, race, religion, geography, age, status or identity need not apply—all are invited.

What Is Wellbeing?

Many modern definitions of wellbeing emphasise *how* we experience life rather than *what* it consists of. The UK Department of Health and Social Care (2023) refers to 'mental wellbeing' in terms of thoughts, feelings and ways of coping with the stresses of everyday life. They also use the term 'positive wellbeing', which involves realising one's own potential, coping with ups and downs, engaging in work productively and forming and maintaining relationships.

Other definitions of wellbeing include:

- 'A state of positive feelings and meeting full potential in the world' (Simons and Baldwin, 2021, p. 983).
- 'A person's subjective evaluation of their own lives' (Rablen, 2012, p. 299).
- How one thinks about their life satisfaction as a whole and how one experiences emotions, moods and feelings that are pleasant (e.g., joy, elation and affection) or unpleasant (e.g., guilt, anger and shame) (Fleming and Manning, 2019, p. 7–8).

Positive psychologist Martin Seligman is renowned as one of the world's leading experts on the study of wellbeing. His work is aligned with salutogenic approaches, moving away from the focus on pathology, which dominated much of the 20th century, and focusing on the determinants of wellbeing and good health. Seligman (2011) has identified five elements that contribute to the construct of wellbeing: positive emotions, positive relationships, meaning, engagement and accomplishment.

Wellbeing exercises: Explore your own experience of the five wellbeing elements

Dedicate some regular time alone, with a loved one, with a therapist or within a supportive group to explore the elements associated with wellbeing. Writing down the answers to each of the following questions can help to solidify your responses and can provide a record of your experience that you can revisit in future. You might also find it helpful to draw pictures, produce electronic resources or create vision boards based on your responses. What is important is that you recognise your own power to explore, identify and revisit positive emotions, relationships, meaning, engagement and accomplishment at any time.

Wherever you are, simply ask yourself one of the following questions, close your eyes and search your mind and body for responses that feel genuine to you. There is no right answer. Your truth is within you!

- How do you experience positive emotion? Is it pleasure, rapture, ecstasy, warmth, comfort or something else? What does it look like for you? Where do you feel it? Does it have a colour or a shape? Are there images, places, people or activities associated with it?
- What do positive relationships look like for you? Do they involve laughter and fun? Are they about giving and/or receiving support? Do they simply involve existing alongside other people? How do you communicate in positive relationships? How do others communicate with you? What are the qualities that you value in others? What do you want others to see and value in you?
- What is meaningful to you? What gets you up in the morning? What drives you to complete daily tasks? What do you value most in life? What gives you a sense of purpose? Looking back on your life to date, what are your most meaningful experiences?
- What engages you? Seligman (2011) uses the term 'flow' in conjunction with engagement. Flow is a state where time stops and self-consciousness is lost during an absorbing activity. When does time stop for you? Which activities do you become absorbed in to the point where self-consciousness melts away? To explore this further, Glazer (2023) recommends asking yourself the following questions: In which non-work environments do you feel highly engaged? In which roles or jobs did you do your best work? What help, advice or qualities do others come to you for? What would you want said about you in your eulogy?
- What gives you a sense of accomplishment? Is it completing daily tasks? Setting and achieving goals? Seeing a smile on someone else's face? Winning a race? Getting a promotion? What does accomplishment look like for you? What had you just done the last time you felt accomplished? What is your greatest accomplishment to date? What would you like to accomplish in the future?

There is a possibility that these questions will invoke memories of perceived failure. Acknowledge that those memories are there—and let them pass. Alternatively, you could explore what you gained from experiences of perceived failure. What did you learn? How did you, or could you, apply what you learned to shape positive next steps?

How can we enhance our own sense of wellbeing?

Over the past few years, I have embarked on a journey of personal and professional discovery, investigating wellbeing through theory, research, observation, real-world application, community discussion, personal therapy and client work. What I have learned, so far, about improving and maintaining a sense of positive wellbeing is that in many ways people in the modern world would benefit from living like our ancestors did! The rapidity of social and technological evolution outstrips our physical evolution by thousands of years, leaving many people's bodies and minds in a state of chaos. By engaging with activities, we are naturally drawn towards when we are well, we can help to restore balance.

In a study measuring levels of 'flourishing', a term closely associated with wellbeing, it was found that only 18% of UK respondents, 33% of respondents in Denmark and 6% of respondents in Russia met the criteria (Seligman, 2011). The Office for Health Improvement and Disparities (2022) acknowledges that a range of social, economic and environmental factors affect health and wellbeing. Social prescribing schemes have been introduced in the UK, which typically involve a link person, in a general practitioner (GP) surgery, signposting or referring to various community-based activities. This can be more effective than traditional services for improving the health and wellbeing of marginalised groups and vulnerable individuals and can reduce GP and accident and emergency visits.

The rest of the chapter will summarise factors associated with positive wellbeing that can be cultivated and practiced in everyday life, without the need for a prescription, a therapy referral or a wealth of specialist skills and training. These factors have been identified by paying attention to what people makes people feel good and what has been shown to be beneficial in relation to positive wellbeing. Each factor will be discussed in turn, and readers will be invited to apply the practices within their own lives, while remaining open and curious about what happens when they do.

While this is not an exhaustive list, the factors that I have explored, tested and feel confident to endorse at this time are as follows: aligning with core values and fostering positive relationships, singing and dancing, spending time in nature, exercising, eating well, getting enough sleep, accepting things as they are, practising gratitude, being compassionate to oneself and others and replacing consumerism with essentialism.

Aligning with core values and cultivating positive relationships

Seligman (2011) states that all five of the wellbeing elements discussed previously are underpinned by strengths and virtues, such as kindness, courage, social intelligence, integrity and humour. However, it can be challenging for individuals to identify their own unique qualities, especially when aspects of 'self' have not been accepted or nurtured by others. In order to identify what is truly meaningful, you are encouraged to explore your individual views and values, dating back to early life (Glazer, 2023). Identifying core values can strengthen a sense of self and can help you to move in directions that align with who you truly are.

While knowing who you are and aligning with your own values can be incredibly empowering, 'no man is an island' (Donne, 1624). There are now more than 400 published studies, from over 20 countries and all six continents, emphasising the importance of group membership for health and wellbeing (Haslam *et al.*, 2018, pp. 9–10). One such study by Holt-Lunstad (2017) found that social support and integration were the most important predictors of mortality in a meta-analysis involving 148 studies and over 300,000 participants. Group membership can facilitate bonding with like-minded people, bridge cultural divides, establish norms of trust and reciprocity, encourage knowledge sharing, promote healthy norms and provide access to social support (Haslam *et al.*, 2018, p. 8).

Invitation 1: Explore your core values and relationships

Glazer (2023) recommends creating a short phrase that summarises your core values and how you approach dealing with problems and situations. If you are stuck, look for common words or themes in what you wrote for the previous wellbeing exercises. Alternatively, make a list of things you cannot stand. Your core values will be the polar opposite of the things on this list, as these are the things that violate your values.

Once you have your core values phrase, consider how your values are aligned with different aspects of your life and your relationships.

How are your values nurtured by your family? Friendship groups? Working relationships? Romantic relationships? Social activities?

Write down your answers to the following questions:

- Who are the people in your life who share and nurture your values the most?
- How can you spend more time with these people?
- Which environments promote and nurture your values the most?
- How can you spend more time in these environments?
- What are the boundaries you could put in place to allow you to live most authentically in line with your values? (You may need different boundaries for different people or environments).

It is also important to remember that relationships are two-way streets! You may wish to repeat the foregoing exercises, considering the ways in which you promote and nurture the values of others. If that feels like too much work, you could also try following the advice of Martin Seligman: 'Find one wholly unexpected kind thing to do tomorrow and just do it. Notice what happens to your mood' (Seligman, 2011, p. 21).

Singing and dancing

People from all over the world, and throughout human history, have come together to dance. In modern western culture this often occurs in nightclubs and at weddings or music festivals, but what draws people to dance together? For many dancing is a way to connect with and tell stories about heritage, tradition, culture, spirituality, nature and emotions. In New Zealand different versions of the Haka are performed for war, at funerals and at other times to celebrate life, in keeping with Māori mythology. A traditional Indonesian dance depicts the struggle between good and evil, and a Barong, protective spirit, restores balance through synchronisation. In an Islamic Sufi tradition from Turkey, long white-skirted dresses are worn as people whirl in circles. This is a form of ecstatic meditation that represents abandoning ego and reaching for enlightenment. Dancing can do so many things for so many people. What does it do for you?

In a recent thematic analysis of responses from 185 singing groups in the Republic of Ireland, Helitzer and Moss (2022) identified a range of benefits to health and wellbeing associated with group singing. The groups reported a sense of community connectedness and social engagement when performing for vulnerable and isolated people. Enthusiastic, professionally trained, committed group leaders were also praised for their ability to motivate, as were group members who offered nonjudgmental peer support. Another benefit was the enjoyment and atmosphere in singing groups. Participants reported feeling safe, relaxed, joyful and included, as well as having a sense of escape from stressful jobs or life situations. The groups receive financial contributions enabling them to continue.

Singing together can have a transformative impact on mood, social skills and the development of a routine. Learning to use the voice as an instrument can also generate a sense of achievement and empowerment (Helitzer and Moss, 2022). The clear structure, organisation and communication in singing groups was highly valued by the participants, as was the use of virtual technologies, which allowed groups to provide alternative ways of singing together during the pandemic. While some members left groups when they moved online, new members found group singing at this time, and positive views were expressed about the adaptability, creativity and flexibility of singing groups that continued to connect at a time when many felt extremely disconnected (Helitzer and Moss, 2022, p. 107).

I attended a singing group for a few weeks as part of the research for this chapter, and I very much concur with this quote: 'There is no doubt that many people arrive frazzled and leave cheerful' (Helitzer and Moss, 2022, p. 108). This activity is highly recommended for lifting the spirits and feeling connected to others. Helitzer and Moss (2022) recommend that group singing is more widely offered on social prescription and that equity of geographical access for people with specific diagnoses is supported. They also point out that 71.6% of participants identified as female, which may have implications for those who identify as other than female. What do you make of this?

According to Ilari, Chen-Hafteck and Crawford (2013), singing is associated with wellbeing in four areas of development: cognitive, physical, social and emotional. Singing cross-cultural songs provide knowledge of music, language and culture, helps people acquire singing and speech skills, contributes to understanding of self and other, and helps to express emotion (Ilari, Chen-Hafteck and Crawford, 2013). The Office for Health Improvement and Disparities (2022) highlights that socially prescribed activities like group singing are holistic, health promoting, community centred and connecting. They can reduce health inequalities and enable participants to take an active role in their own care.

> ***Invitation 2: SING! DANCE!***
>
> Use your voice, move your body and notice what it does for you! I am a lifelong promoter of the natural benefits of listening to music, singing and dancing. It helps me to mobilise and release energy, to regulate my emotions, to express myself and to understand more about the diversity of human experience through rhythm and lyrics. This has informed my personal development and my therapeutic work.

Spending time in nature

Kaplan (1995) suggests that immersion in natural environments promotes indirect attention or 'soft fascination', which is restorative, in comparison to the distractions and directed attention required in everyday activities, such as work and study. The biophilia hypothesis suggests that our relationship to nature is innate and that human identity and personal fulfilment is somehow dependent on it (Wilson, 1984). Ulrich (1983) found that post operative patients had a speedier recovery when they had a view of trees, compared to those with a view of a blank wall, concluding that nature evokes positive affect, calm, relaxation, pleasantness and fascination (cited by Jordan, 2015).

Between 2012 and 2013, 92 community members of Nunatsiavut 'Our Beautiful Land' were interviewed, along with 14 health professionals. Nunatsiavut is a self-governed Inuit re-settlement in Labrador Canada, and the aim of the research was to implement and evaluate public health strategies that consider 'local perspectives, wisdom, livelihoods and socio-cultural realities' (Sawatzky *et al.*, 2019, p. 223). Participants referred to the land as 'healer, teacher, connector and kin' and reported that relationships with family and friends were strengthened by 'going off on the land' together. Getting back to cultural roots and taking part in traditional activities made people feel connected to their community and ancestry. How do you relate to this in your own geographical area?

Outdoor waterscapes and immersion in water have also been found to have restorative, therapeutic and health promoting value. Foley and Kistemann (2015) outline the emotional, physical, and imaginative properties that being in or near water can provide, and they emphasise that these spaces can also be seen to welcome and embrace diverse populations. Autoethnographic research with surfers refers to 'a sense of something bigger', 'feelings of connection', 'states of deep contemplation', 'peak experiences', 'exhilaration, laughing, buzzing and vibration', 'a sense of more than me', 'meditation, rhythms' and 'a sense of wholeness' (Hunter and Stoodley, 2021).

I have practiced cold water swimming and forest bathing in supportive groups as part of the research for this chapter, and have experienced multiple benefits, including a sense of freedom, peace and tranquility, feeling more connected to people and the environment, relief from everyday stresses and an increase in spontaneous interaction and creative thinking.

Invitation 3: Try some of these natures immersing activities

Mindfulness walks in green spaces
Move through a forest or park at a slow pace, practising mindfulness by engaging your senses. What can you see in the distance and nearby? Sit or lie down on the earth. Get up close to a tree or plant. What do you notice now? What can you feel around you? What are the textures like? What do you notice in your body? How do you experience the temperature, the weather, the scents? Stop somewhere safe, close your eyes and tune into the sounds. Imagine they are a piece of music ebbing and flowing around you. What does this feel like to you?

Forest bathing
Find a quiet space to lie down under a tree and look up through the branches. Notice your breath, without doing anything to change it. Mindfully engage your senses as you gaze above. What do you notice? How does it change from moment to moment?

Blue sky gazing
In the Dzogchen Buddhist tradition, it is believed that our minds become clear and open when gazing into a clear blue sky. By practising Tibetan blue sky meditation, it is said our minds can become as unaffected by passing thoughts and feelings, as the sky is by passing weather (Douglas, 2020).

Cold water swimming
There are many groups you can join for sea, lake and river swimming. Be safe and enjoy!

Exercising

Regular participation in moderate intensity physical activity can improve physical and mental health and reduce the risk of chronic diseases (Cooper and Barton, 2016). It is recommended that adults aged 19 to 64 should accumulate 150 minutes or more of moderate intensity aerobic activity per week and should also do strength building exercises twice a week (NHS Inform, 2022). Public Health England (2020) promotes being active in our daily lives, during travel and recreation, as well as participating in informal or organised sport. Aerobic activity can include brisk walking, swimming, cycling, hiking, gardening and mowing, dancing and housework. Strengthening can be achieved through lifting weights or carrying heavy shopping, doing yoga, playing ball games or racquet sports and doing aerobic circuit training (Public Health England, 2020).

According to Sport England (2020) the top five most popular physical activities are walking, fitness, running, cycling and swimming. Swim England promotes swimming as an activity that enhances human and social capital, as well as civic engagement and shared values (Moffatt, 2017). However, sport is often associated with binaried culture and practices, which can generate hostility for transgender and nonbinary bodies. This could impact participation and associated wellbeing benefits (Caudwell, 2021). Caudwell (2021) explored the experience of recreational swimming for 63 members of a transgender social group, as this population is under-represented in research regarding the benefits of physical activity.

Caudwell's (2021) participants attended a number of swim sessions at a privately hired pool. They were asked to create drawings to represent their feelings before, during and after sessions, and they also participated in focus groups and semi-structured interviews. Themes of play, pleasure safety and feeling free arose from the research. The drawings reflected transgender and nonbinary imaginations, allowing space for creativity and self-expression and giving participants an opportunity to forget external worries. This highlights the importance of considering diversity within wellbeing initiatives. How does this apply to you? What barriers do you face regarding exercise, and how could they be overcome? Is there an activity or group tailored to support your individual needs? If not, perhaps you could start one!

Invitation 4: Incorporate exercise in your daily life

Take some time to review the levels of aerobic and strengthening exercise built into your weekly routine. Are you doing too much or too little to support your wellbeing? Going to the gym isn't for everyone, but there is a lot of guided exercise content available for free online, and there are multiple opportunities to build exercise into daily life. You could also combine exercise with other wellbeing initiatives discussed previously. How about listening to your favourite music while cleaning and dancing around the house? Or briskly walking to and from a nearby green or blue space for some mindful relaxation in between?

Eating well

In modern consumerist society we are bombarded with messages about what to eat and how our bodies should look. Social media is saturated with products marketed as miracle cures for the size of our waists, our skin, hair, nails and teeth—the list goes on! In 2022 the global wellness economy was worth $5.6

trillion, representing 5.6% of global economic output (Global Wellness Institute, 2023). It is reported that in the aftermath of the pandemic, most of this global spending was on personal care and beauty, healthy eating, nutrition and weight loss, physical activity and wellness tourism. With public health prevention, traditional and complementary medicine, and wellness real estate also raking in sizeable amounts (Global Wellness Institute, 2023). 'Dieting is a scam, one that bilks Americans out of $50 billion annually' (Seligman, 2011, p. 31).

In 2019, *Healthline* published an article on '8 "Fad" Diets That Actually Work', listing the following: Atkins diet, South Beach diet, vegan diet, ketogenic diet, paleo diet, zone diet, Dukan diet and 5:2 diet (Healthline, 2019). They later acknowledge that, while these may be effective for weight loss, this doesn't mean the weight loss is sustainable long-term. The British Heart Foundation (2023) refers to an article published in the *Independent* in (2014) titled 'Crash diets might not be so bad in beating fat after all' (also reported in the *Mail*, *Telegraph* and *Express*). While 12.5% weight loss was achieved for around half, many of the 200 obese adult participants that these findings were based on dropped out of the study, and 71% had regained the weight within three years. The research also excluded smokers and those with diabetes and did not factor in physical exercise. My body is unlikely to be featured in a magazine, and my weight has fluctuated up and down over the years, yet I have always maintained a weight within the range considered healthy for my age and height, and I have never been on a diet! I have achieved this by loosely following 'The Eatwell Guide' produced by the NHS. The NHS (2022) recommends that we eat at least five portions of fruit and vegetables a day, and that just over a third of the food we eat should consist of starchy carbohydrates, such as potatoes, bread, rice or pasta. We should also eat protein rich foods, such as beans, pulses, fish, eggs or meat. Low fat, calcium-rich dairy products are important for bone health, and energy can be gained from small amounts of unsaturated fats in certain oils and spreads. Foods that are high in fat, salt and sugar are not needed in our diet and should be eaten less often, or in smaller amounts. We should also aim to drink six to eight cups or glasses of fluid a day, with water being the preferred choice.

Invitation 5: Find a sustainable way to eat well

The Eatwell Guide and further NHS guidance is easy to access online. It divides food and drink into five main groups, making it easier to see where you can make small, sustainable changes to your diet. Take a look at this and consider how your diet compares. Have you cut out certain food groups? Are you eating significantly more or less than is recommended from a specific food group? Are you drinking too much or too little? If you are concerned about your eating habits, perhaps you can identify one or two small and sustainable changes you can make to improve your wellbeing.

> To achieve and maintain your weight loss goal it's important to find a healthy way of eating that you enjoy and can follow for life.
> (Healthline, 2019)

Getting enough sleep

Matthew Walker is a neuroscientist, sleep expert, university professor and author of *Why We Sleep: Unlocking the Power of Sleep and Dreams*. Walker (2021) recommends thinking of sleep as an investment for tomorrow rather than a cost. He refers to sleep as 'the elixir of life' and 'the Swiss army knife of health'. With 7–9 hours being the recommended amount of sleep for healthy adults, Walker (2021) urges us to go to bed for longer than we intend to sleep but to avoid activities that create an association between being in bed and being awake. He also recommends:

- Setting a 'go to bed' alarm, providing an 8-hour sleep opportunity. You can even add a snooze alarm buffer.
- Getting ready for bed (washing, cleaning teeth, putting pjs on) an hour before you would actually get in to bed.
- If you wake in the night, go to another room in dim light, without doing activities than you associate with waking up, then return to bed when you feel tired.

> ### Invitation 6: Reflect on your attitudes and behaviours around sleep
>
> Is sleep a priority for you? How do you prepare for it? Do you get more or less sleep than is recommended? Are there ways your sleep could be improved? I suffered with insomnia for many years, and I have worked with many clients who experience sleep disturbance. I have found that some people would benefit from a better sleep routine, while others overdo their sleep preparation rituals, putting excessive pressure on themselves, which further disrupts their sleep. There is a wealth of information online that may help, but getting a better night's sleep is dependent on your own individual needs and challenges. I have found pre-recorded 'sleep stories' very helpful. I also reduce the pressure when I wake in the night by reminding myself that my body is still resting. This has helped me to switch into a cycle where I sleep earlier, wake earlier and feel far more productive in the mornings than I ever felt when I was working late into the night.
>
> The best bridge between despair and hope is a good night's sleep.
> (Walker, 2017)

Accepting things as they are

Acceptance and commitment therapy (ACT) is a form of third-wave CBT that teaches people to accept feelings as appropriate responses to psychological distress. This challenges the cultural norm of treating negative emotions like problems to be fixed. Rather than avoiding, denying or struggling with emotions, the emphasis should be on acceptance, mindfulness and living in accordance with one's values (Hayes, Strosahl and Wilson, 2016). This approach is also echoed in many 12-step programmes and is summed up in the serenity prayer, which is a key spiritual tool of most recovery support groups (Very Well Mind, 2023):

> God, grant me the serenity
> To accept the things I cannot change;
> Courage to change the things I can;
> and wisdom to know the difference.
>
> (Reinhold Niebuhr: 1892–1971)

Despite being a passionate advocate for social justice, I have recently learned to apply principles of acceptance to reduce distress in personal and professional situations that are outside of my control. This approach provides relief from internal battles that are unproductive and harmful and can improve one's overall sense of wellbeing. As an integrated therapist informed by Gestalt principles, I am also guided in life and work by the paradoxical theory of change, which states that 'change occurs when one becomes what he is, not when he tries to become what he is not' (Beisser, 1970).

Invitation 7: *Accept what you cannot change, and change what you can*

Make a list of the things that are currently bothering you and go through the items one at a time. For each item on the list, ask yourself the following questions:

- 'Is there anything I can do to change this?'
- 'If there is something I can do, what does that involve, and am I willing to do it?'
- 'If there is nothing I can do, what do I need to accept about myself, others, or the world, in order to reduce the internal distress associated with this?'

Practising gratitude

After approximately 30 years of research on happiness and wellbeing, previous president of the American Psychiatric Society Martin Seligman (2011) has identified a number of positive psychology exercises 'that work'. One such exercise is gratitude practice, which is simple strategy that anyone can employ without the need for specialist skills or tools. It involves taking a few minutes a day to identify the things that went well—the things you are grateful for. You might have enjoyed a comforting drink, a nice meal, getting home at the end of the day, a positive interaction, or something even more significant. Anything you are grateful for counts! Regularly expressing gratitude for the positives in life can create a shift in mindset, helping to move away from dwelling on problems.

> *Invitation 8: Be grateful!*
>
> Seligman (2011, pp. 30–44) recommends the following exercises:
>
> *What went well/three blessings exercise*
> Every night for the next week, write down three things that went well and why they went well, before you go to bed.
>
> *The gratitude visit*
> Write a letter to someone who once did or said something that changed your life and thank them. Be specific and detailed about what they said, how it affected you and how you often think of it. Then plan to meet them face to face and share it with them.

Be compassionate to yourself and others

Compassion involves an awareness of, and concern for, suffering. This is accompanied by a wish to relieve the suffering and a readiness to help (Gilbert, 2014). People in caring professions often possess a great deal of compassion for others, but they may disregard their own self-care needs. Compassion focused therapy is another form of third-wave CBT, which aims to stimulate resting-energy, feelings of calmness, wellbeing, contentment and safety (Reeves, 2018, p. 141). Learning soothing skills can help people to manage future setbacks in more adaptive ways. However, self-compassion may be difficult at first, as some have learned to associate enjoyment with punishment—go slow (Gilbert, 2014, p. 16).

> *Invitation 9: Give yourself the compassion you offer to others*
>
> Think of a scenario where you criticised yourself for the way you felt, behaved or coped. Revisit the activating event with a magical bag full of resources you didn't have at the time. These could be physical or emotional tools, a different environment, a different background, past experience or learned behaviour. You could also give yourself new forms of social support. What is in your bag? How would these resources have changed the way you felt, behaved or coped at the time?
>
> Other self-compassion exercises include:
>
> - Talking to and treating yourself as you would a good friend.
> - Writing a compassionate letter to yourself about something that makes you feel ashamed or 'not good enough'.

Replacing consumerism with essentialism

Data compiled from 7,250 respondents suggests that the key determinants of wellbeing are the natural environment, relationships, health, what we do, where we live, our personal finance, the economy, education, skills and governance (Office for National Statistics, 2011). The first few determinants on this list have been addressed previously, but factors such as governance, the economy and access to education continue to generate inequalities within society. This is challenging and distressing on many levels. Thankfully, we can apply some of the practices described previously to help! We can also take steps to resist the materialism and consumerism dominating contemporary life and make more considered choices about our personal finances (Fields Millburn and Nicodemus, 2021).

Minimalism is the art of living a fuller life by having less things. Best-selling authors of *Love People, Use Things* encourage us to reduce the amount we consume and to make choices based on deeply held values that are foundational, such as good health and relationships (Fields Millburn and Nicodemus, 2021). Many believe that money buys happiness, yet at the turn of the century, it was reported that wellbeing was no longer growing in response to growth in national income (Easterlin, 1995, 2001, cited by Rablen, 2012). An essentialist view is that many people suffer from 'learned helplessness', and we must not to neglect our opportunities to make choices in life (McKeown, 2014).

Invitation 10: Minimalize your life

Fields Millburn and Nicodemus (2021) suggest taking time to reflect on how consumerism helps you to create a façade and distracts you from the real issues in your life. How much do you prioritise things that are surface, and things that feel important but really aren't, such as answering emails and watching TV? Read the following questions and write down your responses before setting some individual goals. SMART goals are specific, measurable, achievable and realistic. They are also time based, so set yourself a timeframe for this activity and identify a preferable way to reward yourself when your goals are achieved.

- How and where can you be more present?
- How can you avoid accumulating unnecessary debt?
- Can you delete unnecessary apps that distract you for 30 days?
- How can you reserve your time for genuine, positive, empowering relationships and/or avoid those that feel toxic? (Fields Millburn and Nicodemus, 2021)

Minimalists Fields, Millburn and Nicodemus (2021) advise that we separate goods into three piles: essentials (food, basic clothing), useful but not essential (furniture, treasured keepsakes) and junk (sell, donate or throw)

Essentialist McKeown (2014) makes the following suggestions to simplify your life:

- Reject the notion that you should accomplish everything and focus your energy on doing something well.
- Constantly question yourself and consider whether what you are doing is helpful.
- Waste no time putting things into action.
- Give yourself daily space to escape and consider what is essential and concentrate on the bigger picture.
- Eliminate things that slow you down, prepare for things to go wrong and allocate a 50% time buffer for each task.

Conclusion

Throughout this chapter, you have been invited to consider how your own wellbeing can be improved or maintained in alignment with your core values. This might include fostering positive relationships, singing, dancing, spending time in nature, exercising, eating well and getting enough sleep. You have also been invited to practice acceptance, gratitude and compassion, and to replace consumerism with essentialism. In summary, to obtain a greater sense of wellbeing in the modern world, you have been invited to get back to basics and live a life more in keeping with that of our ancestors!

In many ways we are more fortunate than our ancestors. We have better health care, numerous means of communication, less manual labour and more rights than those who came before us, but what has this social evolution cost us as a species? How much time do we dedicate to genuine connection with other people and nature? Are we able to slow down enough to experience moments of joy, to acknowledge meaningful experiences and to feel fully engaged with mindful activity? Are we able to recognise our own accomplishments, however big or small, before moving on to the next items on the to-do list? I hope that some of the practices outlined in this chapter will encourage you to flourish in new ways and will empower you to take charge of your own wellbeing.

References

Beisser, A. (1970), The paradoxical theory of change. In J. Fagan and I.L. Shepherd (Eds.), *Gestalt Therapy Now* (pp. 77–80). New York: Harper and Rowe.

British Heart Foundation. (2023), Do crash diets work? Available at https://www.bhf.org.uk/informationsupport/heart-matters-magazine/news/behind-the-headlines/crash-diets (Accessed February 8, 2023).

Caudwell, J. (2021), Queering indoor swimming in the UK: Transgender and non-binary wellbeing. *Journal of Sport and Social Issues*, 46(4), pp. 1–25.

Cooper, K. and Barton, G. (2016), An exploration of physical activity and wellbeing in university employees. *Perspectives in Public Health*, *136*(3), pp. 152–160.

Department of Health and Social Care. (2023), *Quick read version of the mental health and wellbeing plan: Discussion paper.* Available at https://www.gov.uk/government/consultations/mental-health-and-wellbeing-plan-discussion-paper-and-call-for-evidence/quick-read-version-of-the-mental-health-and-wellbeing-plan-discussion-paper (Accessed May 23, 2023).

Donne, J. (1624), Meditation XVII, in *Devotions upon Emergent Occasions*. https://www.luminarium.org/sevenlit/donne/meditation17.php (Accessed May 23, 2024).

Douglas, F. (2020), *The Nature Remedy: A Restorative Guide to the Natural World*. London: Harper Collins.

Easterlin, R.A. (2001), Income and happiness: Towards a unified theory. *The Economic Journal*, *111*(473), pp. 465–484. http://www.jstor.org/stable/2667943

Easterlin, R.A. (1995), Will raising the incomes of all increase the happiness of all? *Journal of Economic Behavior & Organization*, *27*(1), pp. 35–47.

Fields Millburn, J. and Nicodemus, R. (2021), *Love People Use Things: Because the Opposite Never Works*. New York: Celadon Books.

Fleming, C. and Manning, M. (2019), *Routledge Handbook of Indigenous Wellbeing*. Oxon: Routledge.

Foley, R. and Kistemann, T. (2015), Blue space geographies: Enabling health in place. *Health and Place*, *35*, pp. 157–165. Available at https://doi.org/10.1016/j.healthplace.2015.07.003 (Accessed April 13, 2024).

Gilbert, P. (2014) The origins and nature of compassion focused therapy. *British Journal of Clinical Psychology*, *53*, pp. 6–41.

Glazer, R. (2023), *Discovering and Developing Core Values*. Available at www.robertglazer.com/blinkist (Accessed April 8, 2024).

Global Wellness Institute. (2023), Wellness economy statistics and facts. Available at https://globalwellnessinstitute.org/press-room/statistics-and-facts/ (Accessed December 30, 2023).

Haslam, C., Jetten, J., Cruwys, T., Dingle, G.A. and Haslam, S.A. (2018), *The New Psychology of Health*. Oxon, Routledge.

Hayes, C., Strosahl, K. and Wilson, K. (2016) 2, *Acceptance and Commitment Therapy: The Process and Practice of Mindful Change* (2nd Ed.). Hove: Guilford Press.

Holt-Lunstad, J. (2017), Why social relationships are important for physical health: A systems approach to understanding and modifying risk and protection. *Annual Review of Psychology*. *4*(69), 437–458. https://doi.org/10.1146/annurev-psych-122216-011902

Healthline. (2019), 8 "fad" diets that actually work. Available at https://www.healthline.com/nutrition/8-fad-diets-that-work#TOC_TITLE_HDR_10 (Accessed February 4, 2024).

Helitzer, E. and Moss, H. (2022), Group singing for health and wellbeing in the Republic of Ireland: The first national map. *Perspectives in Public Health*, *142*(2), pp. 102–110.

Hunter, L. and Stoodley, L. (2021), Bluespace, senses, wellbeing and surfing: Prototype cyborg theory-methods. *Journal of Sport and Social Issues*, *45*(1), pp. 88–112.

Ilari, B., Chen-Hafteck, L. and Crawford, L. (2013), Singing and cultural understanding: A music education perspective. *International Journal of Music Education*, *31*(2), pp. 202–216.

Jordan, M. (2015), *Nature and Therapy*. London: Sage.

Kaplan, S. (1995), The restorative benefits of nature: Toward an integrative framework. *Journal of Environmental Psychology*, *15*(3), 169–182. https://doi.org/10.1016/0272-4944(95)90001-2

McKeown, G. (2014), *Essentialism: The Disciplined Pursuit of Less*. London: Virgin Books.
Moffatt, F. (2017), The wellbeing benefits of swimming to communities: A literature review, in report commissioned by swimming and health commission. The health and wellbeing benefits of swimming: individually, societally, economically and nationally. *Swim England*, pp. 106–117.
NHS. (2022), *The Eatwell Guide*. Available at https://www.nhs.uk/live-well/eat-well/food-guidelines-and-food-labels/the-eatwell-guide/ (Accessed April 13, 2024).
NHS Inform. (2022), Types of exercise. Available at https://www.nhsinform.scot/healthy-living/keeping-active/getting-started/types-of-exercise (Accessed April 6, 2024).
Office for Health Improvement and Disparities. (2022), Social prescribing: Applying all our health. Available at https://www.gov.uk/government/publications/social-prescribing-applying-all-our-health/social-prescribing-applying-all-our-health (Accessed February 24, 2023).
Office for National Statistics (2011), *Measuring what matters. National statisticians' reflections on the national debate on measuring national well-being*. https://unstats.un.org/unsd/envaccounting/ceea/archive/Framework/nsreport_wellbeing_uk.pdf (Accessed February 8, 2024).
Public Health England. (2020), *Health Matters: Physical Activity–Prevention and Management of Long-Term Conditions*. Available at https://www.gov.uk/government/publications/health-matters-physical-activity/health-matters-physical-activity-prevention-and-management-of-long-term-conditions) (Accessed February 26, 2024).
Rablen, M.D. (2012), The promotion of local wellbeing: A primer for policymakers. *Local Economy*, 27(3), pp. 297–314.
Reeves, A. (2018), *An Introduction to Counselling: From Theory to Practice* (2nd Ed.). London: Sage.
Sawatzky, A., Cunsolo, A., Harper, S.L., Shiwak, I. and Wood, M. (2019), Chapter 19. In C. Fleming and M. Manning (eds.), *Routledge Handbook of Indigenous Wellbeing*. Oxon: Routledge.
Seligman, M. (2011), *Flourish*. London: Nicholas Brealey Publishing.
Simons, G. and Baldwin, D.S. (2021), A critical review of the definition of 'wellbeing' for doctors and their patients in a post Covid-19 era. *International Journal of Social Psychiatry* 67(8), pp. 984–991.
Sport England. (2020), *Active Lives Adult Survey*. Available at https://sportengland-production-files.s3.eu-west-2.amazonaws.com/s3fs-public/2020-04/Active%20Lives%20Adult%20November%202018-19%20Report.pdf?BhkAy2K28pd9bDEz_NuisHl2ppuqJtpZ (Accessed April 14, 2024).
Ulrich, R.S. (1983), Aesthetic and affective response to natural environment. In I. Altman and J.F. Wohlwill, (eds.), *Behavior and the Natural Environment. Human Behavior and Environment*, vol 6. Boston, MA: Springer. https://doi.org/10.1007/978-1-4613-3539-9_4
Very Well Mind. (2023), What to know about the serenity prayer. Available at https://www.verywellmind.com/the-serenity-prayer-62614 (Accessed April 7, 2024).
Walker, M. (2021), how to improve your sleep and why you should, *Feel Better Live More Podcast*. Available at https://www.youtube.com/watch?v=X_eWDhXxziU&list=PLwAWbIQiqJ0D2gn5UJBPSOzvLROyqSl7f&index=6 (Accessed March 1, 2023).
Walker, M.P. (2017), *Why We Sleep: Unlocking the Power of Sleep and Dreams*. New York: Scribner.
Wilson, E.O. (1984), *Biophilia*. Massachusetts: Harvard University Press.

Conclusion
Moving Forward

Estelle Tarry

Social and therapeutic interventions and strategies for children and young people have been at the heart of this book. Please see the Conceptual Framework (Figure 13.1) giving a visual summary.

The contributors, who specialise in these areas, are passionate and dedicated and have been drawn together to share their experiences and expertise in supporting vulnerable and marginalized children, from different social, cultural, ethnic, religious and economic backgrounds, in schools. These contributors have given a wide range of social and therapeutic interventions targeted to foster these children's psychological, social and emotional wellbeing, which in turn will improve social skills, behaviour and educational development.

We must not underestimate the importance of children's sense of belonging and the consequential mental health and wellbeing, in which teachers, practitioners, parents and communities all have a role to play. Throughout this book the key elements of focus that have been identified, which are universal, permeating throughout, are the importance of a nurturing and safe environment, inclusion and integration, culturally responsive pedagogy, resources, communication and active listening, collaboration and engagement with parents and communities, funding and teacher/practitioner training.

Children need to be prepared for the future. All children need 21st century skills: 'Creativity and innovation critical thinking, problem solving, decision-making, learning to learn, metacognition communication, collaboration (teamwork), information literacy, ICT literacy, citizenship (local and global), life and career, [and] personal and social responsibility including cultural awareness and competence' (Global Partnerships for Education, 2020, p.27). However, without the practitioners' positive mental health and wellbeing, none of this would be possible, so it is vital include the supportive processes for them too!

Hopefully the readers of this book will reflect on their individual and collective role, and the need for compassion, care, understanding and empathy, the building of relationships and connectedness through active listening, discussion, sharing views and perspectives, with a holistic approach in fostering children's sense of belonging.

Social Injustice
Age, gender, race, ethnicity, religion, disability, sexual orientation, sexual identity, education, or any other distinguishing characteristic or trait.

⬇

Marginalised and Vulnerable Children

⬇

Section A: Tackling Social Inequality and Social Justice	Section B: Social Interaction; Social Beings and Relationships	Section C: All Schools and All Practitioners
Examines the relationship between social inequality and globalization, education systems and the role of global governance/ social policy in mitigating drivers of inequality	Through relationship-rich pedagogies children are happier, better adjusted, more engaged at school and more motivated to learn.	Inclusion and inclusive practice and the children's learning and challenges that face the teachers, with a needs-led perspective being at the core.
Race-based terminology and anti-racist pedagogy and the adoption of 'transformative anti-racist activism'.	What is a family? The different family structures, including LGBT families and families with stepparents and lone parents	A positive whole school approach to a mentally healthy culture and the role of the Mental Health Practitioner in schools.
The importance of religion and spirituality in children's sense of self and belonging.	The importance of trauma informed practice, and compassionate care and leadership.	Positive psychology and the application of self-discovery, healing, empowerment and connection.
Unmasking toxic masculinity in early years and primary schools: Exploring the impact on children's socialisation and development	Trauma informed practice specifically targeting asylum and refugee children, highlighting culturally responsive pedagogy.	
	Empowering practitioners and how they can facilitate children to re-connect children with nature.	

⬇

Key Elements
A nurturing and safe environment, inclusion and integration, culturally responsive pedagogy, resources, communication and active listening, collaboration and engagement with parents and communities, funding and teacher/practitioner training

⬇

Sense of Belonging

⬇

Mental Health and Wellbeing

Figure 13.1 Conceptual Framework.

Reference

Global Partnerships for Education. (2020), *21st-Century Skills: What Potential Role for the Global Partnership for Education? A Landscape Review*. Washington: Global Partnerships for Education.

Index

Pages in *italics* refer to figures and pages in **bold** refer to tables

Abuse 53, 106–108, **109**, 113–114, 123
Academic: achievement 72, 83, 95, 100, 126–127, 169–175, 184, 192–193, 204; progress 15, 21, 90, 130–133, 166, 183, 186, 190–195
Acquired Immunodeficiency Syndrome (Aids) 189
Acts: Adoption and Children Act (2002) 88–89; Children's Act (2004) 91, 168; Children and Social Work Act (2017) 86; Civil Partnership Act (2004) 89; Education 2030 Act 10; Equality Act (2010) 13, 23, 28, **30**, 87–88, 99, 164, 172; Gender Recognition Act (2004) 94; Human Fertilisation and Embryology Act (2008) 92–93; Human Rights Act (1990) 164; Local Government Act (1988) 87; Marriage Act (Same-sex couples) (2013) 89; Race Relations Act (1965) 21; Race Relations Act (1976) 21–22; Race Relations (amendment) Act (2000) 22
Adoption 59, 88–92, *217*
Adverse Childhood Experiences (ACE) 91, 108, **109**, 116–126
Africa 127, 131
Ainscow, Melvin 169
Anti-bullying 63–65, 188
Anti-discrimination 22–23, 94–95, 129, 159
Anti-racism 19–**31**, *217*
Anti-racist: early childhood pedagogy 21–23; implementing anti-racist pedagogy 24–28; lens 26; pedagogy 24–28; transformative anti-racist activism 28–29

Anxiety 20, 58, 80, 108, 126, 183, 186–187, 193–194
Assessment 25, 64, 132–135, 165–166, 172–173, 183, 185–186
Asylum seeker 2, 123–136
Attachment 14–15, 108, 114, 199
Attitudes 20–22, 56, 58–59, 73, 77, 94, 99, 166, 176, 199, 209
Attunement 71–72, 78–81
Autism 171

Behaviour 44, 46–49, 55, 57–58, 105–106, 110, 113, 117, 126, 134, 175, 188–199, 216; acceptable 58, 94; aggressive 58–59, 64; criminatory 90; disruptive 80; learned 112; managing 114; modelling 128; racist 22; respectable 25, 63–64; risk taking 95; social 72, 80; trauma response 12; unacceptable 64
Beliefs 1, 22, 35, 37, 40, 42, 44–49, 99–100, 125, 127, 176, 199–200; *see also* Religion; Religious education; Buddhism 39, 206; Christianity 39–40; Hinduism 36, 39, 46–47; Islam 39, 204; Judaism 39; popular 89; Sikhism 39
Bias 58, 64, 135, 162; conformity bias 97–98; cultural 162; heterosexual bias 87; hostile attribution bias 58–59
Binary 94
Bisexual 87, 90, 97, 167
Black Lives Matter 1, 22, 24
Blue sky gazing 206
Bourdieu, Pierre 7, 37
Brain 55, 108
Bricologic 40–41

Bronfenbrenner, Urie 22, 26, 81
Bruner, J 168
Buddhism 39; *see also* Beliefs; Religion; Religious education
Bullying 14, 63–64, 87, 94–96, 98–99, 129, 189; cyberbullying 108

Capitalism 9
Caribbean 127, 164
Children and Young Peoples Mental Health Services **109**
Children's Services and Skills (2021) 183
Children's Society 54, 66, 107
Childhood and Adolescent Mental Health Service (CAMHS) 193
Children and Young Peoples Mental Health Services (CYPMHS) 107
Christianity 40–41; *see also* Beliefs; Religion; Religious education
Circle time 44, 60, 63
Citizenship 2, 7, 161, 164, 174, 216; active 164; digital 163; global 161–162
Cognitive 58, 126, 143, 145, 167; Cognitive Behavioural Therapy 194, 199; cognitive development 8, 126, 205; cognitive language 131; cognitive load 167–168, 176; cognitive orientation 46; cognitive skills 14
Colonization 9
Comparative education 10
Connectedness 1, 74, 83, 216; community 204; nature 145–146; school 14; school attachment connectedness 15; social 15
Consumerism 202, 212–213
Coronavirus 1, 7, 27, 42, 106, 114, 166, 182
Creativity 147, 170, 204, 207, 216
Critical Race Theory 20–21, 24
Cultural lens 3, 132
Culturally responsive 3, 24–26, 127, 131–135, 216, *217*

Dancing 132, 202–205, 207, 213
Dartmoor National Park *142*, 146
Decolonization 27–28
Depression 1, 108, 126, 184, 186, 193–194
Disability 13, 88, 95, 134, 164, 172, *217*
Disorder 87; anxiety 187; eating 183; mental 107
Displacement 1–3, **109**, 123
Displays 24, 59, 61–62, 128

Early Years Foundation Stage 22
Eating well 202, 207–208, 213; disorder 183; healthy 184, 208
Ecology 141–144
Ecosystem 145
Embodiment 141–145
Ethics 79–81
Europe 124, 127
Every Child Matters (2003) 168, 192
Exercise 206–208, 210
Exosystems 89–90
extra curricula activity 168

Floyd, George 22, 24
Forest Bathing 206

Generation alpha 1
Germany 82, 125
Good Childhood Report (2021) 54, 107, 187–188
Governance: educational 10–11; global 9–10, 12, 15, *217*
Gratitude 147, 202, 210–211, 213

Haka 204
Health Care Plan 171–172
Heteronormative 86, 97
Human immunodeficiency Virus (HIV) 88
Hindu 36, 39, 46–47; *see also* Beliefs; Religion; Religious education
Homophobic 54, 88
Homosexual 87
Hong Kong 125

Immigration 1, 131, 133
Indonesia 204
Integrated counsellor 200
Interconnectedness 2, 8, 74, 126, 151–152, 161
Intercultural competencies 132
Intersectionality 11–13, 20
Ireland 204
Islam 39, 204; *see also* Beliefs; Religion; Religious education

Japan 127
Judaism 39; *see also* Beliefs; Religion; Religious education

Kairological time 76–78

Lesbian 88, 98, 167
(LGBT) 86–100
lone parents 93–94, 107, *217*

Masculinity: minimize 57; mitigate 58–59; social implications 54–56; social media 56–57; toxic 2, 54–66, *217*
Maslow, Abraham 99, 126, 168, 174
Mattering 71–83
#MeToo 1
Mental health practitioner 193–195, *217*
Middle East 132, 182
Migration 123, 126, 129, 136
Māori 74, 204
Muslim 41, 44, 46, 48

National Curriculum England 86, 166–169, 175
Natural world 74, 140–141, 143–145
Nature 2, 37, 140–152, 203–206, 213, *217*
New Zealand 74, 204
Nonbinary 94, 96, 100, 207

Outdoors 141–142

Pandemic 165–166; *see also* Coronavirus; post-pandemic 93
Place responsive 141–143
Personal Social and Health education (PSHE) 92, 168
Perspective-taking 61
Piaget, Jean 38, 95
Poverty 7–8, 10–11, 13–115, 161, 165–166, 182
Prejudice 2, 20, 24, 64, 129, 135, 151
Pride 62, 98–100, 165, 185
Problem-solving 3, 169, 171, 175, 189–190, 194
Psychoanalyst 200
Psychologist 200
Psychological Contract 184–187, 193–194

Qualifications 8, 14, 135

Race 1–3, 11, 13, 19–35, 64, 88, 95, 124, 152, 200–201, *217*; *see also* Anti-racist; race-based terminology 19, *217*; racial 19–21, 23, 27–29; racist 189; relations 22
Ramadan 48
Reciprocal restoration 144
Refugee 2, 124–136, *217*
Religion 36–53; *see also* Beliefs; Religious education; Buddhism 39, 206; Christianity 39–40; Hinduism 36, 39, 46–47; Islam 39, 204; Judaism 39; Sikhism 39
Religious education 36–50; *see also* Beliefs; Religion
Resilience 25, 75, 151, 168, 183, 190, 196
Restorative practice 100, 173–176
Risk 118, 124, 126, 171, 191; exclusion 170; factors 106, 184; health 206; high 91, 193; low 170, 174; taking 96
River Dart 146–147

Safeguarding 116, 187
Schumacher College 141–143, 150
Scotland 105, 113–116, 118
School inspector 184, 189–190, 192
Sesame workshop 132
Self: self-awareness 126, 130, 132; self-concept 75, 187; self-confidence 91; self-development 46; self-efficacy 108; self-esteem 75, 96, 98–100, 126, 167, 171, 175–176; self-identity 99; self-knowledge 58, 66; self-reflection 44, 46, 57; Self-worth 99
Senses 37, 82, 206; sensorial 146–147
Sikhism 40; *see also* Beliefs; Religion; Religious education
Singing 79, 132, 202, 204–205, 213
Sleep deprivation 107
Social: cohesion 128–129, 136; inequality 7–15, *217*; justice 7–15, 20, 22, 27, 210, *217*
Sociocultural 73, 146
Special Educational Needs Coordinator (SENCO) 185
Stepparents 88–90, *217*
Stereotype: gender 54, 57–63, 65–66; language 25; masculinity 62–63
Stonewall 87, 96–97
Storytelling 43–45, 60, 62–63, 147
Substance Abuse and Mental Health Services Administration (SAMHSA) 109
Sustainable: changes 209; compassion 110; development 13; Development Goals (SDG) 7, 10, 161; future 11, 127, 135, 208; paradigm 142; race pedagogy **31**
Surrogacy 92–94
Swimming 146, 206–207; cold water swimming 206

Thrive 1, 19, 123, 136
Tibet 206
Toxic masculinity 1, 54–66, *217*
Trafficking 123–125
Transformative: activism 2, 19–35, *217*; anti-racist activism 28–30; learning 142
Transgender 90, 97, 99–100, 207; parenting 94–96, 99; rights 167
Trauma informed practice 114–116, 125–136, *217*
Trust 3, **31**, 83, 90, 130, 174, 195; developing 80, 92, 94, 114, 131–132; norms 203; relationships 13, 74, 128, 136; trustworthiness 113–114, 126–127, 133–134
Turkey 124, 204

United Arab Emirates (UAE) 127
United Nations 9–10, 73, 99, 116, 124, 160, 164
United States of America 21–22, 108, 112, 160

Voice 10, 28, 36, 39, 41, 66, 100, 113, 127, 130–131, 161–162, 170, 190, 204–205
Vygotsky, Lev 170

Wales 74, 86, 106, 108, 113, 115–116, 118
Water 123, 145–148, 205–206, 208
Welfare: child 73, 91; organisation 126; standards 8
World Health Organisation (WHO) 87

For Product Safety Concerns and Information please contact our EU
representative GPSR@taylorandfrancis.com
Taylor & Francis Verlag GmbH, Kaufingerstraße 24, 80331 München, Germany

www.ingramcontent.com/pod-product-compliance
Lightning Source LLC
Chambersburg PA
CBHW071409300426
44114CB00016B/2235